For the People

Left Populism in Spain and the US

For the People

Left Populism in Spain and the US

Jorge Tamames

Lawrence Wishart
London 2020

Lawrence and Wishart Limited
Central Books Building
Freshwater Road
Chadwell Heath
RM8 1RX

Typesetting: e-type
Cover design: River Design
Printing: Imprint Digital

First published 2020
© Jorge Tamames 2020

British Library Cataloguing in Publication Data.
A catalogue record for this book is available from the British Library

ISBN 9781912064441

Contents

Acknowledgements   vii

Prologue by Chantal Mouffe   1

Part I: Landscapes

Introduction
Populists at the Gates   9

Chapter One
Populism and its Discontents   26

Chapter Two
Earthquakes and Countermovements   53

Part II: Faultlines

Chapter Three
The Move to the Market   75

Chapter Four
From Consensus to Crisis: Spain, 1978-2013   106

Chapter Five
From New Deal to No Deal: America, 1977-2014   138

Part III: Landslides

Chapter Six
Storming Heaven: Podemos at Spain's Populist Moment   167

Chapter Seven
Bernie Sanders' Political Revolution   201

Conclusion
Hopes and Prospects for Left Populism   238

Index   254

Acknowledgements

This book would never have been written without the support of Cornel Ban and Chantal Mouffe. Cornel's generous mentorship is behind whatever useful insights on political economy the reader finds within these pages (the book's flaws and limitations, on the other hand, are mine alone). Chantal's inspiration and support were essential to theorising and guiding this project. I am also grateful to other scholars who provided invaluable advice and feedback: Mark Blyth, Oddný Helgadóttir, Aidan Regan and Katrina Burgess, who supervised the initial stages of my research.

In Spain I am indebted to Pablo Bustinduy and the admirable team he gathered at the Secretaría Internacional. Among these, Sirio and Violeta were subjected to – and gracefully endured – a great number of harangues on Karl Polanyi, populism, emancipation, and a variety of unrelated topics. Clara Ramas San Miguel and Guillermo Fernández Vázquez also delivered input with élan. In the US, Claire Sandberg and Winnie Wong transmitted their contagious enthusiasm, which was often badly needed.

Last but not least, I am grateful to friends and family: Camilo, Kathy, Joaco and Pedro for their patience in bearing with my frequently angst-ridden writing. And most of all to Berta, who read the initial draft and answered an essential question: *does any of this make sense?*

Chantal Mouffe

Prologue

The field of 'populism studies' is flourishing in the social sciences, and new publications are constantly being added to the already plentiful literature on this topic. While acknowledging the difficulty of *providing* a definition of populism, the majority of these studies nevertheless converge in asserting that populism's key feature consists in conceiving of society as divided into two antagonistic groups: a pure homogeneous people – that the populists claim to represent – and a corrupt elite that must be discarded. It is on the basis of such a definition that these studies conclude that populism is always incompatible with pluralism, and that it constitutes a menace to democratic societies.

Now, this is clearly to credit populism with a programmatic content that it does not possess. If populism is so difficult to define and has been open to so many divergent interpretations, this is because it does not exist as an entity that may be theorised independently of its different historical forms of expression. To apprehend this political phenomenon, instead of treating it as a doctrine whose principles may be defined, one should examine the political logic that is at play in the different movements that have been characterised as 'populist'. According to this alternative approach, originally elaborated by Ernesto Laclau in *On Populist Reason*,[1] populism should be understood as a discursive strategy, in which a political frontier is constructed that divides society into two camps and which calls for the mobilisation of the 'underdog' against 'those in power'. It not an ideology with any conceptual unity, even a 'thin' one, but rather is a way of doing politics that can take various ideological forms and is compatible with a variety of institutional frameworks. Everything depends on how the political frontier of us/them is constructed, and the historical contexts and socio-economic structures in which it is inscribed.

To be sure, in some cases, the political frontier is constructed on the basis of the opposition of 'morally upstanding people' versus 'corrupt elites', but such an opposition is far from present in all populist movements. It is therefore disingenuous on the part of critics to claim this as a common trait of all forms of populism.

Adopting the discursive approach and scrutinising the particular conjunctures in which populist movements develop allows us to recognise the existence of a variety of forms of populism with specific characteristics and diverse political orientations. It becomes possible to acknowledge the crucial difference between right-wing populism with anti-pluralist, illiberal traits, and left populism, whose aim is to deepen and radicalise liberal-democratic values.

This is the path followed by Jorge Tamames in *For the People*, a book that exemplifies the fruitfulness of the discursive approach to understanding populism. *For the People* is an important contribution to the understanding of the origins of the current 'populist moment' in Western liberal democratic societies, as well as being an outstanding analysis of two examples of left populism in action: Podemos in Spain and the Bernie Sanders movement in the United States.

Tamames's central thesis is that it is only by espousing a long-term approach that takes political economy into consideration that we can understand the emergence of populist movements. As far as current Western forms of populism are concerned, he argues that these cannot be comprehended without taking into account the socio-economic context of the advance of neoliberal policies, and the social and political cleavages that these generated. Far from being a short-term phenomenon linked to the appearance on the political scene of demagogic politicians, they are a consequence of thirty years of neoliberal policymaking, and must be seen as a response to the forces unleashed by economic transformations dating back to the 1970s.

Inquiring into the demise of the 'embedded liberalism' that prevailed during the post-war Keynesian consensus, Tamames shows how this gave way to neoliberalism when the credibility of the Keynesian model began to crumble as inflation increased, jointly with unemployment. The discrediting of Keynesianism contributed to the growing acceptance of the neoliberal paradigm that established its dominance through the coming to power of Ronald Reagan in the US and Margaret Thatcher in the UK. In the years that followed, this new paradigm was progressively adopted in other Western societies, and became hegemonic with the conversion of social-democratic parties to its main tenets. Cemented by the conviction that there was no alternative to neoliberal globalisation, this hegemony remained practically unchallenged for three decades. However, the dislocation that neoliberalism brought about in Western societies created the terrain, both in economics and in politics, for the emergence of various forms of resistance that, after the crisis of 2008, crystallised in a variety of populist movements.

One of the most original aspects of Tamames's book is the way in which he deploys the work of Karl Polanyi, in particular his conception of a 'double movement', to illuminate the rise of contemporary populist movements.

Elaborated by Polanyi in *The Great Transformation*,[2] the notion of the 'double movement' refers to the process through which society defends itself from the advances of commodification by developing a countermovement to restore the relation between the economy and social needs. Interrogating the political and social consequences of the rise of the market from the end of the eighteenth century to the Great Depression, Polanyi shows how this generated a movement of self-protection on the part of society, reacting against the devastation produced by market forces. This countermovement of societal self-protection, he notes, can take different forms, and it is as likely to have a democratic as an authoritarian outcome. Indeed, the 1930s saw the implementation of the New Deal with Roosevelt in the US, alongside Stalinism in the Soviet Union, and Nazism and fascism in Europe.

Tamames convincingly argues that combining the discursive approach – which understands populism as the construction of a political frontier – with the Polanyian framework is particularly useful for grasping the nature and growing success of populist movements in the past ten years. He proposes that we see them as the expression of a countermovement by which liberal democratic societies react to the fragmentation and dislocation caused by the dominance of financial capitalism. The social and economic conditions that are at the origin of this countermovement are the result of neoliberal policies that, with the aim of subordinating society to the dictates of financial markets, have undermined the institutions typical of the 'embedded liberalism' of the post-war welfare state. Financial liberalisation increased the importance of international trade, as well as integration and interdependence between different economies. The social consequences of this process of 'globalisation' have been wide-ranging. Privatisation and deregulation policies have contributed to a deterioration in the conditions of the workers. With the austerity policies imposed after the 2008 crisis, this deterioration began also to affect a part of the middle classes, which has entered a process of pauperisation and precarisation. At the political level, states, expected to bow to market pressures, saw their capacity to intervene in the economy drastically reduced. As far as political parties are concerned, having abandoned their partisan character, they have lost their capacity to integrate and mobilise the citizenry, and have been reduced to what Peter Mair calls 'ruling the void'.[3]

The profound erosion of the democratic values of equality and popular sovereignty that has taken place under the hegemony of neoliberalism is at the origin of the 'post-democratic' condition that has become one of the characteristic features of present-day liberal democratic societies. This hegemony is currently challenged by the populist countermovement, whose aim is to resist the destructive effects of neoliberal globalisation. However, as was also the case in the period analysed by Polanyi, depending on how resistance to post-democracy is articulated, this countermovement can foster either radical right populism or left populism.

In his granular analysis of the left populism of Podemos in Spain and Bernie Sanders in the US, Tamames traces the rise of neoliberalism in both societies and brings to the fore its socio-economic consequences. In the United States, the Carter-Reagan years witnessed the dismantling of the New Deal, and a strong pro-market drift took place as the result of an offensive of the rich against the working and middle classes. The country was thereby transformed into an increasingly precarious society frayed by massive inequality. The Democratic Party colluded with the turn to the markets, and it was during Bill Clinton's presidency that this turn was consolidated. However, from 2011 onwards, thanks to the emergence of new progressive social movements, the neoliberal consensus was broken, and opposition voices began to be heard.

In Spain, the implementation of neoliberalism was less brutal. In the late 1970s and early 1980s, the country was transitioning from dictatorship to democracy, and embraced a 'compensatory' version of neoliberalism that was able to smooth its rougher edges. But the economy had fundamental weaknesses that were highlighted by the combined impact of the financial crash of 2008 and the bursting of the real-estate bubble. The austerity measures imposed by the European Union in 2010 eroded the legitimacy of the governing socialist PSOE, and a climate of intense social contestation signalled the beginning of a countermovement.

Both in Spain with the *indignados* and in the US with Occupy Wall Street, the countermovement was initiated by social movements that advocated a 'horizontalist' strategy and refused to engage with political institutions. But the lack of institutional connection limited these movements' impact, and they lost momentum over time. It was only when resistance to neoliberal policies was translated into a political programme in each case, through the creation of Podemos in Spain in 2014 and through Bernie Sanders's 2016 presidential campaign in the US, that the countermovement acquired an institutional shape in each country and became a significant political force.

To this day, neither Podemos nor the Bernie Sanders movement has been able to attain its goals, and there are some who conclude that the time for left populism is over. But this is to misunderstand the nature of a left populist strategy, and to mistake it for the Gramscian 'war of manoeuvre' when it should instead be conceived as a 'war of position'. Politics is, as Max Weber reminds us, 'a strong and slow boring of hard boards'. This is something that the advocates of left populism need to acknowledge and integrate into their strategy. The socio-economic conditions that call for a countermovement against the devastating effects of neoliberal globalisation are still very much with us. It may take time, but a countermovement is bound to take place, and we cannot allow it to be driven by right-wing populist forces.

It is, therefore, crucial for the left to grasp the nature of the challenge it is currently facing, and this is why this book is extremely timely. Unlike most conceptions of populism, which limit themselves to denunciation and moral condemnation without offering any perspective for positive action, Tamames's analysis provides us with crucial insights, not only for understanding the present conjuncture, but also for envisaging a strategy to recover and deepen democracy.

Notes

1. Ernesto Laclau, *On Populist Reason*, Verso: London, 2005.
2. Karl Polanyi, *The Great Transformation: The Political and Economic Origins of Our Time*, Beacon Press: Boston, MA, 2001 [1944].
3. Peter Mair, 'Ruling the void?', *New Left Review*, 42, November-December 2006, 25-51.

I

Landscapes

Populists at the gates

The tyrant, in all his doings, at least knows what is he about, but a mob is altogether devoid of knowledge; for how should there be any knowledge in a rabble, untaught, and with no natural sense of what is right and fit? It rushes wildly into state affairs with all the fury of a stream swollen in the winter, and confuses everything.[1]

> – Persian satrap Megabyzus, sixth century BC

Well, what then?
How shall this bisson multitude digest
the senate's courtesy? Let deeds express
what's like to be their words: 'we did request it;
we are the greater poll, and in true fear
they gave us our demands.' Thus we debase
the nature of our seats and make the rabble
call our cares fears; which will in time
break open the locks of the senate and bring in
the crows to peck the eagles.[2]

> –William Shakespeare, *Coriolanus*, early 1600s

It's time for the elites to rise up against the ignorant masses.[3]

> –James Traub, *Foreign Policy* columnist, 28 June 2016

Liberal democracy, we are told, is under siege. From the Philippines to Poland, authoritarian demagogues have swept to power, shattering the international order in the process. At the time of writing, in early 2020, the United Kingdom and the United States are still assimilating two unexpected blows from 2016: Brexit and the election of Donald Trump. Where this onslaught is contained, voters are exhorted to participate in round after round of elections, the aim of which seems merely to be to stop the barbarians from storming the gates. When it is temporarily defeated, as with the victory of Emmanuel Macron in France in 2017, the price is a wholesale demolition of the country's political party system.[4]

As the opening quotations suggest, elites have recurrently taken an unsympathetic view toward what José Ortega y Gasset termed 'the revolt of the masses'.[5] Today, however, the object of their disapproval is slippery. Opposition to established politics comes in different forms, but new actors on the left and radical right are often clumped together as fellow travellers in some kind of 'Populist International', even when they oppose one another.[6] Before electing a xenophobic, ex-show-host millionaire as president, US voters flirted with a self-described socialist calling for a political revolution. In France the radical right lost part of its appeal among younger voters to a left populist rallying against Eurozone elites. Perry Anderson's remarks on that country are applicable to others with strong left and radical right populists: 'the two anti-systemic forces, rather than aggregating to a common populist insurgency, largely cancel each other out'.[7]

The equation of such varied – and mutually opposed – parties and movements says as much about the labelling processes as it does about the forces disparaged as 'populist'. But what seems beyond doubt is that, in Europe and the US, the governing socio-economic paradigm is coming under increasing strain. This paradigm combined orthodox guidelines on economic management – the 'stabilise, privatise, and liberalise' mantras of the Washington Consensus, subsequently exported beyond the developing world – with a mildly inclusive social agenda: a configuration that Nancy Fraser terms 'progressive neoliberalism'.[8] This appearance of populist parties and movements, coupled with the ideological differences that separate them, poses urgent questions for researchers, policymakers, and the general public. What explains their surge? Do they present a threat to liberal democracy?

Most academic and journalistic coverage views populism in a sceptical or openly hostile light. While scholars continue to disagree on a working definition of the term, leading accounts present populists negatively: as demagogues duping voters through mass psychology, as an embodiment of democratic excesses that threaten liberal societies, or as incomprehensible catastrophes that beset the citizenry. Consequently, leading researchers grapple with 'how best to deal with populists from a democratic perspective'.[9] If liberal democracy is to survive, the populist virus must be contained.

For me, the puzzle presents itself differently. I am first and foremost interested in the reasons why populist movements have risen to prominence at this particular juncture: that is, during the decade that followed the eruption and management – or mismanagement – of the 2008 economic crisis. Because of this, I consider that their advance may speak to social and economic issues that define the nature of our time, rather than simple political opportunism or skilful electoral tactics. The purpose of this book is to challenge leading accounts of populism, contextualise its rise, and identify the features of and processes within Western liberal democracies that have led to present circumstances. In so doing, my goal is to develop a political economy of populism: a theory of social change that links the rise of new parties and movements to the forces unleashed by economic transformations dating back to the 1970s.

I contend that the rise of populism is not a short-term phenomenon resulting from the sudden appearance of demagogic politicians, but a reflection of a deeper, societal response to growing economic inequality and austerity policies. Drawing on the work of Karl Polanyi, I frame populist parties as part of a 'double movement' that seeks to contain market logic and adapt it to the needs of societies imperilled by its advance. Following Ernesto Laclau and Chantal Mouffe, I view populism as a political logic based on the establishment of internal, agonistic frontiers – an *us* and a *them* – between 'the people' and political and economic elites, and the creation of bonds between different groups that face a common adversary. This logic is susceptible to becoming galvanised under specific social and economic circumstances, generating a populist *moment*. My focus is on left populist movements, which are frequently presented as equatable to their radical right counterparts in spite of immense programmatic and ideological differences. I argue that the former, far from presenting an existential threat to liberal democracy, offer effective alternatives to the processes and policies that have led to economic inequality, political instability, and the rise of the radical right.

None of this makes populist claims inherently inclusive or democratic. The populist logic can be harnessed to mobilise disenfranchised citizens against corrupt elites, but it can just as easily be deployed to inflict violence upon marginalised communities. Radical right populists construct 'the people' as hard-working patriots threatened from above – by cosmopolitan elites – and below – by immigrants and religious and/or racial minorities, as well as the advance of feminism and LGBT rights. Examples abound: from India's Narendra Modi, whose Hindu nationalism goes hand-in-hand with violent persecution of the country's Muslim community, to Jair Bolsonaro and Viktor Orbán, who have cemented their respective holds on Brazil and Hungary through fraught cultural wars waged on exclusionary terms. Against the essentialist narratives of the populist right, populists on the left draw a frontier based on material conditions: economic and political elites on one side, and an inclusively defined 'people' on the other: the 99 per cent versus the one per cent, in the slogan popularised by the Occupy Wall Street movement. Articulating this frontier, however, requires cooperation, solidarity, and the integration into a common project of heterogeneous societal groups, as well as a political style and rhetoric that makes these connections intuitive – no small challenge in an age of increasing social fragmentation.

That populists of all stripes adhere to an adversarial conception of politics tells us less about them than about the brand of politics they oppose – a decades-long consensus between the centre right and centre left, over which time the free market has become increasingly exalted as the optimal arbiter of social relations. We have come to associate this socio-economic model with liberal democracy, but it is a historically contingent arrangement, rooted in the demise of Keynesian economics during the 1970s, consolidated by the left's embrace of 'third way' politics – that is, a tacit acceptance of neoliberalism – and reinforced throughout the 1990s and early 2000s, becoming manifestly untenable – if nevertheless still applied – in the aftermath of the 2008 crash. The importance of this insight cannot be overstated. Accounts of the rise of populism that ignore its long-term socio-economic drivers do so at the expense of explanatory power.

Left populism in Spain and the US

This book examines how economic transformations led to the almost simultaneous appearance of left populist movements in two apparently very different political contexts: Spain and the US. In Spain, we saw the emergence of Podemos, which, in its first two years of existence – 2014 and 2015 – became the country's third-largest political force, winning more than 20 per cent of the popular vote and a similar proportion of parliamentary seats. While it has lost some of its original electoral strength, since January 2020 Podemos has been in government, a junior party to the centre-left Spanish Socialist Workers' Party (PSOE): an unprecedented alliance in Spain's recent democratic history. This government has put forward an agenda that remains within the bounds of traditional social democracy, but which aims to reverse the most damaging aspects of the past decade of economic crisis and austerity policies.[10]

In the US, we have seen the Bernie Sanders campaign, which in 2016 and 2020 blazed a trail of democratic socialism through the Democratic Party's presidential primaries, giving a platform to policies previously well outside the US political mainstream, such as universal healthcare, free public university tuition, and far-reaching reform of the US financial system. Between those electoral tests, the campaign developed into a movement that encompasses a wide range of political actors besides Sanders himself.

While both movements can be viewed as populist, neither espouses the authoritarian and exclusionary agenda associated with radical-right populism. This makes their trajectory particularly useful for highlighting the limitations of the dominant discourse on the subject, which tends to collapse the differences between left and radical right populists, presenting them as equally undesirable.

Why Spain and the US? Recent years have witnessed the appearance of left parties and movements elsewhere: Jean-Luc Mélenchon's France Insoumise, the British Labour Party under

Jeremy Corbyn's leadership, and Greece's Syriza, to name a few. Moreover, the pairing may seem mismatched, with little in common between the two countries. One is a presidential democracy of continental proportions, the other a parliamentary monarchy in Europe's southern semi-periphery. The US is considered one of the world's oldest democracies; Spain's status as a 'paradigmatic' democracy, to use Juan Linz's expression, dates back to the 1975-1982 transition that transformed the country into the poster child of third-wave democratisation.[11] The US has a unique two-party system, with Republicans and Democrats retaining a considerable degree of ideological diversity within their ranks; Spanish parties, like most in Western Europe, are centralised and regimented, with powerful formal bureaucracies and party executives. Thus Sanders, while not a registered Democrat, was able to compete in the party's primaries; Podemos, by contrast, is an independent party that competes against both the right and the PSOE.

These differences are precisely what make the comparison useful. In spite of them, both countries have experienced unprecedented and widely unexpected populist upsurges – from both the left and radical right – in recent years. Using John Stuart Mill's method of agreement, or a 'most different systems' model, as it is known in comparative political science, we can select cases with different background characteristics that nevertheless share one central feature – in this case, the appearance and electoral success of left populists. Comparing otherwise dissimilar cases allows us to ask: what is the common thread? While immediate responsibility for Spain and America's populist 'explosions', as the journalist John Judis calls them, can be placed at the feet of the 2008 financial meltdown, I argue that both developments are impossible to understand without a long-term analysis of political and socio-economic trends dating back to the late 1970s.[12]

Using Mill's method of agreement should enable the differences between cases to strengthen the comparison's explanatory power. It points to the possibility that the mechanism explored and detailed in these pages could be at work in a wide range of intermediate cases; countries that have also experienced political volatility and the emergence of populist forces. France – like Spain, a Eurozone member enforcing unpopular economic reforms; like the US, a presidential democracy – and the United Kingdom – a parliamentary monarchy, but one that retains control over its monetary policy – are cases in point. I stress, however, that the theoretical framework offered in the following pages was conceived as what academics term a middle-range theory: useful for understanding the relationship between political economy and populism in a wide variety of Western European and North American cases, but not designed for application in all regions with populist parties, for example Latin America, Eastern Europe, or South Asia, whose cultural, political, and historical particularities place them beyond the scope of my work.

Given the differences between the political and institutional architectures of Spain and the US, it should come as no surprise that the populist explosion was channelled differently in each. The US witnessed the appearance of anti-system candidates on both the radical right and left, the electoral victory of the former, and the development of a new, populist left at both a grassroots and institutional level during Donald Trump's presidency. In Spain it was left populists who initially monopolised political discontent, but their electoral stagnation from 2016 onwards, coupled with the outbreak of an unresolved constitutional crisis in 2017, led to the appearance and strengthening of the radical right from then onwards. But if the US's bipartisan structures harnessed the populist upsurge along party lines, Spain's two-party system was shattered by it, giving way to a multiparty system. In the US in 2016, Donald Trump defeated Hillary Clinton, the erstwhile favourite for the presidency. In Spain, containment of the populist challenge cemented the country's political establishment and led to a brief period of cooperation between parties of the centre right and centre left, from October 2016 to May 2017.

Containment, internal divisions, and an accumulation of unmet political challenges blunted Podemos' rise and eventually transformed it into a more traditional leftist party, currently hovering around 14 per cent of the vote: half as much as that of the socialists it once sought to eclipse as Spain's leading progressive force. From 2018 onwards, however, the appearance of the radical right and internal changes within the PSOE forced the centre left to reconsider its position and opt for an alliance with Podemos.

Differing trajectories also reflect the institutional and

organisational choices made by each actor. Early on, Podemos coalesced as a tightly run, top-down party geared for electoral competition, placing great emphasis on tactical manoeuvring against its adversaries and developing innovative discourses that allowed it to dominate the news cycle and highlight contrasts with traditional Spanish parties. Initially, this strategy yielded impressive electoral results, although these were insufficient for the party to overtake either the PSOE or the centre-right PP (People's Party). Once the initial enthusiasm generated by Podemos' rise subsided, however, lack of organisational strength led the party to underperform against the PP and PSOE, which could rely on more ingrained voter loyalties and established networks and infrastructure for electoral competition. The Sanders campaign, to a certain extent, followed the opposite strategy: while its discursive commitment to left populism was not as explicit, it placed great emphasis on building a popular movement behind the Vermont senator's candidacy. This pathway did not yield immediate benefits in 2016, when Sanders, in spite of an unexpectedly strong performance, failed to wrest the Democratic nomination from Clinton. In 2020, the impressive groundwork laid by the earlier campaign was still insufficient to beat the Democratic frontrunner, Joe Biden. This time, Sanders' discursive strategy – in particular, his unwillingness to confront his main rivals' flaws in a straightforward, agonistic manner – critically undermined his 2020 bid.

As a Spaniard living alternately in Spain and the US between 2010 and 2017, I had the chance to experience first-hand the left populist upsurge in both countries, through print, online, radio, and television coverage, as well as interviews with politicians, conversations with activists, and direct involvement in party events, policy and campaigns. In Spain, I participated in the *indignados* movement in May 2011, and joined Podemos in 2014. Between then and 2018 I enjoyed an advisory role in the party's international affairs team, providing foreign policy analysis, outreach to US progressive organisations, and occasional edits to party manifestos and legislative proposals. While living in Boston in 2016, I canvassed and phone banked for Sanders' campaign.

The scope of this book goes well beyond my personal involvement in activism with Podemos and the Sanders movement study, however. This book is concerned with the origins, appearance and broad development of these two movements, not the particularities of their policy platforms. As I have hopefully made clear by now, sympathy for left populism is not at odds with acknowledgement that the populist logic, if monopolised by the radical right – or, in fairness, by opportunists on any part of the political spectrum – poses a considerable threat to political pluralism.

Structure, terms, layout, disclaimers

The argument of this book is that the rise of anti-systemic move-ments across the US and Europe can be understood as a reaction to market forces that detach the economy from vital social needs and structures. While left populist movements have appeared in Spain and the US within the past decade, the circumstances that led to their rise should be traced to the past four decades. Drawing on Paul Pierson's meteorological analogies, populism has often been characterised as a tornado: a destructive event with immediate causes and outcomes. I will argue instead that the present trans-formation of Western politics is best understood as resulting from an earthquake. An earthquake has a short time horizon of outcome but a long time horizon of cause, in which socio-economic forces act as tectonic plates.[13]

This book uses the term 'neoliberalism' to denote these forces. While this word has been subjected to considerable conceptual stretching, I follow Cornel Ban in viewing it as:

A set of historically contingent and ideologically hybrid economic ideas and policy regimes derived from specific theo-ries whose distinctive and shared goals are the following: make economic policies have credibility with financial markets, ensure trade and financial openness, safeguard internal and external competitiveness.[14]

An important insight of Ban's for the purpose of this book is that neoliberalism is an ideology with global reach but local thrust, and in the transition from the former to the latter it develops along different domestic economic doctrines and policy choices – a process he refers to as 'grafting'. Therefore, just as there exists an immense volume of academic literature on varieties of capitalism, neoliberalism can be seen as adapting to different countries and contexts. Ban identifies more and less accommodative local translations of neoliberalism, but establishes a litmus test in their common resort to deregulation, spending cuts, and internal devaluation (that is, wage cuts) as default policy tools in the face of economic downturns or crises. The following pages refer to these measures simply as austerity policies.

To return to the earthquake analogy: socio-economic dynamics throughout the past decades have pushed Western societies into precarious terrain, perennially rocked by economic shocks (and, increasingly, by the growing threat of climate crisis). The ideal option would be to push beyond neoliberalism, but this is not a journey that middle-sized countries like Spain can unilaterally embark upon. (The case might be different for the US, which retains an immense economy, its own monetary policy, and a dominant position in the international arena.) Instead, the focus must be on taking preventive measures to minimise the damage caused by these rumblings. As we will see, however, neither Spain nor the US put in place the shock absorbers and countermeasures necessary to shield their societies from the damage unleashed by the 2008 crisis, which compounded three decades of neoliberal drift. For the most part they did the exact opposite, developing growth models that were built on fragile foundations and, once these came crashing down, doubling down on the failed policies of the past. As the 2020 crisis brought about by the Covid-19 virus pandemic makes patently clear, these models are equally brittle in the face of unexpected exogenous shocks. What remains to be seen at the time of writing is whether a second harrowing experience of this sort will lead to the same flawed responses that the 2008 crash did.

To assess the relationship between socio-economic patterns and political discontent, the book returns to the late 1970s to identify critical junctures that point toward the eventual rise of populist forces in Spain and the US. These junctures in Spain were the country's 1975-1982 transition to democracy, which consolidated an economic model that Ban defines as 'embedded neoliberalism', and the signing of the 1992 Maastricht Treaty, which outsourced monetary policy and locked in pro-cyclical macroeconomic governance, such that austerity policies became the default response to economic recessions.[15] In the US, the critical junctures were the economic paradigm shift introduced during the Carter-Reagan years and the Democratic Party's embrace of third-way politics – its neoliberal 'reinvention', to use the term coined by sociologist Stephanie L. Mudge – during Bill Clinton's presidency.[16] In both the US and Spain, the 2008 crisis acts as an intervening variable and the definitive critical juncture, accelerating political and economic processes that were already underway. By 2011, both countries were experiencing a spontaneous societal backlash against this trend: the Occupy Wall Street movement in America, and the 15-M or *indignados* in Spain.

Now is a good time to clarify some further terms used in the book. I employ the word 'liberalism' in its continental European usage – that is, to denote a philosophic doctrine of the enhancement of individual and market freedom – and will therefore refer to US 'liberals' as Democrats, progressives, or leftists, depending on their proximity to the political centre. I consider there to be a crucial distinction between what I view as liberalism's desirable elements – the commitment to individual freedom and civil liberties – and its problematic faith in market logic as a guarantor of social wellbeing. To avoid unnecessary confusion, I will simply refer to the former as 'pluralism' and the latter as 'liberalism'. In a similar way, I distinguish between figures such as Adam Smith, John Stuart Mill, Benjamin Constant, Isaiah Berlin, and John Rawls – to name a few liberals who grappled thoughtfully with the balance between individual liberty and social equity – and the market fundamentalism that contemporary libertarians inherit from Ludwig von Mises and Friedrich Hayek.[17]

As mentioned before, I follow Laclau and Mouffe's definition of 'populism', which I consider more ductile and cogent than those of other leading authors in the field. I refer to Podemos and the Sanders movement as 'left' populists because their agenda, while more ambitious than that of contemporary centre-left parties, is nevertheless reformist and not vastly different from that of a Western European social-democratic party in the early 1970s. Following Mouffe, I view 'radical social democracy' as an adequate way to describe their orientation, even when the behaviour of actually existing social democratic parties can make the term appear an oxymoron.[18] In a similar spirit, *Jacobin* magazine editor-in-chief Bhaskar Sunkara views Sanders as a vehicle to implement an agenda of 'radical reforms' that can push toward and beyond the horizon of social democracy.[19] The challenge, as he sees it, is 'imagining a social democracy that doesn't just try to reshape capitalism in the interests of workers but seeks to permanently restructure economic relations'.[20]

I believe that these goals are achievable within the framework of liberal democracy. The amenability of left populists to liberal democracy distinguishes them from their reactionary counterparts in countries such as Hungary, Poland, and the US, who view the establishment of illiberal regimes as a constitutive element of their agenda.[21] Nevertheless, I draw back from defining these parties and movements as extreme right or neo-fascist. While they often count the latter among their sympathisers and members, and labelling them 'fascist' is common among progressives, I think this choice obfuscates more than it illuminates, and misleads us into viewing events in the twenty-first century through the lens of the 1930s.[22] Following Guillermo Fernández Vázquez, a leading researcher on the subject, I prefer to use the term 'radical right', which underscores the extremist nature of this agenda but helps frame its existence as a political problem rather than a moral catastrophe.[23]

The word 'socialist' can also be a misleading one, depending which side of the Atlantic Ocean one writes from. In Spain, the Spanish Socialist Workers' Party (PSOE) is not an insurgent force but the country's leading centre-left party, occasionally more concerned with checking Podemos' rise than with opposing the right. US socialists, in contrast, present a left challenge to the Democratic Party and resemble Podemos. The word's meaning will therefore vary depending on the national context in which I employ it. Last but not least, I use a series of terms that are common in the Polanyian tradition, which views economic dynamics as traditionally woven into – that is, 'embedded in' – social institutions and processes. Attempts to fully adopt market logics can fray these bonds, eventually generating a societal response – a 'countermovement', 'double movement', or 'pendulum swing' – that renders the fully autonomous – i.e., 'disembedded' – market society a 'stark' and unreachable utopia.

This book began life as an academic project. I have a background in international relations and political communication, and in 2019 I began to research the interplay between changing party systems and macroeconomic regimes, as a doctoral candidate in the Jean Monnet Centre of Excellence in the New Political Economy of Europe, at University College Dublin. This book is neither an academic thesis nor a political intervention, however, but something broader: an attempt to offer insights for theorists and practitioners of left populism, and anyone else concerned with the current predicament of progressive politics.

A final note on the timing of this book, and its relationship to the hopes and prospects of left populist forces in Spain, the US, and beyond. When I first embarked upon this project, in mid 2015, Podemos seemed poised to prove its populist hypothesis and become the leading progressive force in Spanish politics. The Sanders campaign, at the time in its infancy, faced an uphill and seemingly unwinnable battle against the Democratic Party establishment. But it performed unexpectedly well and seemed exceptionally poised to exploit this position as the 2020 primaries loomed closer.

Since then, both have suffered considerable pushback. After its narrow 2016 defeat against the Clinton machine, Sanders and the movement he inspired became increasingly relevant actors in US politics, such that their demands became not just those of the Vermont senator but of an increasingly wide array of activists and politicians: some pushing from his left, such as the Democratic Socialists of America (DSA), or Minnesota congresswoman Ilhan Omar; others more moderate, such as Massachusetts senator Elizabeth Warren. Ultimately, however, his 2020 bid came undone in the face of unwavering opposition from the Democratic Party apparatus, mainstream media, and even a significant part of the centre left – plus the outbreak of the Covid-19 crisis, which effectively made the ongoing contest between Sanders and Biden unviable.

Podemos, following an inspiring performance in its first two years of existence, stagnated from mid 2016 onwards. Facing a hostile political establishment and allowing intraparty fights to spiral out of control, the party witnessed its original, highly innovative style degrade and lose much of its staying power. The 2019 elections – national in April and November, municipal and regional in May – delivered steep losses across the party's key bases of support, both regional – Madrid, Catalonia, and the Basque Country – and demographic – younger voters, culture-sector professionals, and disgruntled centre-left voters. Coupled with the emergence of the radical-right party Vox, these results effectively pushed Spain back toward the traditional axis of left-right competition, now in multi-party rather than two-party format, but with Podemos pigeonholed as the junior partner of a PSOE with a recurrent inclination to swerve toward the centre.

In the course of writing this book, what began as a perhaps somewhat naïve celebration of left populism's virtues has become a more critical review, examining populism's limits and the tactical and strategic mistakes made by Podemos and the Bernie Sanders campaigns. In presenting such a review, my aim is simply to offer a set of pointers that may prove helpful beyond Spain and the US. The challenges that reversed Podemos and Sanders' fortunes are likely to beset other parties and movements fighting for lasting change in a more inclusive and just direction. Eric Hobsbawm once observed that 'nothing sharpens the historian's mind like defeat'.[24] My hope is that his insight holds true in the fight for an emancipatory politics in the twenty-first century, as the needs of our societies remain unmet, and their resolution cannot be postponed for much longer.

The first chapter of left populism's insurgency has come to a close. This moment offers an opportune vantage point from which to not only reflect on the movement's limitations, but also to acknowledge what have been often dramatic and widely unforeseen advances. In the face of a new socio-economic crisis, possibly greater than its immediate predecessor, the legacy of these movements – discursive as well as institutional, because the left is now in a stronger position than it was in 2008 – may be to ensure that, instead of a re-enactment of previous failures, the response is a move towards a more fair and just socio-economic arrangement.

The book is divided into three sections, each three chapters long. The first section, 'Landscapes', outlines the framework I use to offer a political economy of populism. Chapter One surveys mainstream thought, both academic and journalistic, on the subject of populism. It identifies limitations in the dominant approaches taken in the field, and suggests instead that populism is a political logic that can be activated at particular historical and political junctures – a populist 'moment', in Laclau and Mouffe's terminology. Chapter Two unpacks Karl Polanyi's work, laying out a framework for making sense of the rise of populism in increasingly disembedded economies. As I will argue, Polanyi's leading work, *The Great Transformation* – first published in 1944 – offers a powerful theoretical and practical resource for understanding the rise of populism, which draws attention to long-term processes that leading scholars in the field have failed to adequately recognise.[25] This chapter also presents this theoretical framework through a more intuitive metaphor to understand present transformations in Western political landscapes: that of an earthquake.

The next section, 'Faultlines', analyses the structural conditions that preceded the appearance of populist parties and movements. Chapter Three offers an account of the global turn to the markets that took place in the 1970s, examining the case of British Conservative Prime Minister Margaret Thatcher as a paradigmatic example of this transition. Chapters Four and Five outline the local translations of global neoliberalism in Spain and the US, respectively. In Spain, compensatory measures were developed to cushion the blows delivered to the 'losers of globalisation', while in the US a disciplinary variant of neoliberalism prevailed. This section moves from a theoretical to an empirical level of analysis, but remains centred on macro-structural processes.

The final section, 'Landslides', zooms in to describe the abrupt cessation of business-as-usual politics in Spain (Chapter Six) and the US (Chapter Seven) following the 2008 financial crisis. It examines the discursive and electoral strategies that Podemos and the Bernie Sanders movement deployed at this juncture to achieve prominence. I focus on their attempts to electorally harness a populist moment through discursive constructions of 'the people', their tracing of agonistic frontiers through identifying adversaries within their societies, and the development of 'bonds of equivalence' between the different social groups they sought to rally. I also examine the weak links in their strategies that kept them back from their goals – in Sanders's case, winning the Democratic presidential nomination; in Podemos', becoming the leading political actor in a process of national political and economic transformation. In the Conclusion, I trace back through the story of these two populisms to pull out clues as to the conditions and choices that can benefit or smother left populist projects.

Notes

1. Herodotus, quoted in Marco d'Eramo, 'Populism and the new oligarchy', *New Left Review* 82, July-August 2013, p9.
2. William Shakespeare, *Coriolanus*, Act III, Scene I.
3. James Traub, 'It's time for the elites to rise up against the ignorant masses', *Foreign Policy*, 28 June 2016.
4. Edward Luce, 'The siege of Western liberalism', *Financial Times*, 5 May 2017; David Frum and Edward Luce, '"Western liberalism is under siege"' *Vox* Conversations, 7 June 2017; Roger Cohen, 'The death of liberalism', *New York Times*, 14 April 2016.
5. José Ortega y Gasset, *La rebelión de las masas*, Espasa: Barcelona, 1999.
6. For an example of this style, see Anne Applebaum's writing in the *Washington Post*. See also Rubén Amón, 'Le Pen y Mélechon: extremadamente iguales', *El País*, 20 April 2017; José Ignacio Torreblanca, 'El eje de la soberanía', *El País*, 30 January 2015.
7. Perry Anderson, 'The centre can hold', *New Left Review* 105, May/June 2017, p20.
8. Nancy Fraser, 'The end of progressive neoliberalism', *Dissent*, 2 January 2017; see also Suresh Naidu, Dani Rodrik and Gabriel Zucman, 'Economics after neoliberalism', *Boston Review*, 15 February 2019.
9. Cas Mudde and Cristóbal Rovira Kaltwasser (eds), *Populism in Europe and the Americas: Threat or Corrective to Democracy?* Cambridge University Press: Cambridge, MA, 2012, p214; Jan-Werner Müller makes a nearly identical point in his book *What is Populism?* University of Pennsylvania Press: Philadelphia, 2016.
10. See 'El acuerdo de PSOE-Unidas Podemos para un gobierno de coalición, íntegro', *El País*, 31 December 2019.
11. See Juan J. Linz and Alfred C. Stepan, *Problems of Democratic Transition and Consolidation: Southern Europe, South America, and Post-communist Europe*, Johns Hopkins University Press, Baltimore, 1996.
12. John Judis, *The Populist Explosion: How the Great Recession Transformed European and American Politics*, Columbia Global Reports: New York, 2016.
13. Paul Pierson, *Politics in Time: History, Institutions, and Social Analysis*, Princeton University Press: New Haven, NJ, 2004, pp79-83.

14. Cornel Ban, *Ruling Ideas: How Global Neoliberalism Goes Local*, Oxford University Press: Oxford, 2016, p10.
15. *Ibid.*, p33; see also Ban, 'El neoliberalismo integrado y la crisis actual', *Política Exterior*, No. 186, November-December 2018, pp66-78.
16. Stephanie L. Mudge, *Leftism Reinvented: Western Parties from Socialism to Neoliberalism*, Harvard University Press: Cambridge, MA, 2018.
17. See Corey Robin, 'Uninstalling Hayek', *Boston Review*, 3 March 2019.
18. Chantal Mouffe, *For a Left Populism*, Verso: New York, 2018.
19. Cora Lewis, 'The kids are all left', *BuzzFeed*, 27 March 2016.
20. Bhaskar Sunkara, 'The world after capitalism', *Foreign Policy*, 15 January 2020
21. On this subject, see for example Ivan Krastev, 'Eastern Europe's illiberal revolution', *Foreign Affairs*, Vol. 97, No. 3, May-June 2018, pp49-59.
22. For a worthwhile reflection on this subject, see Branko Milanovic, 'This time is different', www.socialeurope.eu/, 17 June 2019.
23. Guillermo Fernández Vázquez, 'Dos estrategias para la extrema derecha', *Política Exterior*, No. 188, March-April 2019, pp68-75.
24. Quoted in Robin, 'Eric Hobsbawm, the communist who explained history', *New Yorker*, 9 May 2019.
25. Karl Polanyi, *The Great Transformation: The Political and Economic Origins of Our Time*, Beacon Press: Boston, MA, 2001 [1944].

Populism and its Discontents

'When *I* use a word', Humpty Dumpty said, in rather a scornful tone, 'it means just what I choose it to mean – neither more nor less'.

'The question is', said Alice, 'whether you *can* make words mean so many different things'.

'The question is', said Humpty Dumpty, 'which is to be master – that's all'.[1]

– Lewis Carroll

It would be easier to list what has *not* been defined as populist. At the same time, as we shall see, the social category from which it has been derived historically, 'the people', has all but vanished from political discourse.[2]

– Marco d'Eramo

To each his own definition of populism, according to the academic axe he grinds.[3]

– Peter Wiles

20 May 1910. The opening lines of Barbara Tuchman's *August 1914* evoke the high tide of Europe's *belle epoque*, when nine European kings gathered in London to head an immense diplomatic delegation at the funeral of Edward VII of England.

In scarlet and blue and green and purple, three by three the sovereigns rode through the palace gates, with plumed helmets, gold braid, crimson sashes, and jewelled orders flashing in the sun. After them came five heirs apparent, forty more imperial or royal highnesses, seven queens – four dowager and three regnant – and a scattering of special ambassadors from uncrowned countries. Together they represented seventy nations in the greatest assemblage of royalty and rank ever gathered in one place and, of its kind, the last. The muffled tongue of Big Ben tolled nine by the clock as the cortège left the palace but on history's clock it was sunset, and the sun of the old world was setting in a dying blaze of splendour never to be seen again.[4]

As the rest of Tuchman's masterpiece about the outbreak of World War I makes clear, that world shattered abruptly in the summer of 1914. Writing thirty years later, Karl Polanyi would open *The Great Transformation* with a blunt summary of what the following decades ushered in: 'Nineteenth-century civilisation has collapsed'.[5]

The atmosphere of Tuchman's parade echoed faintly in the morning of 1st September 2018. The occasion was John McCain's memorial service, held at Washington DC's National Cathedral. The lack of European royalty was made up for by the full display of the US political establishment: two former presidents – George W. Bush and Barack Obama – three former vice presidents – Al Gore, Dick Cheney, and Joe Biden – the Senate's majority and minority leaders, Bill and Hillary Clinton, Alan Greenspan, and an everlasting Henry Kissinger, among many others, gathered to bid farewell to the Republican senator. All of them hailed McCain as an elder statesman above the everyday fray of politics. 'When all was said and done,' Obama proclaimed of his 2008 presidential rival, 'we never doubted we were on the same team'. Bush, who ran a smear campaign against McCain in the 2000 Republican primaries – spreading rumours that the one of the senator's daughters was the product of an illicit relationship – offered affectionate words regarding their former rivalry: 'In recent years, we sometimes talked of that intense period like football players, remembering a big game. In the process, rivalry melted away.'[6] The following days witnessed an avalanche of eulogies for McCain, with whose passing, it seems, went an entire way of conducting politics: more honest and less histrionic, not bound by the narrow ties of partisan affiliation or tribal identities.

One absence from the memorial service, however, eclipsed all the attendees. Donald Trump, who two years earlier won the Republican primaries after systematically humiliating McCain, was not invited to the event. The late senator's true rival, it was repeatedly implied, was none other than the US president.

Now as in 1910, it seems that a world is dying as another one is born. This is the anxious conclusion drawn by a host of journalists, academics, and politicians, many of whom rush to defend the world that McCain seemingly represented – the so-called liberal order – from the populist challenge embodied by Trump. Like the attendees at the memorial, however, they often lack self-awareness. The new always arises from the old; Trump is not a clean break with recent history but a by-product of decades of rightward drift in American national – and particularly Republican – politics. The ideological roots of his rivalry with McCain become less clear when one considers that the two men aligned 83 per cent of the time on their support for actual legislative proposals.[7]

What, then, is this populist insurgency? Does it represent a break with the past? An unprecedented threat to liberal democracy? In the following pages I will review the dominant definitions of populism and explanations for the apparent crisis of liberal democracy, explain why I believe they fail to engage the problem at hand, and offer some ideas for a more fruitful approach. This chapter does not, however, pretend to offer a full review of existing scholarship on populism, a field that is growing rapidly and somewhat haphazardly.

I begin by surveying the history of the term and the conceptual dead ends to which it has sometimes led – notably, the tendency to view populism as a pathology or natural catastrophe, and to present its supporters as misled dupes. I offer a critical overview of prominent accounts, which often present an irreconcilable and unprecedented clash between populism and liberal democracy, and contrast these with the more cogent theory of populism developed by Ernesto Laclau and Chantal Mouffe. My contention is that mainstream accounts pay insufficient attention to two themes key to explaining the rise of populist parties: the importance of time in politics, and the longue durée of socio-economic processes and crises. This means that these accounts fail to situate either left or, for that matter, right populism in historical context. In Chapter Two,

I begin to lay out an alternative approach, through a discussion of earthquake metaphors, inspired by Paul Pierson's *Politics in Time*,[8] and the links between Laclau and Mouffe's definition of populism and Polanyi's writing on political economy.

Popular pathologies, mistaken metaphors

For half a century, 'populism' has been a perennial source of distress in scholarly circles. Ghita Ionescu and Ernst Gellner opened their 1969 seminal volume on the subject warning that '[a] spectre haunts the world: populism'. A 'populist zeitgeist' had spread across the globe in 2004, according to populism scholar Cas Mudde. Three years later, another academic, Ivan Krastev, announced the dawn of an 'age of populism'. Closer to the present, Spanish political scientist José Ignacio Torreblanca stated that Italy's 2016 constitutional referendum, which witnessed the rejection of centrist Prime Minister Matteo Renzi's proposal for a more centralised executive, constituted 'the defeat of one kind of populism (institutional) at the hands of another', represented by both the centre-right Silvio Berlusconi and the anti-system Five Star Movement.[9] Observers might wonder where the perils of populism reside if it turns out that we have been breathing its fumes for decades without even knowing it.

Recurrent angst notwithstanding, this time is different. The decade following the 2008 financial crisis witnessed a wave of new political forces making unprecedented electoral gains across the European Union and the United States. Left parties such as Podemos, France Insoumise, and Syriza in Greece, and radical right ones such as Lega Nord in Italy and Alternative for Germany, have variously been described as protest, anti-system, anti-establishment, or populist parties. For the sake of simplicity, and because it is the most widely used term among these, I will cleave to the last of these terms. The phenomenon must also be distinguished from electoral volatility or political fragmentation, as some new challenger parties, such as Ciudadanos in Spain, are not particularly radical or transformative. Nevertheless, the current rise of populism is not simply a case of observers crying wolf.

Part of the problem in attempting to understand this trend lies in the fact that 'populism' remains a notoriously slippery concept. Half a century after the 1967 London School of Economics (LSE) conference that laid the groundwork for research on the subject – and famously failed to provide a working definition of the term – scholars continue to debate what is it that they study in the first place. It is generally agreed that modern-day populism originates in the nineteenth century, with the People's Party in the US and Russia's Narodniks: progressive movements linked to rural constituencies and, especially in the former case, heterodox economic policies such as a rejection of the nineteenth-century Gold Standard. Beyond that, to paraphrase a US Supreme Court Justice's famous observation on pornography, most researchers seem to know populism 'when they see it'.[10]

Lack of clarity has often gone hand in hand with normative hostility. In a 2013 *New Left Review* essay, Marco d'Eramo argued that the LSE's research agenda established from the start 'a new paradigm of political orthodoxy ... one of whose capstones, together with "totalitarianism", was the term "the people", and it was definitively consolidated in the theory of the "opposite extremes"'. The theoretical framework outlined at the LSE was influenced by Richard Hofstadter's re-interpretation of the US populist tradition in light of the Cold War and the perceived threat of communism. This framework was now being deployed to render 'populism "fascist" and fascism "populist"'. As a result, the term is never a self-definition:

> In its most brutal form, 'populist' is simply an insult; in a more cultivated form, a term of disparagement. But if no one defines themselves as populist, then the term populism defines those who use it rather than those who are branded with it.[11]

The assumption that popular passions are dangerous, of course, precedes Hofstadter and the LSE conference. And it frequently seeps into depictions of the political phenomenon of populism. Going back at least to the beginning of the modern era, popular leaders have often been analysed through the lens of public psychology. The French Revolution and the Paris Commune were sites of emergence of 'the people' as a collective subject in history. This development prompted a hostile and condescending reaction from nineteenth-century crowd theorists: in the work of Gustave Le

Bon, Hippolyte Taine, and Cesare Lombroso, 'the masses' appear as easily befuddled, prone to criminal behaviour, or even vulnerable to collective hypnosis.[12]

Plus ça change, plus c'est la même chose. Social science today continues to draw on psychological accounts of populism. Writing on the website of the World Economic Forum, Molly Crockett, a neuroscientist and experimental psychologist, explains that 'social emotions like anger, envy, and spite...outweigh economic self-interest' and tap into 'the same brain areas that play a role in addiction'. Populist messaging, she claims, 'has been very effective at channelling retributive impulses into votes'.[13] On progressive-leaning website *Vox* – not to be confused with the Spanish radical right party of the same name – Amanda Taub distinguishes Trump voters by their psychological profiles, which cause them 'to express much deeper fear than the rest of the electorate, to seek the imposition of order where they perceive dangerous change, and to defeat those fears with force'.[14] Her description is reminiscent of Marx's writing on Napoleon III, a Trumpian character, and the French peasants who constituted his political base. Marx famously observed that these small landholders, working in alienating conditions and isolated rural environments reminiscent of Trump's voting base,

> cannot represent themselves, they must be represented. Their representative must at the same time appear as their master, as an authority over them, as an unlimited governmental power which protects them against the other classes and sends them rain and sunshine from above. The political influence of the small peasants, therefore, finds its final expression in the executive power subordinating society to itself.[15]

Missing from Taub's account, however, is the analytical depth that endowed *The Eighteenth Brumaire of Louis Napoleon* with lasting value. She suggests, for example, that '[Trump's] followers seem to have come out of nowhere', when in fact they constitute the traditional voting base of the Republican Party.[16] Neither is the text particularly concerned with understanding the social or moral reasoning behind their political impulses, as other authors – such as the sociologist Arlie Hochschild, in her poignant portrayal of poor Trump voters in rural Louisiana – have sought to do.[17]

Another problem with this approach is that defining something as pathological only makes sense in relation to what is assumed to be normal. What, then, is the present benchmark for normality? Without this basic grounding, many psychological explanations for the rise of populism become little more than shallow reiterations of earlier theories of totalitarianism and mass psychology. As Jan-Werner Müller notes, such diagnoses also 'end up confirming [populist's voters'] view of liberal elites as being not just deeply condescending but also constitutively unable to live up to their own democratic ideals by failing to take ordinary people at their word'.[18] To echo Charles Tilly's warning, social scientists risk becoming 'the bearers of nineteenth-century folk wisdom' if they refuse to approach the subject with more empathy, a broader analytical lens, or a combination of both.[19] Psychologising accounts, which often conflate populism and demagoguery, are at best incomplete.

Examples of other counterproductive approaches abound. One of them is attempting to understand populism quantitatively. A case in point is *The Guardian*'s project on 'The new populism', which keeps its readers updated, through an array of sleek graphs and charts, on such questions as 'How to spot a populist', 'The rise and rise of populist rhetoric', and how different leaders 'compare' on a populist chart. (Hugo Chávez scores a 1.9 out of 2, almost four times as much as Jair Bolsonaro. Tony Blair, a guest in the project's speaker series, receives a mere 0.1; Angela Merkel, a 0.) 'How populist are you?' asks an elaborately graded quiz that places Barack Obama and Emmanuel Macron to the left of Bolivia's coup-ousted Evo Morales. Another disquieting nugget, conveyed through another animated chart: 'More than 2bn people in the 40 countries studied now have a leader whose speeches are populist.'[20]

Ranking political processes that unfold at different points in time, in regions with widely different characteristics across a single benchmark is a better recipe for entertainment than analysis. I do not mean to dismiss the entirety of the project nor all quantitative studies of populism, many of which have yielded important insights. But as most scholars conducting them know, analysis on this level requires the sort of contextual and methodological caveats that are noticeably absent from *The Guardian*'s project.

Mainstream media discourses also depict the breakdown of established politics through misleading metaphors. Often, populism is depicted as an epidemic or a virus, spreading internationally and infecting the body politic with demagoguery and polarisation.[21] In France it is common to speak of a 'cordon sanitaire' – quarantines enforced by parties of the left, centre, and centre right to isolate radical-right forces. Regardless of the strategy's merits, the wider tendency to characterise populism as an epidemic presents a series of problems. It can lead to the conclusion that the problem is exogenous: a virus entering the body politic from outside. This is, for example, the unstated reasoning behind most accusations of Russian meddling in the 2016 US elections: 'fake news' wreaked havoc in the minds of 'low-information' voters and generated an unpleasant political outcome that in no way represents what the US truly stands for. Leading Spanish newspapers took a similarly alarmist tone in the aftermath of the 2017 constitutional crisis that followed the Catalan government's unilateral bid for independence. In both cases, a failure on the part of domestic elites to effectively handle a politically explosive situation was deflected, and responsibility for the problem placed at the door of the Kremlin. To be clear, I am not arguing that illicit foreign influence in democratic elections is irrelevant. Moscow's attempts to interfere in US and European politics are well documented, if often incompetent. The point is that the existence of such initiatives, while concerning, should not be used as an excuse to avoid self-criticism.[22] One would hope the aftermath of the 2020 coronavirus outbreak brings a more restrained approach to virus analogies, but the habit is likely to get worse before it gets better.

Another set of mistaken metaphors is tidal. Populism is described as a rising tide or a tsunami about to crash down on the heads of hapless citizens. When populist gains fail to materialise, it means that their 'tide' is not rising anymore.[23] It is easy to see why this metaphor has gained currency: like the previous one, it expresses a complex social phenomenon as an intuitive image. But it also presents contingent social events as natural catastrophes, subject to forces beyond our control. Plagues and floods have a biblical ring to them: thinking of populism in these terms might lead us to imagine political events in terms of some cosmic punishment for debauched societal ways. Most of the problems that we face today result from political choices taken over the past four decades, not the wrath of some vindictive god. They are not inevitable, and their political consequences are not preordained.

Liberal democracy under threat

So much for journalistic clichés. Does current scholarship do better? Recent years have witnessed important advances from researchers attempting to find common, non-normative definitions of populism. Scholars are coalescing around an 'ideational' approach that views populism as a strategy or ideology anchored around people-centrism and anti-elitism.[24] The definition has the merit of being easily applicable and is far more useful than resorting to psychological explanations. But it has its own limitation: a failure to adequately recognise context. Associating the term 'populism' with a set of rhetorical and ideological devices can help us to identify the phenomenon, but does not explain what happens when seemingly non-populist parties adopt these devices, or why populism has emerged at this particular time in history.

To interrogate such approaches further, I will review the work of four leading voices in the field. While their positions differ, these thinkers share characteristics that justify a common critique. They are well-known academics recognised as public intellectuals, and they all offer broad definitions of the phenomenon that are used to conceptualise populism beyond a series of Western European cases. A guiding assumption in all their work is that liberal democracy and populism – in both its left and radical right variants – coexist uneasily. Taking the two to be irreconcilable, these theorists invariably find themselves defending 'the liberal order' against populist challengers. But a lack of contextual references often leaves them theorising in a historical vacuum.

Cas Mudde, a professor at the University of Georgia's School of Public International Affairs, is by far the least normative of the four, and his theory of populism has yielded several useful insights. In their influential 2012 book *Populism in Europe and the Americas,*

Mudde and Cristóbal Rovira Kaltwasser adopt a 'minimal' definition, and describe populism as:

> a thin-centred ideology that considers society to be ultimately separated into two homogeneous and antagonistic groups, 'the pure people' and 'the corrupt elite', and which argues that politics should be an expression of the *volonté general* (general will) of the people.[25]

Being 'thin-centred', populism can attach itself to the host body of a larger ideology like liberalism or socialism, or another 'thin' one, such as environmentalism and nationalism. In such cases, as Spanish political scientist Pablo Simón puts it, populism plays the part of the 'software' to the host ideology's 'hardware'.[26] Mudde and Kaltwasser argue that populism exploits 'moral (i.e. pure vs. corrupt) rather than ethnic, religious, or class cleavages'. Its direct opposites, therefore, are elitism and pluralism.[27] Mudde has also expounded his views across a wide array of media outlets, including writing extensively for the *Huffington Post* and *The Guardian*. His minimal definition has been widely adopted in both academia and journalism, as it provides a flexible and useful set of guidelines for assessing which parties and movements are 'populist'.

The problem is that the definition can be attached to almost any political phenomenon. More importantly, the notion of a 'thin-centred ideology' attached to a larger one raises questions about the nature of the attachment itself, which becomes central to understanding whether political parties are *intrinsically* populist, or whether they simply resort to populism for particular purposes. After all, most mainstream political parties make use of moralistic rhetoric and metonymy, attempting to present the wishes of a small part of the electorate as immensely popular. Are they thus populists for as long as they do so? When employing Mudde and Kaltwasser's definition outside the pages of their book, one discovers that it applies well beyond the spectrum of parties they consider populist.

A glance at actually existing cases – and at Mudde's journalistic, rather than his academic, writing – highlights the limitations of this approach. Neither the pre-Trump Republican Party nor Spain's main right-wing party, the PP, seem to be viewed by Mudde as 'populist'. What to make, then, of the Republican Party's recurrent moralising claims – skilfully portrayed by journalist Thomas Frank in *What's the Matter with Kansas?* – to represent true, hard-working Americans?[28] Do Spanish conservative politicians appeal to a 'pure people' when they depict their voters as 'well-meaning Spaniards' (*españoles de bien*)?[29] It might be argued that these parties are not populist because they do not proclaim their embodiment of 'the people' at every single rally or press briefing. But then neither does Syriza in Greece, which Mudde repeatedly identifies as intrinsically populist. Bernie Sanders, on the other hand, is no populist: his critique of the status quo is, Mudde says, 'institutional' and 'built around class interests', in a way that the Greek Coalition of the Radical Left's (aka Syriza) apparently is not.[30] Also populist was Occupy Wall Street, which espoused exactly the same slogan as Sanders (the 99 per cent vs the 1 per cent), but showed itself to be populist but focused excessively, in Mudde's view, on 'the morality of that division'.[31] The comparison, if anything, reveals a lack of familiarity with the subject at hand. Sanders occasionally describes himself as a populist and his campaigning has been based, per his own account, on the introduction of 'a radical concept of morality'.[32]

Seemingly distressed by the fact that the media plays fast and loose with 'the p-word' and perhaps aware that his own work contributes to this trend, Mudde has in recent years sought to offer some adjustments. 'We are thinking about populism in the wrong way', he admonished in an article published after the 2017 Dutch elections.[33] The problem, Mudde explained, is that 'we see too much and too little' of it – a predictable consequence, one might imagine, of living under the populist 'zeitgeist' he depicted back in 2004. 'Populism' went underreported in the Netherlands, even while political parties framed the contest as a choice between 'good' and 'bad' versions of it.[34] During the Brexit process and the 2016 US elections, however, it was overemphasised – in a column published after Trump's election, Mudde asserts that 2016 was 'just another presidential election'.[35] While his work seeks to avoid drawing distinctions on an ad hoc basis, and provides useful clues to understanding the relationship between populism and mainstream political ideologies, the picture that emerges from Mudde's reading is confused.

Princeton professor Jan-Werner Müller takes a darker view. In *What is Populism?* (2016), he describes the phenomenon as a 'particularly moralistic imagination of politics', that sets a pure, unified people 'against elites who are deemed corrupt or in some other way morally inferior'.[36] Populists are anti-pluralist because their claim to exclusive representation is distinctively moral. Once in power, they hijack the state, filling public institutions with friends and cronies, and engage in mass clientelism. Because they are 'fine with representation, as long as the right representatives represent the right people to make the right judgment', they tend eventually to suppress civil society.[37] Müller has developed these views in a number of journalistic articles, most of them published in the *London Review of Books* and *The Guardian*.

Borrowing from the Austrian legal theorist Hans Kelsen, Müller argues that the notion of a popular will, as constructed by populists, is a meta-political illusion. Populists are instead indebted to Kelsen's arch-rival, the German jurist and Nazi sympathiser Carl Schmitt, who famously theorised the 'friend-enemy' distinction as the fulcrum of politics. While drawing parallels between today's radical right parties and 1930s Europe is relatively common, Müller takes this reasoning a step further and reverses its linearity: he argues instead that fascism and national socialism 'need to be understood as populist movements'.[38] Perhaps his sharpest insight is that populism constitutes the reverse mirror image of technocracy, and its rise is a reaction to the technocratic drift of liberal democratic regimes:

> Technocracy claims that there is only one correct policy solution; populism claims there is only one authentic will of the people...For neither technocrats nor populists is there any need for democratic debate. In a sense, both are curiously apolitical.[39]

Unlike authors who bundle together all opposition to the status quo under the rubric of populism, Müller establishes a clear distinction between left and radical right anti-establishment parties in Europe, pointing out that Syriza and Podemos share very little in common with the French radical right. But he also argues that 'there can't be such a thing as left-wing populism by definition', because populism is concerned with moral claims rather than with policy content.[40] Bernie Sanders, he argues, is not a populist.[41] While Müller is right to point out that the policies and moral visions defended by left and radical-right populists diverge hugely, and while much of his analysis holds for radical-right populist movements – especially those in government – this assertion that left anti-establishment parties cannot be 'populist' flies in the face of statements from both Podemos leaders and their leading detractors, who have defined that party as progressive politically, and their guiding strategy as populist.[42] Müller's misconception stems from insufficient engagement with left theories of populism, and from a Eurocentric conceptualisation of the phenomenon – in Latin America, where populism has an older and richer history, it is more often than not linked to leftist politicians.

Many of the characteristics Müller views as populist are in fact core features of the political right more broadly. In *The Reactionary Mind*, political theorist Corey Robin argues persuasively that the impulse to simultaneously rally and demobilise 'the people'; regressive impulses driven by the sense of losing one's privilege; and even contempt toward the status quo, are features of right-wing thought in both its moderate and radical iterations.[43] Donald Trump's brand of populism, which pits supposedly victimised 'genuine' Americans against the political establishment and undeserving minorities, is heir to Richard Nixon's 'Southern strategy', subsequently fine-tuned by Ronald Reagan. Extolling the virtues of real, 'heartland' – to use Paul Taggart's term – Americans exploited by coastal elites is thoroughly ingrained in Republican discourse.[44] In Spain, the first party to explicitly define itself as 'populist' was the predecessor of the country's current leading party of the right, the PP – at the time effectively an offshoot of the Franco regime.[45] While Müller correctly views the traditional right as complicit in enabling populism, his decision to view the latter as an exceptional phenomenon linked almost exclusively to the radical right, rather than as a political logic than is prevalent across the party spectrum, blunts potentially useful insights.

The claim that those political actors anathemised as populists are unique in denying the legitimacy of their rivals also collapses under close scrutiny. It was mainstream Republicans who led visceral opposition to Barack Obama, urging him to 'learn to be an American' and abandon 'Kenyan, anti-colonial behaviour'.[46] The tendency to fall for conspiracy theories is universal, as shown by many Democrats' ongoing allegations that Trump is on the Kremlin's payroll and owes his 2016 victory to Russian disinformation campaigns, rather than to his rival's decision not to campaign in key swing states like Wisconsin, to cite one alternative explanation.[47] In Spain, after unexpectedly losing power in 2004, the PP joined right-wing media outlets in undermining José Luis Rodríguez Zapatero's centre-left government by suggesting that the PSOE was complicit in the Madrid bombings that killed close to 200 people and tilted the election results – mostly because the preceding government falsely claimed that Basque separatist terrorists, not Islamic extremists, were behind the attack.[48] The centre-right party Ciudadanos (Citizens), which used to brand itself as centrist, technocratic, and anti-populist, has repeatedly denounced the current prime minister, who initially won power through a no-confidence vote, as an illegitimate ruler supported by a 'gang' of political parties intent on subverting the Spanish constitution.[49] In increasingly polarised democracies, overblown rhetoric and hyperbolic accusations are the norm of mainstream political discourse, not an exclusive feature of populist parties and leaders.

Yascha Mounk – Associate Professor at Johns Hopkins School of Advanced International Studies, Contributing Editor at *The Atlantic*, Senior Fellow at the German Marshall Fund, and 'one of the world's leading experts on the crisis of liberal democracy and the rise of populism', per his own website – describes just such a scenario in his grandiosely titled 2018 book, *The People vs Democracy: Why Our Freedom is in Danger and How to Save It*. (The cover of the Spanish edition features two sheep, perhaps representing 'the people', staring blankly at the viewer).[50] Mounk begins by observing how, when Juan Linz and Alfred Stepan laid out their well-known theories on transitions to democracy and democratic consolidation, they assumed these processes to be irreversible in any relatively prosperous country. Today, however, 'democratic regression' threatens more and more wealthy societies.[51] Absent the conditions that underpinned liberal democracies in the post-war period (improving life standards, ethnic and cultural homogeneity, and a relatively controlled media environment, according to Mounk), twenty-first century governance faces a series of critical challenges.

The conundrums that the book outlines and its proposals for resolving them follow a familiar pattern. Mounk begins by acknowledging the existence of a series of problems that cause social disaffection, goes on to explain how complex – if not outright impossible – their resolution is, and proposes a series of modest reforms. His discussion of social networks is a case in point. While recognising that these have increased disinformation and polarisation to dangerous levels, Mounk does not consider promoting a different model of internet governance – perhaps one that is tightly regulated, as Cathy O'Neil has suggested; or one that treats data as a public good and infrastructure, as Evgeny Morozov and others have argued.[52] Instead, his main suggestion is that Silicon Valley give self-regulation a chance. What is not immediately clear is why a data monopoly such as Facebook would voluntarily give up its business model without a political struggle. Similarly, one may wonder whether this technical fix would be enough to placate voters of anti-system parties, whom Mounk attempts – but sometimes fails – to address without condescension.

The book's strongest observation concerns the relationship between democracy and liberalism. Mounk points out that these traditions interlocked at a specific historical juncture. Today, however, we find democratically elected politicians who trample on individual rights and liberties: illiberal democracies such as Viktor Orbán's regime in Hungary or, increasingly, Trump's America. But we also witness undemocratic liberalism: regimes that do not respect the decisions of sovereign electorates. Mounk's clearest example is the European Union's 2015 standoff with Syriza in Greece, which ended up with the imposition of a punitive austerity agenda against the explicit wishes of more than 60 per cent of Greek voters.

The tension between liberalism and democracy is an important one to understand, and it has been abundantly theorised in the past. One of the leading references in this regard is Chantal Mouffe's *The Democratic Paradox*, which, borrowing from Carl Schmitt, examines the 'constitutive tension' at the heart of liberal democracy.[53] 'Using Schmitt against Schmitt', Mouffe depicts the friction between liberalism – with its emphasis on individual rights – and democracy – grounded upon popular sovereignty – as one that, far from condemning liberal democracies to instability (as Schmitt had argued), makes them ideal for political combat: a space where opposed worldviews face each other through a process of institutionalised competition. Mouffe terms this dynamic 'agonism', in contrast to the antagonism that Schmitt depicted as ultimately dooming liberal democracies. Similarly, she posits the existence of political adversaries: combatants seeking their opponents' political defeat, not irreconcilable enemies to be eliminated. Liberal democracy is thus always an open game, subject to different reconfigurations.

Mounk avoids citing Mouffe altogether. It is not hard to see where they diverge. Mouffe places the blame for the rise in radical-right populism at the door of the 'third way' politics adopted by centre-left politicians in the 1980s and 1990s, which effectively involved the abandonment of the post-war consensus on the centrality of the welfare state and Keynesian economic management in favour of neoliberal policies. One of the third way's pioneers is Tony Blair, in whose Institute for Global Change Mounk was an executive director at the time *The People vs Democracy* was written. The book is hamstrung by that contradiction. Whenever the author identifies and seems ready to tackle an actual driver of social disaffection, he pulls back and calls for patches.

Finally, Steven Levitsky and Daniel Ziblatt, both of Harvard University, provide an unambiguous defence of liberalism in the face of democratic regression. In *How Democracies Die*, the authors develop Levitsky's pioneering work on competitive authoritarianism and hybrid regimes and apply some of his insights to the ongoing crisis of liberal democracy.[54] As is the case with Mounk's book, *How Democracies Die* boasts thematic range as a leading source of appeal, comparing a variety of past and present democratically elected politicians and actual dictators: Hugo Chávez, Augusto Pinochet, Mussolini, Rodrigo Duterte, and Trump, among others. For audiences in search of concise definitions, however, this scattergun approach is not always useful.

In keeping with the spirit of the book's title, the authors begin by outlining the magnitude of the problem at hand. It is not just societies such as Venezuela, Turkey, or Russia that are succumbing to democratic regression, they argue, but the prosperous democracies of the European Union and US. In most cases, democracies die in similar fashion: elected strongmen come to power with the intention of changing the institutional rules of the game. They do so by undermining liberal democracy – i.e., checks and balances, the rule of law, and other minoritarian institutions that contain executive power – from within and rendering it void.

Faced with such threats, their argument goes, it is not enough to erect institutional safeguards or defend a given constitution. The answer lies in a more ethereal realm: that of democratic norms, of due institutional respect, and the search for cross-party consensus among responsible political elites. According to *How Democracies Die*, the abandonment of such norms lies at the heart of democratic backsliding across different countries. This view is dearly held by centrist elites in the US (if only there were more politicians like John McCain, who once chastised a Republican voter for musing out loud that Obama was an undercover Muslim!), but it flounders as soon as the authors apply it to reality. They suggest, for example, that Augusto Pinochet's coup in Chile was a consequence of the disrespectful treatment that Christian Democrats and Socialists dished out to each other following Salvador Allende's election in 1970.[55] A more plausible and hardly novel interpretation is that Allende's ouster, followed by the imposition of a radical austerity programme, were dictated by the logic of Cold War politics, Chile, like Italy, being a country in which a communist party could not be seen to be winning democratic elections, much less governing successfully.[56]

Within the US itself, it is also worth asking whether norms and civility actually form the keystone of democratic politics. Following the work of political scientists such as Norman Ornstein and Thomas E. Mann, Levitsky and Ziblatt identify the Republican Party's radicalisation and drift toward the radical right as the main driver of political polarisation across the US.[57] But they also fault Barack Obama for responding to a gridlocked Congress and an unconditionally hostile opposition with executive orders. It is a strange accusation, considering that Obama was one of the most deferential presidents in recent US history, with a permanent disposition to treating his rivals respectfully, a constant willingness to 'reach across the aisle' in the pursuit of some quixotic grand bargain that Republicans were invariably uninterested in negotiating, and a lack of personal scandals tarnishing his presidency. Obama's speech at McCain's funeral – highlighting his sympathy for the senator and his belief that they fought 'on the same team' – exemplifies his political style. In spite of this, his administration gave way to Donald Trump's. Instead of wondering whether Obama was sufficiently deferential to his rivals, a more appropriate line of inquiry might begin with the question that *No Country for Old Men*'s Anton Chigurh poses to one of his hapless victims before shooting him in the head: 'If the rule you followed brought you to this, of what use was the rule?'

A potential solution, according to the authors, lies in the adoption of a less plebiscitary form of liberalism.[58] Their defence of using legal vetoes against anti-system parties and their criticism of democratic primaries suggest that they think the problem resides first and foremost with voters. As is well known, but worth noting at this point, Trump lost the popular vote by roughly three million votes and the key to his victory – as to that of George W. Bush in 2001 – was the Electoral College, which effectively introduces a right-wing bias into US presidential elections. Similarly, a number of polls and studies suggest that Sanders may have defeated Trump in the Midwestern states where Clinton lost.[59] But his campaign for the presidential nomination was hampered by a series of explicitly undemocratic measures taken by Democratic Party elites – the types of measure that Levitsky and Ziblatt consider useful to limit the destabilising effect of internal party democracy. In short, both the proposed origins of the problem and the prescriptions the authors invoke to address it seem off course.

The above approaches to the question of populism are usually decontextualised in a deeper sense. While the 2008 financial crisis and austerity in the Eurozone are sometimes presented as causes of the rise of populism, long-term, structural processes that change the content of liberal democratic regimes are rarely taken into account. In fact, and as we will see, Western societies exhibited troubling features well before the rise of populist parties, as a result of growing economic inequality, rising political apathy, and an ongoing fragmentation and atomisation of social life. The left's often-uncritical embrace of pro-market policies has collapsed important differences between conservatives and progressives and blurred the lines of political competition. As a result, and as the Irish political scientist Peter Mair pointed out some years ago, 'the political class itself has become an issue of contention'.[60]

Most scholars ignored Mair's warning. They have attempted to understand populists assuming that actually existing liberal democracy is an uncontested and unproblematic point of departure, whereas it in fact accumulates decades of profound transformation. Unsurprisingly, establishing this departure point has often ended up predetermining their conclusions.

Populism as a political logic

An alternative to presenting populism as pathology or as an existential threat to liberal democracy is to view it as a constitutive element of democratic politics, articulated through public discourse. This approach is associated with the Essex School of discourse analysis and the work of Ernesto Laclau and Chantal Mouffe. In his landmark *On Populist Reason* (2005), Laclau, a post-Marxist Argentinian sociologist, contended that populism is not just a discursive technique but, 'quite simply, a way of constructing the political'.[61] Because of this, treating the phenomenon with disdain risks leading to 'the dismissal of politics *tout court*', in favour of technocratic management.[62] One should, therefore, not approach the phenomenon by dividing up a political landscape between populists and their opponents, but by asking to what extent different actors embrace populism in the first place.

> Is populism really a transitional moment derived from the immaturity of social actors and bound to be superseded at a later stage, or is it, rather, a constant dimension of political action which necessarily arises (in different degrees) in all political discourses, subverting and complicating the operations of the so-called 'more mature' ideologies?[63]

As the preceding pages show, parties that are not explicitly populist frequently use techniques and discourses commonly associated with populism. Once the phenomenon is understood as a political logic, we can think of it as a spectrum on which parties sit differently at given points in time, rather than in terms of a binary opposition between populist and normal politicians. This is not to say that a party cannot be labelled as populist from outside, or itself adopt a populist strategy at a given point in time, as Podemos did explicitly and the Sanders movement in a tacit way.

For Laclau, populism is also a way of constituting the unity of a given group. The departure point of his analysis is not the group itself, however, but the popular and democratic demands that he and Mouffe, in their post-structuralist reading of Antonio Gramsci's work, view as eventually constitutive of the group itself. 'Demand' is, as Laclau points out, an ambiguous word: 'it can mean a request, but it can also mean a claim'.[64] In the transition from request to claims, the first defining features of populism appear. As unfulfilled democratic demands develop an 'equivalential chain' between them, they lead to the formation of 'a people'. Benjamín Arditi summarises the process as follows:

> (1) When a series of demands cannot be absorbed differentially by an institutional system, they become (2) unsatisfied demands that enter into a relationship of solidarity or equivalence with one another and (3) crystallise around common symbols that (4) can be capitalised by leaders who interpellate the frustrated masses and thus begin to incarnate a process that (5) constructs 'the people' as a collective actor to confront the existing regime with the purpose of (6) demanding regime change.[65]

How would this dynamic work out in real life? Consider the case of a democracy coping with rising disaffection and a series of unresolved social problems: economic inequality, crumbling infrastructure, unemployment, racist police brutality, evictions, sexism, lack of public safety, deteriorating public services. In conditions of normality, a functioning system can absorb and defuse the demands associated with each of these separately: public transport is a technical issue related to mobility, police brutality may be resolved by improving 'race relations', unemployment and inequality might be understood as the consequences of wrong individual choices, and fixable through better educational schemes, etc. As the problems pile up, however, the system is unable or unwilling to deliver clear solutions. Since the demands remain unfulfilled, an agonistic frontier is created between the different people formulating them and the system that denies their resolution. In the process, equivalential chains may be built between the different demands, such that they are no longer formulated in isolation from each other, and become 'popular' instead of democratic: they are no longer claims made by atomised citizens or interest groups with a narrow goal, but instead become representative of social ills affecting the entire body politic. Citizens no longer view themselves as simply unemployed, evicted, or victims of police brutality; rather, they come to view their experiences as different expressions of a common oppression, and develop affective ties that bind them as a movement. The result is a community mobilising to protest against an entire status quo, not merely asking for a few policy tweaks: in the process, the different demands are unified.

In order to bring about this transformation, however, would-be populist leaders must develop discursive strategies to frame different problems as part of a larger whole. This operation is metonymical: it employs a series of symbols and signifiers – often the populist leaders themselves, or the notion of 'the people', or, as is common in Latin America, a country's flag – to represent the sum of demands being formulated. One important question is where and how the frontier between 'the people' and 'the elites' is drawn. The process I have described might articulate an emancipatory, progressive movement – pitting the 99 per cent against the 1 per cent – but it could as easily represent an illiberal project that pits 'the people' against immigrants, feminists, and George Soros, to name a few perennial scapegoats of the radical right.

Laclau and Mouffe's notion of 'articulation' – the process through which different democratic demands become, through the creation of affective bonds, part of a common popular agenda – is useful analytically, because it describes a political logic that has been applied by many successful parties, not just explicitly populist ones. It is also valuable to the left strategically, because it offers an alternative to the Scylla of 'workerist' essentialism – which, economistically, views all social and political phenomena as byproducts of a class conflict – and the Charybdis of a degraded 'intersectional' politics, in which different demands are understood in terms of personal identities and addressed in isolation from, or even as if at odds with, one another.

Laclau and Mouffe are not without their critics. On the left, Slavoj Zizek finds the populist hypothesis problematic.[66] Perry Anderson has repeatedly taken issue with Laclau's reading of Gramsci: Podemos, following in the late Argentinian thinker's erratic trail, is, he muses, 'a long way from the prisoner of Bari'.[67] A more common objection to their work is that it is both 'extremely abstract' and 'so vague and malleable it loses much of its analytic utility', as Mudde and Kaltwasser put it.[68] At issue is the equation of populism with politics, which they find problematic. The resulting framework is, in their view, 'not helpful for undertaking empirical analysis'.[69] There are several reasons to reject this dismissal, however. *On Populist Reason* itself notes that 'vagueness and indeterminacy are not shortcomings of a political discourse about social reality, but, in some circumstances, inscribed in social reality as such'.[70] The vagueness surrounding populism is constitutive of the phenomenon as such, as it attempts to grapple with a social reality that is often complex and contradictory. More to the point, if the above charges are to stick, scholars of populism must offer their own working definitions of the term. As we have seen, they have not been successful so far. Furthermore, Laclau and Mouffe's work is of special interest because it has explicitly informed the discursive strategies of a number of left European parties, including Podemos, France Insoumise, Syriza, and Jeremy Corbyn's Labour.

In the following pages, I will approach populism through the prism of Laclau and Mouffe's definition of it as a political logic. I also follow Mouffe in acknowledging the central role of agonism in democratic practice – an insight that helps us to understand the alleged stridency of populist parties in terms of an attempt to repoliticise the body politic. The core work of this book is to integrate Laclau and Mouffe's understanding of populism into the logic of Karl Polanyi's 'double movement', and thereby gain a deeper understanding of the phenomenon from the vantage point of long-term processes in the field of political economy. My guiding assumption is that left populism is more clearly viewed from the outsider's trenches than it is from the battlements of a centrist fortress. This is because the liberal-democratic centre from which political theorists and social scientists take swings at the populist threat is no neutral vantage point. To better understand how and why this is so, we need to stop thinking about epidemics, tides, or thin-centred ideologies, and reach instead for a more helpful set of metaphors.

Populism is, first and foremost, about constructing a political subject or *demos*, as well as about identifying the adversary that resists its demands. It speaks in the name of the people, but 'the people' remains a social construction, not an ontological reality. Populism becomes an intuitive political response to the present juncture because of the atomising, individualistic drive of neoliberalism, which has eroded the social fabric of Western countries, such that the notion of a *demos* can no longer be taken for granted. As Marco d'Eramo points out, 'the social category from which [populism] has been derived historically, "the people", has all but vanished from political discourse'.[71] Yet this concept is still easier to recover than traditional left categories, such as the proletariat. This is because, as we will see in Chapters Two and Three, the institutions that constructed a sense of belonging and unity for left constituencies – most notably trade unions, but also neighbourhood associations, churches, and a variety of civil-society institutions – have been greatly weakened by contemporary economic arrangements, and they cannot channel electoral support or contribute to building political identities with the effectiveness they once did. Absent these traditional categories, progressives are left with 'the people' as the main rhetorical vehicle for framing their demands. It is one that, properly employed, can yield outstanding electoral results.

Notes

1 Lewis Carroll, *Through the Looking-Glass*, Hayes Barton Press: Raleigh, NC, p72.

2 D'Eramo, 'Populism and the new oligarchy', *New Left Review*, 82, July-August 2013, p6.

3 Peter Wiles, 'A syndrome, not a doctrine: Some elementary theses on populism', in Ghita Ionescu and Ernest Gellner (eds), *Populism: Its Meanings and National Characteristics*, Macmillan: New York, 1969.

4 Barbara Tuchman, *August 1914* [published in the US as *The Guns of August*] Constable: London, 1962, p13.

5 Karl Polanyi, *The Great Transformation: The Political and Economic Origins of Our Time,* Beacon Press: Boston, MA, 2001 [1944], p3.

6 For the entire event, see 'FULL VIDEO: John McCain's Memorial Service | NYT News', YouTube, 1 September 2018.

7 'Tracking Congress in the age of Trump', https://fivethirtyeight.com, last updated 23 July 2018.

8 Paul Pierson, *Politics in Time: History, Institutions, and Social Analysis,* Princeton University Press: New Haven, NJ, 2004.

9 Ionescu and Gellner, 1969, p1; Cas Mudde, 'The populist zeitgeist', *Government and Opposition,* Vol. 39 No. 3, 2004, pp541-63; Krastev, 'The populist moment', www.eurozine.com/, 18 September 2007; Torreblanca, https://twitter.com/jitorreblanca/status/805558078611607553, 4 December 2016.

10 I owe this analogy to Benjamin Moffitt, 'Guess who's coming to dinner? Populism as the awkward dinner guest of democracy', at 'Connected Globe, Conflicting Worlds', University of Melbourne, 27-29 September 2010.

11 D'Eramo 2013, pp5-28; see also d'Eramo, 'They, the people', *New Left Review,* 103, January-February 2017, pp129-38.

12 Ernesto Laclau, *On Populist Reason,* Verso: New York, 2005, pp21-64.

13 Molly Crockett, 'How populism taps into the human desire for punishment – a psychologist explains', www.weforum.org, 5 January 2017.

14 Amanda Taub, 'The rise of American authoritarianism', *Vox,* 1 March 2016.

15 Robert C. Tucker (ed), *The Marx-Engels Reader,* W. W. North: New York, 1978, p608.

16 Taub 2016.

17 Arlie Hochschild, *Extraños en su propia tierra,* Capitán Swing: Madrid, 2018.

18 Müller, *What is Populism?* University of Pennsylvania Press: Philadelphia, 2016, p16.

19 Charles Tilly, *Big Structures, Large Processes, Huge Comparisons,* Russell Sage Foundation: London, 1984, p13.

20 See 'The new populism', *The Guardian.*

21 For recent examples, see 'British politics is being profoundly reshaped by populism', *The Economist,* 16 November 2017; Adrián Mateos, 'Pons: 'El populismo es un virus capaz de matar la democracia y los principios europeos', www.abc.es/, 11 June 2019.

22 On this subject, see Jorge Tamames, 'Moscú en la red: la nueva injerencia rusa', https://elordenmundial.com/, 4 October 2018; Tamames,

'Desinformación y los límites de la injerencia rusa', https://elorden-mundial.com/, 17 October 2018; Tamames, 'El atolladero, en España y Estados Unidos', www.politicaexterior.com, 15 November 2017.

23   For recent examples, see Richard C. Schneider, 'Europe's far-right populists didn't get their tsunami. But they're still as dangerous as ever', *Haaretz*, 27 May 2019; Pablo R. Suanzes, 'Europa espera poner dique a la marea populista', *El mundo*, 26 May 2019.

24   Matthijs Rooduijn, 'State of the field: How to study populism and adjacent topics? A plea for both more and less focus', *European Journal of Political Research*, Vol. 58, No. 1, pp362-372.

25   Quoted in *ibid.*, p8.

26   Quoted in Pedro Vallín, 'Podemos sí es populista', *La vanguardia*, 20 November 2016.

27   Mudde and Kaltwasser 2012, p9.

28   Thomas Frank, *What's the Matter with Kansas? How Conservatives Won the Heart of America*, Henry Holt and Co: New York, 2004.

29   See, for example, Ignacio Escolar, 'Los españoles de bien', *El diario*, 17 April 2013.

30   Mudde, 'Syriza's second year in power: From being isolated to being ignored', *Huffington Post*, 30 January 2017; Mudde, 'The power of populism? Not really!', *Huffington Post*, 13 February 2016; Mudde, *Syriza: The Failure of the Populist Promise*, Palgrave Macmillan: London, 2017.

31   Mudde, 'We are thinking about populism wrong', *Huffington Post*, 20 March 2017.

32   Bernie Sanders, *Our Revolution: A Future to Believe In*, St. Martin's Press: NY, 2016, p88.

33   Mudde 2017 (*Huffington Post*).

34   *Ibid.*

35   *Ibid.*

36   Müller, *What Is Populism?* University of Pennsylvania Press: Philadelphia, PA, 2016, pp19-20.

37   *Ibid.*, p25; Müller, 'Real Citizens', *Boston Review*, 26 October 2016.

38   Here Müller evokes a strand of thought that dates back to Hofstadter and seeks to, as d'Eramo pointed out in his 2013 essay, render 'populism "fascist" and fascism "populist"'. Müller does so less than two pages after criticising that very tradition.

39   Müller, *What is Populism?*, p97.

40   *Ibid.*, p93.

41   Müller, 'Please stop calling Bernie Sanders a populist', *New York Times*, 23 January 2020.

42   Müller, 'Populism and the people', *London Review of Books*, 23 May 2019.

43 Robin, *The Reactionary Mind*, Oxford University Press: New York, 2011.

44 Frank 2004.

45 Antonio Maestre, 'El PP, el partido que se definió a sí mismo como populista en su ideario', www.lamarea.com, 28 November 2016.

46 For a compilation of insults hurled by Republicans at America's first black president, see Jason Duaine Hahn, 'The most insulting things politicians have said about President Obama', www.complex.com/uk, 23 January 2015.

47 For a detailed account, see Matt Taibbi, 'It's official: Russiagate is this generation's WMD', https://taibbi.substack.com, 23 March 2019.

48 Irene Castro, 'El PP alimentó la teoría de la conspiración del 11M con cientos de preguntas parlamentarias', *El diario*, 15 March 2017.

49 Following these accusations, a leading US political scientist working on Spain observed that 'Of all of the speeches given over the past week, by far the most populist was from Citizens. This is the party that most criticises populism. Populism scholars take note.' Bonnie N. Field, https://twitter.com/BonnieNField/status/1154468641372401664, 25 July 2019.

50 Yascha Mounk, *The People vs Democracy: Why Our Freedom is in Danger and How to Save it*, Harvard University Press: Cambridge, MA, 2018.

51 See Mounk and Stefano Foa, 'The signs of deconsolidation', *Journal of Democracy*, Vol. 28, No. 1, pp5-16.

52 Cathy O'Neil, *Armas de destrucción matemática. Cómo el big data aumenta la desigualdad y amenaza la democracia*, Madrid: Capitán Swing, 2018; Evgeny Morozov, 'Digital socialism?' *New Left Review*, 116/117, March-June 2019, pp33-67. For a practical attempt to realise some of these measures, see Amy Lewin, 'Barcelona's Robin Hood of data: Francesca Bria', https://sifted.eu, 16 November 2018.

53 Chantal Mouffe, *The Democratic Paradox*, Verso: New York, 2009; see also Mouffe, *The Return of the Political*, Verso: New York, 2005.

54 Steven Levitsky and Daniel Ziblatt, *How Democracies Die*, Random House: New York, 2018.

55 *Ibid.*, pp134-8.

56 For a well-known overview, see Naomi Klein, *The Shock Doctrine: The Rise of Disaster Capitalism*, Knopf Canada: Toronto, 2007.

57 Thomas E. Mann and Norman J. Ornstein, 'Let's just say it: The Republicans are the problem', *Washington Post*, 27 April 2012.

58 Levitsky and Ziblatt 2018, 175-7.

59 On this subject and for 2016, see Gideon Resnick, 'Trump's pollster: Bernie would've won', www.thedailybeast.com, 31 October 2017; for 2020, see Steve Phillips, 'Bernie Sanders can beat Trump. Here's the math', *New York Times*, 28 February 2020.

60 Peter Mair, 'Ruling the void?', *New Left Review*, 42, November-December 2006, pp25-51.

61 Laclau 2005, p.xi.

62 *Ibid.*, p.xi.

63 *Ibid.*, p.x.

64 *Ibid.*, p18.

65 Benjamín Arditi, 'Populism is hegemony is politics? On Ernesto Laclau's *On Populist Reason*', *Constellations*, Vol. 17 No. 3, 2010, p489.

66 Slavoj Zizek, 'Against the populist temptation', *Critical Inquiry* 32, Spring 2006, p556.

67 See Perry Anderson, 'The heirs of Gramsci', *New Left Review* 100, July-August 2016, p83. A partial answer to Anderson's objections is that the good is the enemy of the best. Populism as a political logic and strategy is indeed riddled with contradictions, as I will show in the second half of this book. But this is the nature of political action, against which a stance of doctrinal punctiliousness will not achieve much. At the same time such criticism should be welcomed, as the roadmap for a 'radical social democracy' defended by Mouffe is a strategy that leaves space for, and can be complemented by, approaches to its left.

68 Mudde and Kaltwasser 2012, p7.

69 *Ibid.*, p6.

70 Laclau 2005, p67.

71 D'Eramo 2013, p6.

CHAPTER TWO

Earthquakes and Countermovements

When an earthquake happens deep underground a crack will start to open on a pre-existing line of weakness in the Earth's brittle crust. This crack will then grow larger and larger, relieving built-up stress as it goes.[1]

– British Geological Survey

The experience of an earthquake can be destabilising, not just physically but also philosophically ... To no small extent, earthquakes force us to ask what we mean by 'land' in the first place, including how we define architecture when the ground it stands on moves like the sea.[2]

– Geoff Manaugh, New York Times

To allow the market mechanism to be sole director of the fate of human beings and their natural environment ... would result in the demolition of society.[3]

– Karl Polanyi, The Great Transformation

California experiences constant seismic activity, but the earthquake that struck San Francisco in the early hours of 18 April 1906 remains the most devastating in the state's history. Reaching roughly eight out of ten on the Richter scale – modern estimates place it between 8.2 and 7.7 – the earthquake and the ensuing firestorm, which lasted for three days, ravaged 500 blocks and 25,000 buildings throughout the city. 'Downtown everything is a ruin,' The

San Francisco Call-Chronicle-Examiner stated. 'Not a business house stands. Theatres are crumbled into heaps. Factories and commission houses lie smouldering on their former sites'.[4]

In the aftermath of the city's destruction, San Francisco's civic leaders chose to tell the country a different story. During the following weeks, they presented an alternative account of events, describing the earthquake itself as a relatively minor incident, and the ensuing fire as the real culprit behind the catastrophe. As David Ulin writes in *The Myth of Solid Ground*, 'the most important narrative was that of San Francisco rising from the ashes to be reborn'.[5] The reasoning behind this presentation was simple: fires had damaged other American cities, for example Boston and Chicago. Fire offered the general public a set of familiar images and references, as well as an awareness that the destruction they wrought could be repaired. Earthquakes, on the other hand, loomed incomprehensible and terrifying.

Today we face a similar situation. We can choose to tell ourselves – as in discourses of the kind outlined in the previous chapter – that our problems stem from the spread of 'fake news', or from the erosion of parliamentary norms and politeness, or from our fellow citizens' psychological impediments. Addressing an issue such as the digital spread of misinformation, for example, would no doubt make our societies better places to live in, but our problems will linger if their root causes remain unaddressed. The 1906 catastrophe was a consequence of San Francisco being situated on the San Andreas fault, not of its buildings being flammable. Accepting this, however, would have required acknowledging an unsettling reality.

Instead of talk of viruses, tides, or psychopathology, we should use the language of the earthquake to analyse the transformations of Western societies. The failed responses to the 2008 economic crisis led to the appearance of parties and movements claiming to speak and fight for 'the people' – but the origins of these movements lie much further in the past. My contention is that, much as the discovery of plate tectonics represented an enormous advance in our understanding of how earthquakes happen, Polanyi's conceptualisation of the interaction between markets and society as a 'double movement' offers a powerful long-range guide to the origins and development of populism.

Landslides, fault lines, and the dream of control

The idea that earthquakes offer a useful metaphor for social change is by no means my own. In *Politics in Time* (2004), Paul Pierson develops a useful set of meteorological analogies that social scientists can apply to the objects of their study.[6] His key variables are an event's 'time horizon of cause' (i.e., the time it takes to build up) and its 'time horizon of outcome' (how long before its effects become noticeable). Climate change, for example, has long horizons of cause and outcome: it has taken centuries to become an existential threat, but even now its impact is slow and cumulative rather than immediate. Contrast this to tornados, which have short time horizons of cause and outcome: they form abruptly and cause instant damage. When social scientists, journalists, or politicians depict populism in the ways described in the previous chapter – as a pathology, an epidemic or a rogue wave, or a simple product of demagoguery – they are effectively conceiving the phenomenon as a tornado. It came out of nowhere, and, hopefully, it will vanish within a few years.

Earthquakes are different. Their impact is also immediate, but they have long time horizons of cause, which result from the underground movement of tectonic plates. In other words, while their effects are seen in the short term, their irruption is a consequence of long-term movements and underground rumblings not always perceptible to humans. (The opposite of an earthquake, according to Pierson, is a meteor strike: its impact upon our planet is sudden, but its full effects take time to develop.)

The earthquake's long causal time horizon is comparable to the way that economic transformations that took place more than four decades ago led to the present breakdown of established politics. The seismic analogy also helps us parse out structural conditions from contingent events. We know that earthquakes usually take place along fault lines, but their outbreak remains frustratingly hard to predict. As a seismologist explains to Ulin, again resorting to a meteorological analogy,

You have climate, which is what you can expect in the long-term history of a place. And you have weather, which is what you're predicting for tomorrow. We can do earthquake climate.

Give me 100,000 years, and I'll tell you what earthquakes are going to happen. That's not random. That's deterministic, and it's driven by plate tectonics. Which subset of them are going to happen in our lifetime is completely random.[7]

Seeing as the advance of populism in Western Europe and the US responds to socio-economic forces and processes, it should be easy to pinpoint places where it is likely to develop. Predicting the precise location of an actual populist tremor, never mind its ideological orientation, is an entirely different matter.

Some birds and dogs can hear the p-waves that precede actual shocks, but their panicked responses are inadequate as an early warning system, because they come too late for anyone to act on them. An alternative to prediction is prevention: developing measures that will kick in to minimise the damage from the moment the shock is unleashed. In relation to earthquakes, the solutions reside in architecture, urban planning, and educating the population to undertake basic security routines. In the case of economic management – as I will explore in more detail later – the main shock absorbers are public regulation, redistributive and predistributive policies, and an activist welfare state, all of which require a countercyclical management of the economy in order to remain sustainable. Our governing economic paradigms, however, limit and sometimes actively bar these measures, forcing instead policies that only compound previous damage.

A second insight from earthquakes is that not only their outbreak, but also their consequences are hard to prevent. The San Francisco tremor caused a devastating fire. The Great Lisbon earthquake that demolished Portugal's capital in 1755 had its epicentre in the Atlantic Ocean, and thus its damage was magnified by tsunamis that flooded the city's docks and rushed up the Tagus estuary. The consequences of socio-economic crises are not fires and floods, but the parallel is that radically different kinds of populism emerge in response to the same crisis: some left, some radical right, others, like Italy's Five Star Movement or Germany's Aufstehen, an opportunistic and confused hodgepodge of both.[8]

When considering which kind of populism is more likely to develop in a given place, the quote from the British Geological

Survey at the beginning of this chapter provides a helpful cue: 'a crack will start to open on a pre-existing line of weakness in the Earth's brittle crust'.[9] Lines of weakness will vary according to each society. In the US, a long history of nativism and structural racism facilitated the success of a candidate like Donald Trump. At the same time, a widespread understanding of the country's founding as revolutionary allows Sanders to present his programme as a 'political revolution' without mainstream observers becoming immediately alarmed. In Spain, the powerful legacy of the 2011 protest movements – which delivered a resonant critique of austerity policies and Spain's leading political parties – made it less likely that migrants and other vulnerable groups would be scapegoated during the 2008 crisis; instead, political and economic discontent was channelled against the country's banks and elites. Conversely, Spain's history of fraught politics around the administrative status of regions with distinct languages and cultural heritages means that a reactionary brand of centralising Spanish nationalism can be easily galvanised in response to regional claims for independence, as happened in relation to Catalonia from 2017 onwards.

Nevertheless, the cracks that develop along these lines of weakness are not predetermined. A given country's history or makeup does not mean that only certain kinds of political expression and discourses can resonate with the public. Skilful populist parties and movements are still able to frame the prominent problems of the day in ways that suit their worldview, whether reactionary or progressive. Regardless, these lines of weakness offer pre-formed routes to channel a given crisis, in progressive or reactionary ways.

A final lesson concerns the psychological impact of seismic activity. As Geoff Manaugh wrote in the aftermath of the July 2019 Ridgecrest tremors in California, earthquakes can be philosophically as well as physically unsettling: they 'mock the very idea of solid ground, of trustworthy geology'.[10] Ulin, in his account of earthquakes and their impact upon everyday Californian life, remarks that he was 'captivated most by uncertainty, an open-ended quality of being caught in something I could not control'.[11] But most people resent being caught in social and economic circumstances in which their desires and actions become meaningless. It is probably no coincidence that the idea of *control* is emphasised by populists of all ideological leanings, even if what each means by 'control' varies. The feeling that people have of losing their agency and place in the world can undergird the appeal of different populist movements, both when these address economic discontent and when they focus on cultural grievances – which are, of course, not always separate or mutually exclusive domains.

In writing of the impact of economic transformations in seismic terms, I am not implying that left populism itself is a destructive force that wreaks havoc with people's lives in places like Spain and the US. The driving force in these destructive transformations, creating fault lines and dangerous tremors, is an economic paradigm that subordinates social needs to those of the 'self-regulating' market. It is my contention that out of this juncture, left populism can emerge – dramatically, apparently out of nowhere – as an unexpected guarantor of stability. To realise its potential to do this, however, it must successfully address the root causes of social discontent.

Similarly, I do not suggest that because fault lines exist and, indeed, entire societies are built upon them, we are doomed to suffer an unending succession of crises and our only option is to endure, ameliorate, or contain their damage. It is true, of course, that a medium-sized economy such as Spain cannot singlehandedly change an international economic order, much less neutralise a threat such as global warming. (The US is in a different position, as it retains considerable resources and sovereignty at its disposal.) But lasting change will only take place if and when enough states align and cooperate to effect a socio-economic paradigm shift on an international level. I am aware that, as the late critical theorist Immanuel Wallerstein highlighted, nation states are a limited vehicle for effecting global, systemic change. Adam Tooze similarly notes, in the introduction to his landmark study of the 2008 crisis, that unlike in the preceding era of Keynesian capitalism, today's leading economic units are not states, but globally integrated supply chains.[12] The international dimension of the agenda of populism-driven transformation is, thus, one that transcends individual nation-states. The key point is that countries such as Spain retain the capability to blunt the sharpest edges of neoliberal economic management, and it would be foolish for left and progressive forces to dismiss them because they are not far-reaching enough. In order to understand these means in more detail, as well as the situation in which populism has taken root, we must turn first toward political economy.

The double movement

The years since the 2008 financial crisis have witnessed a renewal of academic and journalistic interest in the work of Karl Polanyi (1986-1964). Among the authors who have made use of him are Fred Block, Nancy Fraser, Sheri Berman, and Mark Blyth in the US, and César Rendueles and Carlos Fernández Liria in Spain.[13] In the UK, Jonathan Hopkin has employed a Polanyian framework to contextualise Brexit and, more recently, to examine the differences between populist parties in the Eurozone core and periphery; former Podemos Member of Parliament Manuel Monereo interprets his party's rise in similar terms, noting that 'behind a "populist moment" there is always a "Polanyi moment"'.[14]

The Great Transformation also occasionally appeals to progressive liberals, since its author's popularity partially reflects, in Daniel Luban's words, 'the desire of the non-Marxist left for a champion of its own to compete with that other Karl'.[15] Polanyi's popularity should come as no surprise to students of the Austro-Hungarian thinker's 1944 magnum opus, *The Great Transformation*. While the text is particularly useful for scholars, activists, and policymakers of the left, adopting a Polanyian normative framework also offers a clear path for contextualising the rise of radical-right populist movements.

Polanyi is known for his theory of the 'double movement', the process by which a society imperilled by the advance of commodification – the 'move to the market' – pushes back in a protective 'countermovement', readapting the economy to social needs. The fulcrum of Polanyi's work is his understanding of the relationship between society and the economy. Against the grain of the liberal tradition, he viewed the economy as traditionally 'embedded' in social structures. Throughout history, the reach of markets was consistently curtailed by moral and communal institutions – custom, religion, and political action (or inaction). In this regard, nineteenth-century Europe's market economy was historically unprecedented. Far from being firmly grounded on humanity's supposed natural propensity to 'truck, barter, and exchange', in Smith's classic terms, or resting on the pleasant bed of Montesquieu's *doux commerce*, liberalism was erected on hubristic and precarious foundations: the attempt to extricate the economy from society and submit the latter to the imperatives of the market.[16]

In its drive to commodify all aspects of social life, Polanyi argues, nineteenth-century liberalism ran into three unsurpassable obstacles. Labour, land, and money could not accommodate its advance. This is because none of these are marketable goods in any standard reading of the term, and they can only be integrated into a system of exchange as 'fictitious commodities':

> Labour is only another name for a human activity which goes with life itself, which in its turn is not produced for sale but for entirely different reasons, nor can that activity be detached from the rest of life, be stored or mobilised; land is only another name for nature, which is not produced by man; actual money, finally, is merely a token of purchasing power which, as a rule, is not produced at all, but comes into being through the mechanism of banking or state finance.[17]

Because it depended on violence to uphold these fictions, market economy was ultimately a 'stark utopia'.[18] It could never come into full being, as its complete realisation required an unbearable amount of social dislocation and environmental destruction. A paradoxical consequence of this utopian character is that market society could not develop on its own. In order to uphold the fictional character of land, labour, and money as commodities, economic liberalism was forced to summon the full force of the state. Thus the state is redeployed as an active agent of deregulation and coercion, with its social protection role correspondingly diminished – a subject to which I will return.

The Great Transformation narrates the destruction of nineteenth-century European civilisation through its attachment to the chimera of a self-regulating market, expressed in the institution of the international gold standard. But Polanyi posited that, with Roosevelt's New Deal, the Soviet Union's first five-year plan, and the onset of fascism in Central Europe, the age of the self-regulating market had finally come to an end. As they had done during the second half of the nineteenth century, societies were mobilising spontaneously to re-embed the market into social structures, this time for good. The examples he gave, however, indicate that the process was not bound to be democratic. Needless to say, neither Stalinism nor Nazism oversaw the expansion of personal liberty that was the intent (if not always the outcome) of the New Deal and Roosevelt's 'four freedoms' – of speech, of worship, from want, and from fear.[19]

Polanyi's work contains a series of insights that shed critical light on the current relationship between economic arrangements, social protest, and the rise of populist parties and movements. The first is that the global turn toward markets produced a countermovement on a global level. The second is that these responses took radically different expressions in different societies. We find a similar dynamic in contemporary times if we look back to the protest movements that swept the world throughout 2011. They began in the Middle East and Northern Africa, crossed the Mediterranean and reached Europe in the spring, and landed in Zuccotti Park in New York by the autumn of 2011. 'If these movements were globally connected', Michael Burawoy has observed, 'it was their national framing that drew their distinctive momentum'.[20] The 2011 protests, as I will show in the second half of this chapter, should be viewed as a textbook example of a Polanyian countermovement. Instead of being confined to pre-determined economic classes, as orthodox Marxists would perhaps anticipate, they attracted wide swathes of society and framed their grievances in socio-political terms.

A second insight concerns the spontaneous nature of such protests. In his response to liberal critics who blamed the countermovement's success on secret cabals of protectionist elites, Polanyi stressed the spontaneous nature of the revolts that took place across Europe in the second half of the nineteenth century, and contrasted them with the state-enforced process of marketisation: 'While laissez-faire economy was the product of deliberate State action, subsequent restrictions on laissez-faire started in a spontaneous way. *Laissez-faire* was planned, planning was not.'[21] Not only were the revolts spontaneous; they also arose across widely contrasting European countries. Similarly, the actors that since 2008 have taken to the streets – from the *indignados* and Occupy protesters to Black Lives Matter activists – have done so with remarkable spontaneity.

A third insight concerns the particular role that the gold standard's rigidity played in leading Europe down the path of destruction. During the decades that preceded the First World War, political elites unanimously supported this inherently deflationary monetary arrangement. In the interwar years, the gold standard was re-established without taking into consideration the burden it imposed upon the societies that adopted it. Polanyi's account of this period stressed how the austerity policies that accompanied the gold standard's return were connected to the rise of fascism in Europe. In his discussion of the institution's failures, we find considerable similarities with the recent history of the Eurozone periphery:

> The repayment of foreign loans and the return to stable currencies were recognised as the touchstone of rationality in politics; and no private suffering, no restriction of sovereignty, was deemed too great a sacrifice for the recovery of monetary integrity. The privations of the unemployed made jobless by deflation; the destitution of public servants dismissed without a pittance; even the relinquishment of national rights and the loss of constitutional liberties were judged a fair price to pay.[22]

Unlike those of Italy and Greece in 2011, Spain's prime ministers have not been forced out of power by European elites attempting to ensure 'the return to stable currencies'.[23] As we will see, however, Spain's signature of the 1992 Maastricht Treaty and entry into the European Monetary Union constitute one of the critical junctures that help us understand the impact of the 2008 crisis. Polanyi acknowledged that an abrupt departure from the gold standard would not have solved the problems faced by most continental economies. In his discussion of León Blum's Popular Front, he observed that a French New Deal 'never had a chance since the government was tied on the crucial question of currency' – whereas Roosevelt's New Deal could prosper after abandoning the gold standard because the US had an immense domestic economy that was not dependent on foreign trade. For European countries, however, 'going off gold involved no less than dropping out of the world economy ... and thereby sacrificing industries dependent upon imported raw materials, disorganising foreign trade upon which employment rested'.[24] In short, then with the gold standard as now under the constraints of the euro, neither uncritical acceptance nor unilateral withdrawal offer easy solutions to the challenges faced by peripheral European economies.

Populism as countermovement

The general contours of Polanyi's idea of the double movement are well known. Other aspects of his book remain less familiar, but offer us crucial help in understanding the present juncture. *The Great Transformation* pays close attention to the dimension of time in politics. In the previous chapter I compared the outbreak of World War I to Donald Trump's 2016 victory – both apparently putting an abrupt end to placid eras of politics-as-usual. Much as there are countless short-term explanations for Trump's victory (his own demagoguery, political polarisation, Facebook, Russian interference), all belonging to the school of populism-as-tornado, the debate about World War I's origins has traditionally remained centred on military and diplomatic affairs in the run-up to the war.

Polanyi comes at the subject from a different angle. Rather than focusing on short-range politics and military matters, he thoroughly analyses the previous century of European economic history and the structural forces that built up against, and ultimately shattered, the 'peace interest' that had accrued throughout the nineteenth century. He is, as Fred Block has pointed out, a 'theorist of discontinuity' who 'provides us with a historical narrative marked by radical turns and fundamental breaks in the patterns of social organisation'.[25] His insights are all the more valuable in an age of generalised political uncertainty.

While stressing the importance of the double movement in checking the advances of the market, Polanyi never lost sight of its potential perils and the fact that 'fascism, like socialism, was rooted in a market society that ceased to function'.[26] As a man of the left who participated in various progressive, socialist, and populist movements, in his theoretical work, he noted critical differences between them. He defined socialism as the tendency to 'transcend the self-regulating market by subordinating it to a democratic society'; he viewed fascism, on the other hand, as 'a reform of market economy achieved at the price of the extirpation of all democratic institutions'.[27] While today's radical right is not outright fascist, the nature of its move is similar. Furthermore, and barring a few cases where it has genuinely adopted a stance of welfare chauvinism – in France, for example – it is ultimately more interested in repressing its enemies – immigrants, feminists, 'globalists', and leftists – than in challenging markets. The Trump administration is a case in point. Protectionism is the most anti-establishment plank of its economic agenda, but it is not new – Ronald Reagan's trade policy, featuring steep steel tariffs and diplomatic agreements that forced Japan and West Germany to modify their trade surpluses, was also interventionist – nor is it unpopular among political elites, as leading Democrats have echoed the White House's concerns about China's trade policies. In other respects Trump's administration has overseen an intensification of the policies traditionally embraced by Republicans and viewed as hallmarks of neoliberalism, such as tax cuts, deregulation, and upward wealth redistribution.

Polanyi's approach therefore recognises the link between the liberal utopia of the self-regulating market and the arrival of fascism, which the former ostensibly opposes: 'in order to comprehend German fascism, we have to revert to Ricardian England'.[28] There are echoes of this in the relation of present-day radical-right populism and the turn to neoliberalism in the 1970s. *The Great Transformation* therefore provides tools for understanding populism without framing 'cultural backlash' and 'economic anxiety' as its binary drivers. This approach, which has gained traction in recent years, has become associated with Pippa Norris and Ronald Inglehart.[29] In their view, it is mainly the former that feeds 'authoritarian populist' projects such as Trump's presidency and Brexit. A possible reading of their work is that economic anxiety should be addressed, but that the cultural grievances of older generations toward multiculturalism belong to the past – and that, in any event, populists should not be entrusted to deliver, because they are authoritarians. As with the mainstream analytic frameworks analysed earlier, this one is excessively centred on radical-right movements and struggles to explain left populism.[30]

It is worth lingering on this binary – that of cultural vs economic demands, or 'material' vs 'identitarian' approaches to politics – as it recurrently generates heated arguments across the left. Polanyi's approach to the subject is more elegant than those that seek to divide and reify the two. It can be summarised in his observation that 'the essence of purely economic progress...is to achieve improvement at the price of social dislocation'.[31] Modulating the speed and extent of that dislocation, and therefore its cultural as well as its economic impact, is the main task he entrusts to government. In his discussion of the Industrial Revolution and the unprecedented urban poverty it generated, Polanyi praises the philanthropic industrialist Robert Owen for understanding that 'what appeared primarily as an economic problem was essentially a social one'. He goes on to explain the effects of economic transformation in a compelling way – and indeed a way that would not displease conservative thinkers who retain a critical view of the market society:

> In economic terms the worker was certainly exploited: he did not get in exchange that which was his due. But important though this was, it was far from all. In spite of the exploitation he might have been financially better off than before. But a principle quite unfavourable to individual and general happiness was wreaking havoc with his social environment, his neighbourhood, his standing in the community, his craft; in a word, with those relationships to nature and man in which his existence was formerly embedded. The Industrial Revolution was causing a social dislocation of stupendous proportions, and the problem of poverty was merely the economic aspect of this event.[32]

Sensitivity toward the socio-cultural aspects of economic change is therefore ingrained in Polanyi's thought. It was rooted in his training not just in the field of political economy but also in economic history and anthropology. Writing from the vantage point of the mid-twentieth century – and, when in Vienna, *contra* Ludwig von Mises' libertarian theses – Polanyi could also challenge orthodox Marxism for its economically deterministic outlook: 'the interests of a class most directly refer to standing and rank, to status and security, that is, they are primarily not economic but social'.[33] His description of the nineteenth century's countermovements ends on a note that applies to the global 2011 protest cycle: 'It appears reasonable to group our account of the protective countermovement not around class interests, but around the social interests imperilled by the market.'[34]

Polanyi's worldview, as Block and Margaret Somers have pointed out, begins and ends with an analysis of the social, into which he infused – or, to put it in his own terms, embedded – economic, cultural, and political considerations. This approach allowed for many rewarding moves. One of these, in anticipation of our time, was his observation that market society would spell catastrophe not just for human beings but also for their environment. The idea of a self-adjusting market, he points out, could 'not exist for any length of time without annihilating the human and natural substance of society; it would have physically destroyed man and transformed his surroundings into a wilderness'.[35]

All of the above makes Polanyi, as Sheri Berman notes, a theorist of the 'primacy of politics'.[36] Concern with practical political action courses through his work and is especially clear in his depiction of market society as a 'utopia' – a charge intended to invert the standard accusation that socialist and emancipatory political projects are not 'realist'. Block and Somers draw important conclusions from these insights: they describe Polanyi's worldview as one with 'no telos', in which there is no final resolution to the struggles between society and the market.[37] This is another aspect of his thinking that brings him close to Laclau and Mouffe. As noted above, the latter's notion of agonistic democracy understands political struggle as a constitutive element of liberal democratic regimes, and rejects end-of-history worldviews in which the free market reigns supreme or a classless society overcomes its contradictions. Laclau and Mouffe's analysis, like Polanyi's, also departs from orthodox strands of Marxism in its defence of the autonomy and critical importance of political action, which is not always determined by the iron laws of economics or the ownership of the means of production. Taken together, these elements endow theirs and Polanyi's writing with a striking explanatory power to address the relationship between populism and neoliberalism.

Bolshevik soul, Fabian muzzle?

Polanyi did not, of course, get everything right. Writing in 1944, he assumed that market society had suffered lasting defeat, not a temporary setback from which it would recover in the span of three decades. By the late 1970s, the dismantling of the Bretton Woods system of exchange rates linked to the gold standard via the US dollar, and a crisis in the post-war, Fordist model of capitalism – which had been characterised by unionised workforces and a growing welfare state – paved the way for a neoliberal counter-offensive that seemed intent on proving his expectations misplaced. The content of this move was explicitly anti-Polanyian, with many of its leading figures arguing that the market, not government or the welfare state, constituted the best mechanism for governing human relations. Polanyi's concern that a self-regulated market 'could not exist for any length of time without annihilating the human and natural substance of society' was dispatched with Margaret Thatcher's famous assertion that 'there is no such thing as society' in the first place.[38]

While Polanyi did not intend to offer an explicitly cyclical theory of change, Michael Burawoy has identified a historical pattern of moves to the market (of which this neoliberal turn was of course one), followed by protective countermovements (Figure 2.1). His chart is especially interesting because it factors in the impact of ecological catastrophe – a concern that, as we saw, was already present in *The Great Transformation*.

Inability to anticipate the future is not Polanyi's only shortcoming. As we have seen, the dynamic of the double movement, much like Mouffe and Laclau's theorisation of populism, sits uneasily with orthodox Marxism, which Polanyi criticised as deterministic and taking a narrow view of class as a primarily economic formation. Polanyi's focus on 'society' makes him vulnerable to the opposing line of attack: while most agree that such a thing does in fact exist, it is a slippery concept to choose as one's main unit of analysis. I have no conclusive answer to this criticism, other than insisting that I do not view indeterminacy as a critical shortcoming. To return to Laclau's contention that 'vagueness and indeterminacy' are often 'inscribed in social reality as such', analysis on a societal rather than

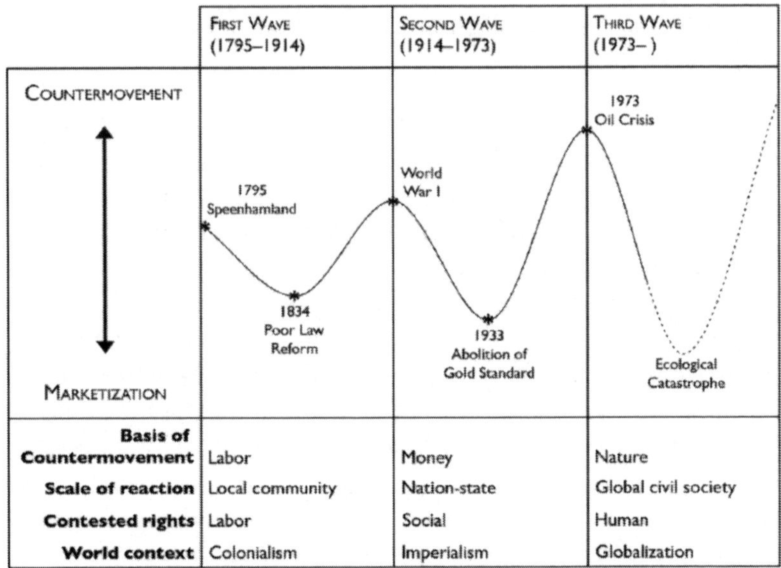

2.1: There and back again: the 'double movement' throughout history. Source: Michael Burawoy, 'Facing an unequal world', *Current Sociology*, Vol. 64, No. 1, p25.

class level can be useful to understand a wave of movements such as those that rose spontaneously in 2011.[39] More to the point, and as I will detail further below, the nature of neoliberal growth models is such that wide swathes of society, not just specific classes, have reasons for disaffection, even as their preferred course of action in response will vary.

Polanyi's work has also been subjected to minor edits. Burawoy submits that 'knowledge' constitutes a fourth fictitious commodity, while Nancy Fraser proposes the importance of 'emancipation' as a third movement that cannot be fitted in either the move toward the market or the protective countermovement.[40] I disagree with the latter: Polanyi, in his discussion of 'the meaning of liberty in a complex society', a subject of profound interest to him, offers an understanding of liberty as non-domination that can be actualised to encompass many of the emancipatory struggles Fraser refers to.[41] Similarly, and as Fraser herself has persuasively argued, movements such as feminism and anti-racism should not proceed in isolation from larger questions of social justice and economic redistribution.[42]

A final criticism of *The Great Transformation* is that, in spite of its obvious merits, it is vulnerable to co-optation by reformist projects that do not seek to deliver structural changes or modify the nature of capitalist accumulation. Polanyi's biographer wrote of the conflict between his 'Bolshevik soul' and his 'Fabian muzzle', such that his work 'can legitimately be read either as an anti-capitalist manifesto or a social-democratic bedtime story'.[43] I consider it a sterile pastime to judge Polanyi's – or, for that matter, any thinker's – work through the prism of its co-optation by opposed political traditions: right-wing activists like Grover Norquist and Steven Bannon are, after all, fervent admirers of Lenin, while Andrew Breitbart was a right-wing Gramscian. And as the second and third sections of this book make clear, a project of radical social democracy, while not advocating for revolutionary takeover of power or a classless utopia, presents a series of demands that neoliberalism is presently incapable of absorbing.

Instead, I follow sociologist Michael Burawoy in seeing Polanyi and Antonio Gramsci – another thinker of the left whose thought has had a profound influence on the right – as the seminal thinkers of a sociological Marxism that rejects economic determinism and approaches society, culture, and ideas as serious objects of inquiry. There are, in fact, suggestive parallels between the two thinkers' lives. While coming from radically different class backgrounds – Gramsci a Sardinian peasant; Polanyi born to a prosperous Jewish family in Budapest – their origins placed them as partial outsiders in Italy and the Austro-Hungarian Empire, respectively. Both were politicised by an intense experience of left municipal projects: the former in Turin's revolutionary worker councils, the latter in red, interwar Vienna. Striking similarities also exist in their views on subjects such as public regulation – both emphasised that its absence constitutes an explicit political choice, rather than a natural state of affairs – and the economism of orthodox Marxism.[44] As we will see in Chapter Six, Podemos' theoretical underpinnings owe much to Gramsci's theory of hegemony and the latter's overlap with Polanyi needs to be explored in the context of this anti-austerity party's development.

Notes

1. British Geological Survey, 'Seismic waves', www.bgs.ac.uk/discover-ingGeology/hazards/earthquakes/seismicWaves.html.

2. Geoff Manaugh, 'We thought we lived on solid ground: California's earthquakes changed that', *New York Times*, 8 July 2019.

3. Polanyi, *The Great Transformation: The Political and Economic Origins of Our Time*, Beacon Press: Boston, MA, 2001 [1944], p76.

4. David Ulin, *The Myth of Solid Ground: Earthquakes, Prediction, and the Fault Line Between Reason and Faith*, Penguin: New York, 2005, pp12-14.

5. *Ibid.*, p20.

6. Paul Pierson, *Politics in Time: History, Institutions, and Social Analysis*, Princeton University Press: New Haven, NJ, 2004, pp79-83.

7. Ulin 2005, pp106-7.

8. On Aufstehen, see Quinn Slobodian and William Callison, 'Pop-up populism: The failure of left-wing nationalism in Germany', *Dissent*, 8 July 2019.

9. British Geological Survey, 'Seismic waves'.

10. Manaugh 2019.

11. Ulin 2005, p23.

12. Adam Tooze, *Crashed: How a Decade of Financial Crises Changed the World*, Penguin Random House: New York, 2019.

13. For academic debate on Polanyi in Spain, see 'La Gran Restauración: sociología económica de la crisis global y actualidad de la crítica de Karl Polanyi al liberalismo', *Revista Áreas*, No. 31, 2012; Polanyi, *Los límites del mercado*, Capitán Swing: Madrid, 2012. For journalistic coverage, see Víctor Lenore, 'El pensador más peligroso de la izquierda (más que Zizek, Monedero, o Varoufakis)', www.elconfidencial.com, 10 July 2017; José Ignacio Torreblanca, 'Capitalismo de emociones', *El País,* 8 February 2018.

14. Jonathan Hopkin, *Anti-System Politics: The Crisis of Market Liberalism in the Rich Democracies*, Oxford University Press: Oxford, 2020. Manolo Monereo, '¡Que se vayan todos! El retorno del "momento populista" que nunca se fue', www.cuartopoder.es, 29 July 2019; Monereo and Héctor Illueca, *España: Un proyecto de liberación*, El Viejo Topo: Barcelona, 2017.

15. Daniel Luban, 'The elusive Karl Polanyi', *Dissent*, 2 April 2017; see also Torreblanca 2018.

16. On this subject, see Albert Hirschman, *The Passions and the Interests: Political Arguments for Capitalism Before its Triumph*, Princeton University Press: New Haven, 2013.

17. Polanyi 2001, pp136-8.

18. Polanyi 2001, p3.

19. One critique of the New Deal, which draws on Ira Katznelson's account, is that it deliberately marginalised black Americans as a result of Roosevelt having to compromise with Southern Democrats. See Touré F. Reed, 'Between Obama and Coates', *Catalyst*, Vol. 1, No. 4, Winter 2018.

20. Michael Burawoy, 'Facing an unequal world,' *Current Sociology*, Vol. 63, No. 1, 2015, p16.

21. Polanyi 2001, p147.

22. *Ibid.*, p148.

23. See Perry Anderson, 'The Italian disaster', *London Review of Books*, Vol. 36, No. 10.

24. Polanyi 2001, pp237-8.

25. Fred Block and Margaret R. Somers, 'Karl Polanyi in an age of uncertainty', *Contemporary Sociology*, Vol. 46, No. 4, June 2017, p380.

26. Polanyi 2001, p248.

27. *Ibid.*, pp242-5.

28. *Ibid.*, p32.

29. Pippa Norris and Roland Inglehart, *Cultural Backlash: Trump, Brexit, and Authoritarian Populism*, Cambridge University Press: Cambridge, MA, 2019.

30. For a piercing critique of the Norris-Inglehart approach, see José Fernández-Albertos, *Antisistema. Desigualdad económica y precariado político*, Catarata: Madrid, 2018, pp40-52.

31. Polanyi 2001, p36.

32. *Ibid.*, pp134-5.

33. *Ibid.*, p160.

34. *Ibid.*, p169.

35. *Ibid.*, p3.

36. Quoted in Somers and Block, 'The return of Karl Polanyi', *Dissent*, April 2014.

37. *Ibid.*

38. Margaret Thatcher, 'Interview for *Woman's Own*, 23 September 1987', www.margaretthatcher.org.

39. Ernesto Laclau, *On Populist Reason*, Verso: New York, 2005, p67.

40. Michael Burawoy, 'Facing an unequal world', *Current Sociology*, Vol. 63, No. 1, pp5-34.

41. Polanyi 2001, pp257-68.

42. See for example Cinzia Arruzza, Tithi Bhattacharya and Nancy Fraser, *Feminism for the 99%: A Manifesto*, Verso: New York, 2019.

43. Gareth Dale, *Karl Polanyi: A Life on the Left*, Columbia University Press: New York, 2016, p286.

44. Burawoy, 'For a sociological Marxism: The complementary convergence of Antonio Gramsci and Karl Polanyi', *Politics and Society*, Vol. 31, No. 2, June 2003, p193-261. Polanyi's thought is also compatible with Michael Heinrich's 'new reading' of Marx. See for example Pablo Batalla Cueto, 'La vuelta de Marx a un mundo en crisis', https:// elcuadernodigital.com, October 2018; Clara Ramas San Miguel, *Fetiche y mistificación capitalistas*, Siglo XXI: Madrid, 2018.

II

Faultlines

CHAPTER THREE

The Move to the Market

The difficulty lies, not in the new ideas, but in escaping from the old ones, which ramify, for those brought up as most of us have been, into every corner of our minds.[1]

– John Maynard Keynes

They are casting their problems on society, and who is society? There is no such thing! There are individual men and women and there are families, and no government can do anything except through people and people look to themselves first.[2]

– Margaret Thatcher

The age of party democracy has passed. Although the parties themselves remain, they have become so disconnected from the wider society, and pursue a form of competition that is so lacking in meaning, that they no longer seem capable of sustaining democracy in its present form.[3]

– Peter Mair

Donald Trump's presidency may seem shocking today, but this is hardly the first time the US has been governed by a demagogue speaking in the name of the people. Eighty years before Trump's election, in 1936, a presidential hopeful took the stage at Madison Square Garden promising a 'crusade to restore America for its own people'. He went on to blame – in the 'paranoid style' that Richard Hofstadter would describe at length – all the country's problems on allegedly powerful interests and enemies deep within the establishment: 'financial monopoly, speculation, reckless banking, class antagonism, sectionalism, war profiteering'.[4] After that, he engaged in the polarising rhetoric that all populists have a weak spot for: 'Never before in all our history have these forces been so united against one candidate as they stand today. They are unanimous in their hate for me – and I welcome their hatred.'[5]

Who was this charlatan claiming to represent the entirety of his people? Why did he attempt to divide society instead of bringing it together? And how did he get away with criticising moneyed interests when he was himself a member of 'the establishment', born to a wealthy New York family and related to a former president? This rabble-rouser was Franklin Delano Roosevelt. Three days after making that speech, he won the greatest electoral victory in US presidential history: above 60 per cent of the popular vote and every state except Maine and Vermont. By the time Dwight Eisenhower took the White House from Roosevelt's successor Harry Truman, the Democratic Party had spent two decades (1933-53) in the White House and had fundamentally transformed the structure of the US – and indeed, the world – economy.

While his rhetoric would have signalled him as an undesirable populist today, scholars of the US presidency continue to view Roosevelt as the most successful US president of the twentieth century.[6] Earlier in 1936, he had expressed his outlook in even more powerful terms:

> For too many of us the political equality we once had was meaningless in the face of economic inequality. A small group had concentrated in their own hands an almost complete control of other people's money, other people's property, other people's labour – other people's lives. For too many of us life was no longer free; liberty no longer real; men could no longer follow the pursuit of happiness.
>
> Against economic tyranny such as this, the American citizen could only appeal to the organised power of Government. The collapse of 1929 showed up the despotism for what it was. The election of 1932 was the people's mandate to end it. Under that mandate it is being ended.[7]

The passage has a Polanyian ring to it, denouncing the expropriation of labour, land, and money (*The Great Transformation*'s triad of fictitious commodities), linking economic needs to social aspirations, and highlighting public action as the route by which societal wrongs might be righted. Having fled Nazism and writing in Vermont at the height of the New Deal period, Polanyi did in fact witness first hand an unprecedented attempt on the part of the US state to subordinate markets to social imperatives. As Mark Blyth and Sven Steinmo summarise it,

> The Works Progress Administration (WPA), perhaps the most iconic program of Roosevelt's first term, put nearly eight million people to work building bridges, roads, schools, post offices, museums, swimming pools, parks, community centers, zoos, botanical gardens, gyms, universities, and much more. There was hardly a community in the country that did not witness the immediate, visible benefits of public action. By 1938, the United States had spent more on social welfare than any country in the world, including the United Kingdom and even Sweden.[8]

Galvanised by the unprecedented wartime mobilisation and subsequent victory over fascism, the original New Deal impulse led to the establishment of a macroeconomic consensus that lasted until the late 1970s. From then onwards, however, Polanyi's pendulum swung back toward the markets, which mounted an impressive and successful counteroffensive. While attempts to counter marketisation have grown in intensity, we still live in the shadow of the 1970s.

It is no coincidence that the New Deal was launched in 1933, the same year that witnessed the onset of Nazism in Germany and the launch of Stalin's second five-year plan, and one year after Great Britain abandoned its hopes to re-establish the international gold standard. The economic crisis of 1929 had shattered the fragile faith that remained in the nineteenth-century world order, which had been largely destroyed during the First World War but painfully reconstructed to a degree in its aftermath. The attempt to build a new economic order in which the reach of markets was successfully curtailed, however, did not take full shape until the aftermath of the Second World War. This countermovement, then, depended on a multiplicity of conditions, among which FDR's election was a necessary but not sufficient one. This chapter will take us through the international emergence and consolidation of the post-war consensus, followed by the move to the market in the 1970s, and the social and political consequences of this shift. It will home in on Margaret Thatcher's Britain, as a national example of this transition that offers political lessons well beyond that country's borders. The two subsequent chapters will tell the story of how neoliberalism rose and consolidated itself in the two countries that form the focus of this book: Spain and the US.

Embedded liberalism

At the time FDR made his Madison Square Garden speech, he had already been president for an entire term. This period had witnessed an ambitious attempt to counter the damage caused by the 1929 crisis with government activism – the American tradition of evaluating political leaders after their first 100 days in office dates back to the barrage of measures and directives Roosevelt undertook in this period of time. But his work was far from done. In 1937-38, in fact, he attempted to reverse course and balance the budget by cutting 17 per cent of government expenditure – an effort that sent the US economy into a second recession.[9] Failure on this front, coupled with ongoing pressure to his left from the American labour movement, meant that the New Deal impulse was eventually sustained. But it was not until late 1941, with the US's entry into the Second World War, that a monumental public spending programme in the form of the war effort lifted the US economy and unleashed its full potential.[10] From 1945 onwards, the New Deal provided a powerful model for the politico-economic consensus that became entrenched in the US and Western Europe, where it was expanded under the mantle of social democracy.

What were the defining elements of the international economic order in this period? Its origins are typically traced to the 1944 Bretton Woods conference. This seminal meeting, which lay the foundations of the post-war international monetary order – underpinned by the US dollar, itself linked to gold, but reliant on a more flexible system of rates than the nineteenth-century gold standard – saw the creation of the International Monetary Fund and the World Bank. Bretton Woods's key architects were John Maynard

Keynes and Harry Dexter White, who represented the UK and US delegations respectively. Perhaps the best way to describe the world inaugurated at Bretton Woods is as, following John Ruggie, 'embedded liberalism'. The conference's goal was to establish an international monetary regime that would:

> safeguard and even aid the quest for domestic stability without, at the same time, triggering the mutually destructive external consequences that had plagued the interwar period. This was the essence of the embedded liberal compromise: unlike the economic nationalism of the thirties, it would be multilateral in character; unlike the liberalism of the gold standard and free trade, its multilateralism would be predicated upon domestic interventionism.[11]

The paradigm was 'embedded' because it allowed for a considerable degree of national intervention in the economy and relied on Keynesian demand management. Strong labour unions, often benefitting from corporatist arrangements, extracted important demands from both capital and the state. As a result, this period also witnessed the development and establishment of modern welfare states, especially in Western Europe. At the same time, the arrangement remained 'liberal'. Cross-border financial flows were actively regulated and states frequently enforced capital controls, but international trade expanded during the post-war recovery and subsequent economic boom. The period therefore witnessed an internationalisation of production and finance – an expansion of the commodifying dynamics that Polanyi warned against. For this reason, many on the left view the post-war arrangement as a failed one, bound to give way to a cruder, less state-centric configuration of capitalism, as it effectively did from the late 1970s onwards.

Ultimately, understanding how the post-war settlement came into being is more important than establishing whether it was ideal or flawed. The exceptional nature of the circumstances under which embedded liberalism came into being highlights the extent to which subordinating markets to society requires both favourable structural conditions and determined political action.

Perhaps the greatest variable at play was wealth redistribution. As

Thomas Piketty, Emmanuel Saez and Anthony Atkinson's research has showed at length, the two world wars effected an extraordinary destruction of private wealth, such that, in 1945, wealth inequality in Western capitalist economies was at an all-time low. Even in the US, which did not experience either war's impact with the intensity that European countries did, the 1940s brought about a 'great compression' of national incomes as a result of the 1929 crisis, the New Deal, the war effort and post-war reconstruction.[12] The destruction of private wealth and the levelling of national incomes on such a large scale meant that the societies that emerged from the Second World War did not resemble their more hierarchical and unequal predecessors of the late nineteenth century.

The wartime period witnessed a parallel increase in states' structural capacities. Managing increasingly complex areas of the economy – seemingly impossible at the beginning of the twentieth century – was a task governments performed routinely by 1945. Having launched immense war efforts, states were then forced to take the reins of economic and industrial planning, nationalising entire sectors of the economy in order to carry them forward. An intuitive conclusion was that, if they had proved capable of systematically destroying Europe in two world wars, governments could at least take the trouble to rebuild their countries and provide infrastructure, education, healthcare, and employment for their citizens in times of peace. These commitments would require states to expand their fiscal capacity, especially in the form of progressive taxation, but this development had already begun to take place during the war years. Just as importantly, the fight against fascism generated solidarity across social classes and facilitated pursuing redistributive agendas on a national level. To quote Blyth and Steinmo again,

> Back in 1931, the top tax rate (on incomes of more than $100,000) was not far from what it is today, 25 per cent. Immediately upon entering office, Roosevelt raised the rate on incomes of more than $1 million to 63 per cent. In 1932, he raised that rate to 79 per cent [...] By 1944, even the lowest-income earners in the United States paid taxes at a rate of 23 per cent, and those at the top paid an astounding 94 per cent.[13]

A macro-structural development of this sort is brought to life in popular culture about the period. Consider the British TV series *Downton Abbey*, which begins in 1914 and presents a landowning, aristocratic family struggling to adapt as its traditional position gives way to a modern, more egalitarian world. Or Ken Loach's 2013 documentary, *The Spirit of '45*, which depicts the climate of social and political mobilisation that paved the way for the key achievements of the British welfare state, including the National Health Service, in the aftermath of victory against the Axis powers. Both reflect a key observation of one of the leading historical studies of the period, Tony Judt's *Postwar*: 'World War One destroyed old Europe; World War Two created the conditions for a new Europe.'[14]

In this new Europe, expansion of state provision had strong popular backing. This was partly due to the fact that attempts at re-establishing nineteenth-century liberalism in the inter-war years had failed disastrously, and were widely perceived as having fuelled the rise of fascism. There was little appetite to return to the mistaken policies of the past after the immensity of the struggle against the Axis powers, and the huge sacrifices made for victory.[15] And no country had sacrificed as much or contributed as decisively to the destruction of the German war machine as the Soviet Union. In 1945, Moscow retained control over Eastern Europe and represented an alternative – still a relatively inspiring one – to business-as-usual. Communist parties in France, Italy, and Yugoslavia had been mainstays of resistance against fascism. Thus the presence of communism – in Western Europe, as well as Eastern Europe and East Asia – was a key factor determining the choices of economic and political elites as they formulated a social-democratic settlement that softened the sharpest edges of capitalism.

Across Western Europe and the US, embedded liberalism delivered unprecedented growth that benefitted a majority of the population, but especially the middle and working classes. The post-war reconstruction effort generated a lasting economic boom. Mass middle classes emerged for the first time in history. Economic prosperity was taken for granted to the extent that British Prime Minister Harold Macmillan could proclaim that people had 'never had it so good', and not appear out of touch or complacent.[16] In France, *'les trente glorieuses'* (the thirty glorious years) witnessed an extraordinary expansion of the *dirigiste* state, especially under the leadership of Charles de Gaulle. And just as the centre left would accept neoliberalism in the 1970s, it was the political right who absorbed and submitted to the hegemonic ideas of the day. As Eisenhower – a Republican president, whose administration raised marginal tax rates for top income earners up to 90 per cent – pointed out in a letter to his brother Edgar,

> Should any party attempt to abolish social security, unemployment insurance, and eliminate labour laws and farm programs, you would not hear of that party again in our political history. There is a tiny splinter group, of course, that believes you can do these things ... Their number is negligible and they are stupid.[17]

I have deliberately painted a rosy picture of embedded liberalism in order to better qualify it. This period, while inspiring at the level of economic management and successful in both channelling social demands and producing new, bolder ones, was riddled with contradictions. On an international level, it coexisted with the high Cold War and a massive build-up of nuclear and conventional military capabilities in the US and the USSR. Colonial wars in Indochina and Algeria, CIA-sponsored coups in Iran and Latin America, as well as US interventions in Vietnam and the Korean peninsula, made for a brutal international order. Western European countries such as Spain and Portugal never properly experienced embedded liberalism, because they remained under the heel of US-supported dictators. On the other side of the Iron Curtain, armed interventions in Hungary and Czechoslovakia projected a bleak and ruthless image of Soviet communism.

Domestically, embedded liberalism faced unmet social demands and often failed to deliver precisely where it claimed to be strongest. Issues such as women's oppression, racism toward migrants from former colonies and black Americans, and the societal critiques implicit in student activism were little heeded by the managers of Western welfare states. For their many merits, these operated as massive, lumbering bureaucracies that treated citizens in an alienating or overbearing manner: an orientation that Stuart Hall, to whose work I will return, defined as statism.[18] Post-war Keynesianism was also eventually bound to run into a contradiction first identified by the Marxist economist Michał Kalecki: full employment in a heavily unionised workforce would likely generate a constant upward pressure on median wages. As a result, he presciently warned,

> A powerful bloc is likely to be formed between big business and rentier interests, and they would probably find more than one economist to declare that the situation was manifestly unsound. The pressure of all these forces, and in particular of big business, would most probably induce the Government to return to the orthodox policy of cutting down the budget deficit.[19]

Just as importantly, a model of consumption-driven growth that is oblivious to environmental considerations is not viable today, when climate change has become the greatest threat that we face as a species. In short, we have much to learn from past attempts to subordinate markets to social needs. But we must avoid nostalgia and conceive alternatives that push beyond the horizons of embedded liberalism.

The onset of neoliberalism

When diagnosing present times, it is common to search for the origins of our problems in two decades: the 1960s or the 1980s – or, occasionally, both. The social movements of the 1960s initiated sweeping cultural changes, some of which our societies are still far from assimilating. This is seen to be the root of many enduring conservative grievances. The alternative optic focuses on the 1980s, which witnessed the transformation of the dominant economic paradigm in a period dominated by the figures of Reagan and Thatcher. Thirty-odd years later – as seen from either view – the 'losers from globalisation' are restless.

Both views shed light on important questions, but they miss the most important story. It was during the 1970s that an inflection point came, and embedded liberalism gave way to neoliberalism.[20] This term is widely employed in political economy, sociology, political theory, philosophy and other disciplines, although its meaning often varies according to the discipline. The term is so widely and loosely used that it has almost become a synonym for most things economic that leftists and progressives dislike. It is sometimes claimed that the term is just an insult and there is no such thing as 'neoliberalism'.[21] It is therefore worth unpacking its origins, and explaining what I mean when I use it.

By the beginning of the 1970s, the Bretton Woods system was coming under increasing strain. The US, which in 1945 enjoyed a position of economic supremacy, was beginning to run commercial deficits against the now-recovered economies of Western Europe and Japan – a position it was to an extent structurally forced into, as the dollar's role as the world reserve currency pushed the country to adopt inflationary monetary policies and provide liquidity on a global level.[22] The problem, in the aftermath of the huge public expenditure required to sustain both Lyndon Johnson's Great Society programme and the Vietnam war, was that the US was effectively exporting inflation to the rest of the world, abusing what one French finance minister and future president called the dollar's 'exorbitant privilege'. In 1965, de Gaulle announced his decision to trade France's dollar reserves in gold, as under the Bretton Woods system the dollar was nominally convertible and valued at $35/ounce. These pressures reached a tipping point in August 1971, when Richard Nixon ended the dollar's convertibility to gold and effectively put an end to the Bretton Woods system.

The rest of the embedded liberal order began to falter as inflation, compounded by the 1973 and 1979 oil shocks, increased hand in hand with unemployment. The phenomenon, known as stagflation, was particularly disconcerting because it contradicted one of the guiding assumptions of the existing economic paradigm: that there was an inversely proportional relationship between inflation and full employment, and public policy should concentrate on ensuring the latter, rather than preventing the former. With both inflation and unemployment climbing to double digits across Western Europe and the US, embedded liberalism's credibility began to crumble. It was in this context that a series of business and finance groups, organised business and industrial lobbies and neoclassical economists, supported by a dense network of new think tanks and publications, mounted an ambitious counteroffensive – detailed in Chapter Five – against the hegemonic ideas of the day.

In a context of economic malaise and instability, this lobbying effort proved enormously successful, and led to the ascent of neoliberalism between the late 1970s and the mid 1980s: first by pressuring political leaders and parties and thwarting left alternatives to the ongoing economic impasse, then by effectively dictating governing agendas, and finally by colonising states and multilateral institutions such the World Bank and the International Monetary Fund – which was possible largely as a result of the disproportionate influence that the US and UK wielded over these institutions.

What were the characteristics of this new paradigm? For Mark Blyth and Jonathan Hopkin, neoliberalism, like embedded liberalism, can be viewed as an international macroeconomic regime with 'hardware' (specific managing institutions) and 'software' (policy commitments), which generate specific outcomes. Embedded liberalism's hardware consisted of corporatist arrangements and domestic markets; its policy commitments, Keynesian demand management and full employment. This setup generated a labour-friendly set of outcomes: moderate inflation, an unprecedented share for labour in GDP, low inequality and corporate profits, strong trade unions, weak international markets and central banks. Neoliberalism, in contrast, is guided by the hardware of independent central banks and international finance; its software is a commitment to maintaining price stability, and this translates into a series of market-friendly outcomes: low inflation, a rise in capital's share of overall GDP, stagnant wages, weak trade unions, and high capital mobility, to name but a few.[23]

Following Cornel Ban, I define neoliberalism as an ideology centred on three key tenets: the need for policy to win the approval of financial markets, the importance of an open economy, and the enforcement of internal and external competition. I also recognise sociologist Stephanie Mudge's point that, under neoliberalism, 'economic life needed as much management as ever, but the understanding of what was to be managed was wholly different. International markets, not the domestic economy or the interest conflicts therein, were the objects of management'.[24] We should therefore not expect to witness a withering away of the state under neoliberalism, but rather its reconfiguration to achieve a different set of purposes. In short, and as the historian Quinn Slobodian points out, neoliberalism is a theory of state design, not a theory of markets.[25]

As we have seen, the second of Ban's characteristics needs some qualification in the current moment. Recent years have seen an increase in protectionism in the US, which its trading partners then mirror whenever they are affected by new tariffs or sanctions. This is one of the ways that the Trump presidency has pushed at the boundaries of contemporary economic orthodoxy – seeking a reconfiguration toward a more nationalist and autocratic variant of neoliberalism, but not superseding it with a different paradigm. Yet it is simply not the case that advanced economies embraced free and open trade before Trump's presidency. Steep tariffs and subsidies to sectors of the economy deemed politically or socially sensitive have long been standard practice across the West, as testified by Reagan's steel tariffs and the EU's Common Agricultural Policy. The principle of commercial openness is generally enforced in opportunistic ways: small or weak economies are expected to abide by the principle, but great powers like the US interpret it with latitude. In any event, financial deregulation and openness, far from being restricted by the arrival of the radical right in the White House, has continued unabated since 2017.

Ban's definition is also useful for implicitly highlighting elements of neoliberalism that were viewed as vital in the 1970s and 1980s and have subsequently been abandoned. The most notable example is monetarism: formulated by Milton Friedman, popularised by Thatcher, and enforced dramatically by chairman of the Federal Reserve Paul Volcker in a series of interest rate shocks in the 1980s that paved the way for the internationalisation of neoliberal principles, it subsequently went out of vogue in both the US and UK.[26] Notice again that Ban's definition does not mention the state playing a decreasing role in economic management, which is often assumed to be a guiding tenet of this macroeconomic regime. As Polanyi and Gramsci both pointed out, de-regulation is itself a form of regulation, actively enforced by the state and demanding the deployment of specific legal frameworks.

Ban also emphasises that neoliberalism is an ideology with global reach but local thrust. Since it is national governments that are pre-eminently tasked with adopting it, they graft neoliberalism onto domestic economic traditions and conditions. This makes his definition useful for comparing different neoliberal economic regimes and growth models. Consider Scandinavia. While its countries are far from homogeneous, they are nevertheless well known for being small, open economies with competitive export sectors that have developed extensive welfare states and other social protection measures. As such, they tend to be held up as exemplars by the left, centre left, and even the centre right in countries like Spain.[27] Does this make 'coordinated market economies', as they are known in the academic literature, less neoliberal than 'liberal market economies' like the US and UK? Not exactly. If we look at a different set of variables, we find that Scandinavian countries enforce much more orthodox policies than do their Anglo-Saxon counterparts. Fiscal and monetary policy are a case in point. Where northern European economies adopted a hardline, stringent and ultimately disastrous position vis-à-vis the European Central Bank's capacity to support countries in the Eurozone periphery, British and American central banks embraced a much more activist stance that helped to mitigate the impact of the 2008 crisis, both nationally and globally.[28] Public research is another example. As Mariana Mazzucato has pointed out, we tend to think of EU states as more dynamic than the US, and they are in fact much more active when it comes to welfare provision; but America remains far ahead of Europe when it comes to public investment in research and development.[29]

What this means, then, is that Scandinavian countries have done a much better job of embedding their economy in social needs, even while they adapted to neoliberalism. To be clear, while I do argue that huge improvements can be made even within the boundaries of the existing economic paradigm – contrast the US or Spain to Denmark – I am not arguing that our societies' challenges and contradictions can be solved through a more inclusive model of neoliberalism. Even in Scandinavia, inhabiting this paradigm means that austerity, internal devaluation, and deregulation will remain the default policy tools in the face of economic downturns.[30]

What are neoliberalism's social and economic effects? To begin with, it has accelerated trends that were beginning to be visible in the late 1970s. One is the increasing importance of international trade and the corresponding dislocation effects: manufacturing jobs are offshored and relocated, leading to the creation of globally integrated supply and production chains; across the US and Europe, deindustrialisation and a gradual move toward the service sector have been accelerated by automation and rapid technological change. Financial liberalisation further increased integration and interdependence between different economies – the process commonly known as globalisation. Because these transformations take place in an environment in which states are expected to conform to market pressures rather than vice versa, and because they effectively limit their capacity to intervene in the economy and secure revenues through progressive taxation, government's choices are often reduced to adopting compensatory versions of neoliberalism (i.e., those that provide social protection to citizens displaced by economic transformations) or disciplinary ones, where the 'losers of globalisation' are ignored, and punished when they voice their discontent. As we will see, Spain adopted the former strategy until 2012, while the US has largely enforced the latter.

Perhaps the clearest way of examining neoliberalism's impact is by measuring the evolution of wealth and income inequality. A good departure point is Oxfam's annual report on the matter. In 2019, this survey established that the world's twenty-six richest billionaires owned as many assets as the poorest half of the world – 3.8 billion people. In the decade that followed the financial crisis, the number of global billionaires almost doubled. Throughout 2018, the world's 2,200 billionaires witnessed their wealth increase by an average of 2.5 billion dollars per day, while the poorest half of the world experienced its wealth contract by 11 per cent during the year. Following the Credit Suisse Global Wealth Report, another leading reference on the matter, Oxfam bases its calculations on individuals' net asset positions. This is an imperfect benchmark, as it could rank an indebted Harvard Business School student 'poorer' than a Bangladeshi textile worker with no debts. Nevertheless, the picture of global inequality that it lays out is in line with that of other leading publications, such as the World Inequality Report. And while these figures can seem somewhat abstract, inequality has tangible effects: the Oxfam report also notes that 10,000 people die every day due to lack of access to healthcare.[31]

Thomas Piketty's ground-breaking 2014 study, *Capital in the Twenty-first Century*, tells a similarly alarming story. It can be roughly summarised in the form of a U-curve (Figure 3.1) that measures income inequality in the US across the length of the twentieth century. The U-curve shows the period between 1914 and 1945 as a period of unprecedented destruction of private wealth, as incomes that derived exclusively from capital – i.e., those of the top one per cent – plummeted and the country saw a 'great compression' of incomes during the two world wars. Between 1945 and 1980, embedded liberalism held a relatively equitable distribution in place: economic recovery meant the return of private wealth, but high and inclusive growth rates also improved the relative position of middle and working classes. The U-curve's two peaks are the Gilded Age at one end, characterised by disproportionate levels of inequality; at the other, the post-1970s world, which is rushing to resemble the past in terms of the extreme concentration of wealth. Under neoliberalism, public policies designed to facilitate the accumulation of capital – deregulation, privatisation, tax cuts on capital and top incomes, and the rise of tax havens, to name a few – vastly accelerate this process of upward redistribution. A similar evolution has therefore taken place in Europe, although the Belle Époque was even more unequal than the Gilded Age, and inequality today remains lower than in the US, thanks largely to the survival of social-democratic welfare states.

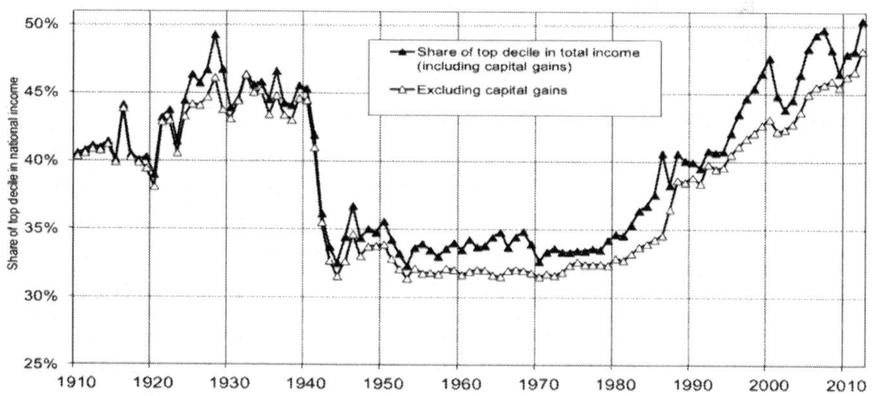

3.1: Income inequality in the United States, 1910-2010. Source: Thomas Piketty, *Capital in the Twenty-first Century* (Harvard University Press, Cambridge, MA, 2014), P291.

Who benefits from this economic regime? The obvious answer is the rich, but a more detailed look at the numbers tells a slightly different story. In most countries, the richest decile of the population splits between a top one per cent that has witnessed its wealth grow exponentially – the trend becomes extreme if we focus on the top 0.1 per cent or 0.01 per cent – and the remaining nine per cent, which has kept modestly ahead of average growth trends. The bottom 90 per cent has seen its position stagnate or simply deteriorate.[32] This is an important fact to bear in mind, as it suggests that the 'losers of globalisation' are not a few Appalachian coal miners or former Detroit autoworkers, but the overwhelming majority of citizens across Western societies. This, in turn, helps us to understand why the 2011 protests were not limited to the working class (which for Piketty would constitute the five lower deciles of wealth distribution, against the next four for the middle class and the top one for the upper), in line with the Polanyian framework I laid out in the first section of the book.

A brief look at the evolution of the global distribution of incomes illustrates how my framework provides a middle-range theory, rather than one with universal application. The phenomenon I have described has not affected the emerging middle classes of countries like Brazil, India, or, most importantly, China, which over the course of recent decades has grown at a pace unprecedented in history (while refusing to abide by neoliberal development guidelines). The disparity in growth patterns is captured in Christoph Lakner and Branko Milanovic's 'elephant chart', which traces the growth of global incomes by each decile (Figure 3.2). The elephant's back and head represent the growing middle classes of emerging economies, while the tip of its snout stands for the ballooning incomes amassed by the top one per cent. This study is concerned with the beginning and middle of the snout, that is, with the eightieth and ninetieth deciles, which represent the working and middle classes of Western Europe and North America. Over the course of the last three decades, they have witnessed their incomes stagnate or grow at a negligible rate.[33] A similarly shaped chart was developed by the World Inequality Database team in a 2017 report (Figure 3.3).

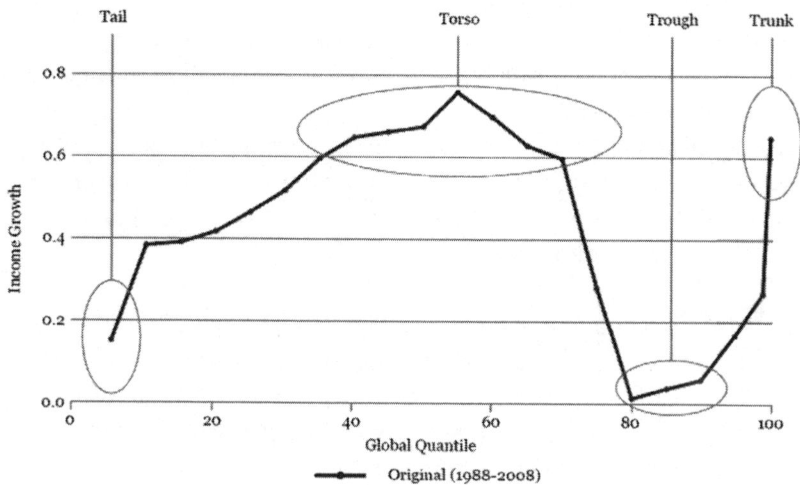

3.2: Lakner and Milanovic's 'elephant chart'. Source: Homi Kharas and Brina Seidel, 'What's happening to the world income distribution? The Elephant Chart revisited', Global Economic and Development Working Paper 114, Brookings, April 2018.

Total income growth by percentile across all world regions 1980–2016

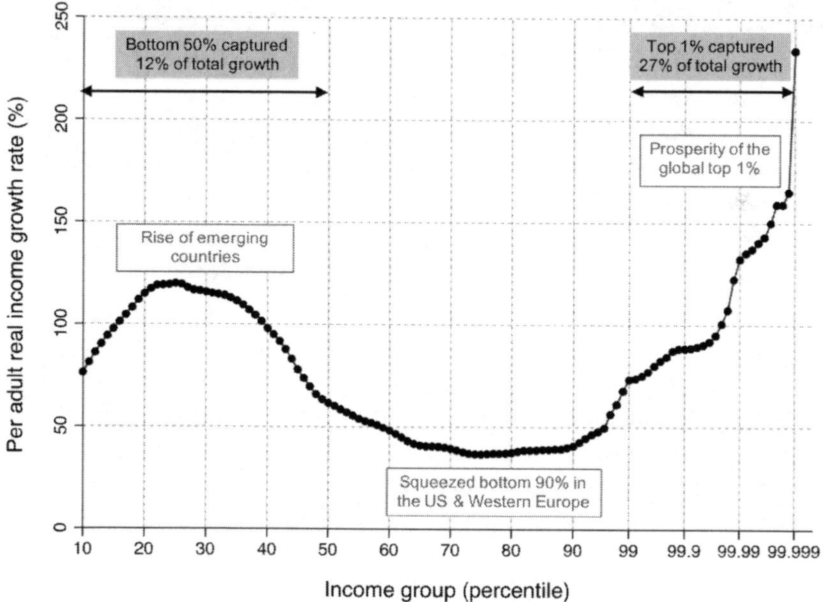

3.3: The World Inequality Database's 'elephant chart'. Source: Facundo Alvaredo et al., 'The Elephant Curve of global inequality and growth', December 2017. https://wid.world/document/elephant-curve-global-ine-quality-growth-wid-world-working-paper-2017-20/

Piketty's story, then, concerns the decoupling of the top one per cent from the rest of Western society, which is left in an increasingly tenuous position. He also observes that, absent ambitious pre- and re-distributive policies, as well as economic growth, market economies gravitate toward a position where the rate of the return on capital is greater than the growth rate (his famous equation, r > G). Under such conditions,

> the past tends to devour the future: wealth originating in the past automatically grows more rapidly, even without labour, than wealth stemming from work, which can be saved. Almost inevitably, this tends to give lasting, disproportionate importance to inequalities created in the past, and therefore to inheritance.[34]

This environment – aggravated by the increased capacity for the wealthy and multinational corporations to avoid fiscal pressure by resorting to tax havens – makes it easier for the well-off to become rentiers and live on inherited wealth rather than work, as was common in nineteenth-century Europe. In Balzac's novels, which Piketty is fond of quoting, it makes more economic sense for the less well-off to attempt to marry into wealth than to play by the 'rules of the game' and work hard. This is what the future holds for post-crisis Europe and the US as long as inequality continues to increase and growth is either anaemic (a juncture of 'secular stagnation,' to use Larry Summers' expression) or concentrated among top earners.[35] This drift toward oligarchisation is worth noting, because we live in societies that are fond of extolling the virtues of meritocracy. (Often, in fact, it is the same people whose wealth grants them unearned advantages who wax poetic about the virtues of thrift and diligence.) The belief that one can do well simply by working hard, while undercut by a growing body of empirical evidence, remains essential to sustaining the social contract in capitalist democracies.

Disembedded economy, fragmented society, political void

Until 2008, the effects of inequality were partially softened by financialisation. Beginning in the 1980s, the deregulation of

Wall Street and European financial sectors unleashed a flood of cheap consumer credit that muffled concerns about inequality or increasing precarity. In 2008, as is well known, that period came to an end. Citizens were compelled, in the words of the Communist Manifesto, 'to face with sober senses the conditions of life' under neoliberalism.[36]

The conclusions to be drawn about these conditions, however, were not immediately clear. Countries subjected to neoliberalism have witnessed a slow but steady erosion of communal bonds and institutions – a breakdown of social capital and civic engagement, to use the terms of Robert Putnam's classic 2000 study, *Bowling Alone*.[37] One of the consequences of this dynamic is that the organisations, institutions, and even parties that traditionally channelled popular demands into political action and public policy are substantially weakened, if not absent altogether. As political scientist José Fernández-Albertos has shown, most citizens who are especially negatively impacted by neoliberal policies also find themselves at an organisational disadvantage when it comes to expressing their electoral preferences. Fernández-Albertos describes those caught in this negative feedback loop as 'politically precarious' (*precarios políticos*).[38] While they are often the target audience of populist parties on both the left and the radical right, more often than not they simply drop out of a political process where they consider, not unreasonably, that their voices have become meaningless.

A useful example of how social atomisation conditions contemporary politics, which I will explore at length further on, is that of labour unions. Previously instrumental not just for centre-left parties but for economic governance, coordination with other forms of activism, and socialising workers into clear political choices, unions have seen their influence decrease dramatically over the past four decades – partly from the transition of Fordist, industrial economies into service-based ones, but also as a result of stringent labour market reforms and anti-union legislation.

Unlike the previous configurations of capitalist development – Fordism, which delivered numerous (and eventually unionised) jobs in the manufacturing sector; or even financialisation, which offered an unsustainable mirage of prosperity – the current wave of economic 'disruption' brings about a combination of precarious jobs, labour arbitrage (Uber), and rent-seeking (Airbnb), coupled with the growing threat of automation. Technological changes that take place within the framework of neoliberalism compound the tendency toward segmentation and atomisation: social networks become ideological eco-chambers, dating apps make searching for a partner resemble grocery shopping, allegedly ground-breaking innovations like Uber and Deliveroo amount to vehicles for labour arbitrage, Netflix allows broke millennials to spend their weekends saving money by 'nesting' inside their increasingly unaffordable apartments, and so forth.[39]

It is one thing to say that neoliberalism causes a series of measurable effects and to observe that populist parties have done well in recent years, quite another to link economic tendencies to social and political events – or, to put it in academic jargon, identify a 'causal pathway' through which one leads to the other. I have already pointed out how social fragmentation relates to the past decades' economic drift. But what about actual politics? At this point, the work of American sociologist Stephanie Mudge and the late Irish political scientist Peter Mair, both of whom analysed the changing nature of Western party systems, becomes crucial to understanding how a disembedded economy and a fragmented society have led to the emergence of populist politics – in other words, to finish welding Karl Polanyi's work to that of Ernesto Laclau and Chantal Mouffe.

As Hopkin and Blyth point out, macroeconomic regimes generate political party systems that are compatible with their defining features. Under embedded liberalism, the dominant political organisation in Western capitalist democracies was the catch-all party, which emphasised economic management and the provision of public goods as key components of its identity. In order to compete electorally, these parties – in Europe, mainly social democrats and Christian democrats, representing the centre left and centre right respectively – 'mobilised large numbers of citizens in activities remote from elections, from social clubs to youth events to study groups'.[40] Developing strong ties to other social actors was a prerequisite for successful electoral competition: as noted above, labour unions were especially important allies for social-democratic parties, as they proved especially adept at mobilising voters, providing electoral muscle in the form of both funds and volunteers.

This social embeddedness allowed centre-left parties, as Mudge points out, to 'cultivate not only progressive policies but also progressive political identities'.[41] In her landmark study of social democracy's twentieth-century reinventions (from socialist to Keynesian, and from Keynesian to neoliberal), Mudge stresses the importance of centre-left parties' provision not only of cultural infrastructure and policy expertise, but also their capacity to intermediate between different social sectors. She identifies the Keynesian 'economic theorist' as the lynchpin of centre-left parties in the heyday of Keynesianism. This figure combined the academic credentials of a professional economist and university professor with a strong and interdependent relationship with centre-left parties and unions. Economic theorists were therefore able to navigate across and mediate between the worlds of academia, party politics, and organised labour. Guided by a 'Keynesian ethic', they provided centre-left governments with the technical know-how to reconcile the demands of their leading constituencies with stable macroeconomic governance.[42]

The onset of neoliberalism put an end to the conditions in which catch-all parties prospered. Absent an environment with an ever-expanding supply of public goods, they had to adapt in three important ways. Discursively, they endorsed Thatcher's mantra that 'there is no alternative' to marketisation, and rushed to proclaim their commitment to open markets. Institutionally, they externalised policymaking – for example, by promoting central bank independence and the dominance of monetary over fiscal policy, which effectively absolved governments of responsibility for managing the economy. Electorally, they detached themselves from other social actors and allies – which now became a burden rather than an asset – in order to cultivate an image of technocratic expertise in increasingly media-driven electoral competitions.[43]

As Mudge points out, this transformation brought internal shifts within social democratic parties. The most notable of these was the replacement of the Keynesian economic theorist by a new figure: transnationalised, finance-oriented economists (TFEs). Guided by a 'neoliberal ethic', TFEs have a much lower capacity for intermediation, and they speak 'on behalf of an object that operate[s] beyond economists, parties, and domestic policies: the market'.[44]

Their prescriptions have brought centre-left parties into conflict with their electoral base, which has slowly morphed over time. As Daniel Oesch and Line Rennwald point out in their influential study of the relationship between occupational status and voting patterns across Europe, social democratic parties have shifted from being the representatives of precarious or low-skilled workers to courting socio-cultural professionals – the salaried middle classes, state employees in sectors such as education and healthcare – as their primary constituency.[45] To the extent that conforming to a neoliberal agenda continues to take its toll on the centre left's electoral performance, these parties have complemented the role of TFEs with new kinds of experts: policy wonks and spin doctors with a permanent eye to crafting media narratives.[46]

Taken together, these changes have transformed catch-all parties into cartel parties. Mair and Richard Katz first theorised this party model as one under which:

> the goals of politics become self-referential, professional and technocratic, and what substantive intra-party competition remains becomes focused on the efficient and effective management of the polity. Competition between cartel parties focuses less on differences in policy and more ... on the provision of spectacle, image, and theatre. Above all, with the emergence of cartel parties, the capacity for problem-solving in public life becomes decreasingly politicised and is less and less embodied in the competition of political parties.[47]

By 2006, Mair began to take a dim view of the viability of cartel party systems. In an ominously titled *New Left Review* essay, 'Ruling the void', he warned that Western democracies were suffering from a 'mutual withdrawal' that threatened to hollow out their political substance. For their part, political elites were detaching themselves from society, pursuing careers in state, multilateral, and corporate institutions in relative isolation from electorates. But voters too were disengaging, becoming less and less active. Party affiliation and identification were decreasing, so that with less participation came higher electoral volatility. Mair's claims were backed by a wealth of empirical evidence from Western European democracies in the

1990s. He linked the trend to economic and cultural transformations leading to social atomisation: 'With the increasing individualisation of society, traditional collective identities and organisational affiliations have become enfeebled.'[48]

The distances between parties were shrinking as a result of their common acceptance of similar policies. At the same time, party-voter distances were stretching as electorates grew disenchanted with these relatively undifferentiated political options. 'What remains is a governing class', Mair observed, such that 'opposition, when structurally constituted, increasingly comes from outside conventional party politics, in the form of social movements, street politics, or popular protests'.[49] Organisational and technological changes reinforced this tendency:

> In early 2002, Anthony Giddens pointed to the watershed that had been passed in mass media entertainment through the growing popularity of reality TV. 'Previously television was something that reflected an external world which people watched. Now television is much more a medium in which you can partici-pate.' In conventional politics, by contrast, the shift has been the other way around. Previously, and probably through to at least the 1970s, conventional politics was seen to belong to the citizen, and something in which the citizen could, and often did, participate. Now, it has become part of an external world which people watch from outside: a world of political leaders, separate from that of the citizenry. It is the transformation of party democracy into 'audience democracy'.[50]

Mair developed these insights in a book with the same title as his 2006 article, published posthumously in 2013. It opened on a similarly sombre note: 'Although the parties themselves remain, they have become so disconnected from the wider society, and purse a form of competition that is so lacking in meaning, that they no longer seem capable of sustaining democracy in its present form.'[51] Mair stressed that, with the decline of parties' representative functions (that is, their capacity to integrate and mobilise the citizenry, as well as to act as articulators and aggregators of social interests), only their procedural ones – i.e., their capacity to establish patronage networks and organise parliamentary and governing activity – remained. As a result, cartel parties were accelerating an ongoing tendency across Western societies: the privileging of the constitutional, at the expense of the popular, dimension of democracy (or, to use Mouffe's terminology, the liberal over the democratic tradition).

As in 2006, *Ruling the Void* warned that 'the widening gap between rulers and ruled has facilitated the often strident populist challenge that is now a feature of many advanced European democracies'.[52] Interestingly, Mair identified Tony Blair as an early symptom of this double drift toward technocracy and populism. As Britain's prime minister embraced the so-called 'third way' and took the Labour Party fully into the neoliberal consensus, he was fond of reminding the public that 'I was never really into politics ... I don't feel like a politician even now.' A member of his cabinet un-ironically stated that 'depoliticising of key decision-making is a vital element in bringing power closer to the people'.[53] The UK, as we will see, provides the clearest example of how the enforcement of a particular macroeconomic regime produced lasting socio-political change.

Paradigm shifts and authoritarian populism: The case of Thatcherite Britain

British Prime Minister Margaret Thatcher, a figure of enduring negative resonance for the contemporary left, was a pioneer of the move to neoliberalism in Western Europe, blazing the path followed by Ronald Reagan and the Spanish ambassadors of neoliberalism, among others. Her eleven years in power (1979-1990) remain the clearest example of a national transition to global neoliberalism. As Mouffe has pointed out, Thatcher also offers an interesting template for making dramatic economic transformations fit into a wider, hegemonic political project – and, as such, a potential model for the left.[54]

Her agenda was lucidly dissected by two thinkers with the same surname. The first of these, Peter Hall, trained his sights on the most prominent outworking of Thatcher's project: the economic transformations it brought about. He described these transform-ations as a 'paradigm shift'. Normal policymaking involves first- and second-order changes: modifying the settings of instruments considered necessary to achieve a given policy goal (for example, targeting inflation at a different rate) or, at the most, changing both the settings and the instruments used to achieve the goal (targeting inflation at a different rate, through wage repression instead of interest rates). Paradigm shifts involve third-order changes, in which not just the instruments settings and the instrument themselves change, but also the hierarchy of goals guiding the policymaking process. This was the case in the transition from embedded liberalism to neoliberalism:

> Inflation replaced unemployment as the preeminent concern of policymakers. Macroeconomic efforts to reduce unemployment were rejected in favour of balanced budgets and direct tax reductions. Monetary policy replaced fiscal policy as the principal macroeconomic instrument, and it was reoriented toward fixed targets for the rate of monetary growth. Many regulatory instruments associated with state intervention, such as incomes policies, exchange control, and quantitative limits on bank lending, were eliminated.[55]

Peter Hall's seminal article on paradigm shifts notes that the move to monetarism had in fact been foreshadowed by Thatcher's Labour predecessor, James Callaghan, following the International Monetary Fund's 1976 emergency loans to the UK and the 1978-79 'winter of discontent' crisis. The failure to manage the country's economic crisis with Keynesian prescriptions, followed by the application of austerity policies by a centre-left government, contributed to legitimising Thatcher's pursuit of a radically different agenda, promoted at the time by her economic adviser Keith Joseph through a budding network of think tanks, journals, and media outlets. The move toward neoliberalism in the UK concluded with the Labour Party's full acceptance – and reinforcement – of this paradigm during Tony Blair's tenure (1997-2007). Centre-left politicians such as Bill Clinton, Felipe González, François Mitterrand, and Gerhard Schröder played similar roles in their respective countries. Their contribution to ending embedded liberalisms is important to recognise, as it challenges the standard narrative that our current economic order dates back to the right's offensive during the 1980s.

As Thatcher's example shows, neoliberalism both predated her arrival and consolidated in her aftermath.

Peter Hall's account also addresses the extent to which market liberalisation in the UK was the result of deliberate and forceful state action, not a spontaneous process. But it was not limited to a series of economic directives. Because he grounded his notion of paradigms on Thomas Kuhn's influential work on the subject, Peter Hall was aware that the process of replacing one paradigm with another always depends on the development of specific normative and political conditions. 'The ensuing struggle to replace one policy paradigm with another', he wrote, 'was a societywide affair, mediated by the press, deeply imbricated with political competition, and fought in the public arena'.[56]

It was the second Hall, Stuart, who theorised this process at length in a series of insightful essays that discerned Thatcher's strengths at a time when many of her critics – among them Eric Hobsbawm – fatally underestimated her.[57] Borrowing from Gramsci as well as from Laclau and Mouffe's theorisation of populism, he defined Thatcherism as a project of 'regressive modernisation': reactionary in intent, but capable of harnessing a popular will – and therefore consent and electoral majorities – toward a series of common goals. As the term itself suggests, the project was inherently volatile, conjoining liberal economic ideas with organic English conservatism – a tension symbolised in the equation 'free market, strong state'. While this narrative projected a vision of society that was appealing to a critical mass of voters, Thatcherism relied on force as well as consent: the events that cemented her – initially floundering – tenure were, after all, the 1982 Falklands war and the 1984-85 miners' strike, crushed in violent, antagonistic terms: Arthur Scargill and the National Union of Mineworkers she defined as an 'enemy within' more dangerous than the Argentinian 'enemy without'.[58]

In order to enforce its contradictory programme, Thatcherism successfully articulated a series of popular notions and grievances – the demand for rule of law, discontent with taxes, essentialised notions of race and citizenship, the perceived need for an aggressive foreign policy, fear of 'creeping collectivism' following embedded liberalism's incapacity to recover from stagflation – in a reactionary direction, framing Britain's socio-economic woes as a national and moral crisis. Against this backdrop, it offered an entirely different vision of society – a hegemonic project, in Gramsci's terms – and never lost sight of the larger picture, setting 'the national-moral question *above* the economic one'.[59] Thatcher acknowledged this herself in a moment of lucidity: 'economics are the method: the objective is to change the soul'.[60]

Stuart Hall described this project as 'authoritarian populism'. Indeed, Thatcher's discursive and operational strategies are a reactionary variant of the ones Laclau and Mouffe had not yet theorised when she came to power:

> This is a high-risk strategy for the right ... 'The people' must be mobilised if they are to join the party in the crusade to drive from the temples of the state the creeping collectivists, trendy Keynesians, moral permissiveness and soft appeasers who have occupied it in the era of the social-democratic consensus. Yet in order to prevent a populist mobilisation from developing into a genuinely popular campaign, the arousal of populist sentiment must be cut off at just the correct moment and subsumed or transformed into the identification with authority, the values of traditionalism and the smack of firm leadership. It is a strategy of authoritarian populism.[61]

The left, both Marxist and social democratic, was incapable of appreciating this 'delicate and contradictory ideological exercise' because it analysed events through an economistic prism that rendered it incapable of grasping the subtleties behind Thatcher's strategy. 'Anti-Marxist as it is in its political orientation, Labour is profoundly "economistic" in its outlook and ideology. It really does suppose that economic facts transmit themselves directly into working-class heads, without passing through the real world.'[62]

It does not follow, however, that progressive politics was doomed from the moment the 1970s crisis began to take shape. As Stuart Hall also acknowledged, up until the 1984-85 crushing of the miners' strike, working-class mobilisation, the experience of the Greater London Council, and Tony Benn's rise within the Labour Party sketched out what a viable left alternative to the end of embedded liberalism might have looked like in the UK. In fact, this period witnessed a high-water mark of labour strikes and mobilisation across the UK, but also in the US, and indeed in Spain – where they proved decisive in paving the way for the country's transition to democracy following Francisco Franco's death in 1975. Ultimately, as we will see, it was not enough to prevent the onset of neoliberalism.

Notes

1. John Maynard Keynes, preface to *The General Theory of Employment, Interest, and Money*, Wordsworth: London, 2017.
2. Thatcher, 'Interview for *Woman's Own*, 23 September 1987', www. margaretthatcher.org.
3. Peter Mair, *Ruling the Void: The Hollowing out of Western Democracy*, Verso: London, 2013, p1.
4. Richard Hofstadter, 'The paranoid style in American politics', *Harper's Magazine*, November 1964.
5. 'October 31, 1936: Speech at Madison Square Garden', https://miller-center.org.
6. See Steve Benen, 'Scholars' rankings offer good news for Obama, bad news for Trump', www.msnbc.com/, 19 February 2018.
7. Franklin D. Roosevelt, 'Acceptance Speech at the Democratic National Convention (1936)', 27 July 1936, https://teachingamerican-history.org.
8. Mark Blyth and Sven Steinmo, 'Can a pandemic defeat the politics of austerity?', *Foreign Affairs*, 22 April 2020.
9. 'When a turn toward austerity turned to disaster', www.npr.org, 16 July 2011.
10. In fact, and as Christina Romer has argued, the New Deal's original impulse was carried forward through monetary rather than fiscal policy. See Christina D. Romer, 'What ended the Great Depression?', *Journal of Economic History*, Vol. 52, No. 4, December 1992, pp757-84. I am indebted to Pálma Polyák for this insight.
11. John Gerald Ruggie, 'International regimes, transactions, and change: Embedded liberalism in the postwar economic order', *International Organization*, Vol. 36, No. 2, Spring 1982, p393.
12. Claudia Goldin and Robert A. Margo, 'The Great Compression: The wage structure in the United States at mid-century', *Quarterly Journal of Economics*, Vol. 107, No. 1, February 1992, pp1-34.
13. Blyth and Steinmo 2020.
14. Tony Judt, *Postwar: A History of Europe since 1945*, Penguin: New York, 2006, p6.

15. *Ibid.*; see also Eric Hobsbawm, *The Age of Extremes: The Short Twentieth Century, 1914-1989*, Abacus: London, 2006, pp109-77, 257-86.

16. '1957: Britons "have never had it so good"', On This Day: 20 July, BBC website.

17. Quoted in Jacob S. Hacker and Paul Pierson, *Winner-Take-All-Politics: How Washington Made the Rich Richer – And Turned its Back on the Middle Class*, Simon & Schuster: New York, 2010, p189.

18. Stuart Hall, *The Hard Road to Renewal: Thatcherism and the Crisis of the Left*, Verso: London, 1990.

19. Michał Kalecki, 'Political aspects of full employment', *Political Quarterly*, Vol 14, No. 4, pp322-31. Quoted in Jonathan Hopkin and Mark Blyth, 'The global economics of European populism: Growth regimes and party system change in Europe', *Government and Opposition*, Vol. 54, No. 2, December 2018.

20. On this subject, see Hacker and Pierson 2010, pp1-8.

21. On this subject, see Matt Bruenig, 'Neoliberals used to call themselves New Democrats', *Jacobin*, 22 December 2017.

22. This problem was named the 'Triffin dilemma', after Robert Triffin, the American-Belgian economist who first theorised it.

23. Hopkin and Blyth 2018.

24. Stephanie L. Mudge, *Leftism Reinvented: Western Parties from Socialism to Neoliberalism*, Harvard University Press: Cambridge, MA, 2018, p300.

25. https://twitter.com/zeithistoriker/status/1184171555150020608.

26. Samir Sonti, 'The world Paul Volcker made', *Jacobin*, 20 December 2018.

27. For an example of the latter, see Luis Garicano, *El dilema de España. Ser más productivos para vivir mejor*, Península: Barcelona, 2014.

28. On this subject, see Adam Tooze, *Crashed: How a Decade of Financial Crises Changed the World*, Penguin Random House: New York, 2019.

29. For a brief explanation, see Francisco de Zárate, 'Innovación: "La desigualdad seguirá aumentando si permitimos que las empresas se queden con todos los beneficios"', https://retina.elpais.com, 27 April 2019.

30. On Sweden's transition to neoliberalism, see Blyth, *Great Transformations: Economic Ideas and Institutional Change in the Twentieth Century*, Cambridge University Press: Cambridge, 2002.

31. Oxfam, 'Public good or private wealth?', www.oxfam.org/en, 21 January 2019.

32. Thomas Piketty, *Capital in the Twenty-First Century*, Belknap Press: Cambridge, MA, 2014.

33. See for example Dylan Matthews, 'Are 26 billionaires worth more

than half the planet? The debate, explained', www.vox.com, 22 January 2019.

34. Piketty 2014, p378.

35. Lawrence H. Summers, 'US economic prospects: Secular stagnation, hysteresis, and the zero lower bound', *Business Economics*, Vol. 47, No. 2, 2014, pp65-73.

36. Karl Marx and Friedrich Engels, 'Manifesto of the Communist Party', in Robert C. Tucker (ed), *The Marx-Engels Reader*, W. W. North: New York, 1978.

37. Robert D. Putnam, *Bowling Alone: The Collapse and Revival of American Community*, Simon & Schuster: New York, 2000.

38. José Fernández-Albertos, *Antisistema. Desigualdad económica y precariado político*, Catarata: Madrid, 2018..

39. On this subject, see Cathy O'Neil, *Weapons of Math Destruction: How Big Data Increases Inequality and Threatens Democracy*, Random House: New York, 2016.

40. Hopkin and Blyth 2018, p197.

41. Mudge 2018, p42.

42. Mudge 2018.

43. *Ibid.*

44. *Ibid.*, p374.

45. Daniel Oesch and Line Rennwald, 'Electoral competition in Europe's new tripolar space: Class voting for the left, centre right, and radical right', *European Journal of Political Research*, Vol. 57, No. 4, November 2018, pp783-807.

46. Mudge 2018.

47. Quoted in Mair 2013, p83.

48. Mair, 'Ruling the void?', *New Left Review*, 42, November-December 2006, p46.

49. *Ibid.*

50. *Ibid.*, p44.

51. Mair 2013, p1.

52. *Ibid.*, p19.

53. Quoted in Mair 2006, p26.

54. Chantal Mouffe, *For a Left Populism*, Verso: New York, 2018.

55. Peter A. Hall, 'Policy paradigms, social learning, and the state: The case of economic policymaking in Britain', *Comparative Politics* Vol. 25, No. 3, April 1993, p284.

56. *Ibid.*, p287.

57. See Perry Anderson, *Spectrum: From Right to Left in the World of Ideas*, Verso: London, 2007, p317. Anderson defined Hall's writing on Thatcherism as 'what remains the most clairvoyant single example

of a Gramscian diagnostic of a given society on record'. Anderson, *The H-Word: The Peripeteia of Hegemony*, Verso, London, 2017, p86.
58. 'Speech to the 1922 Committee ("the enemy within")', www.margaretthatcher.org.
59. Hall 1990, p85.
60. 'Interview for *Sunday Times*', www.margaretthatcher.org.
61. Hall 1990, p72.
62. *Ibid.*, p208.

CHAPTER FOUR

From Consensus to Crisis: Spain, 1978-2013

'Consensus' is an evasive term, notoriously close to euphemism, that parades rather than defines a democratic will. Its usage is best confined to the elites that like to talk of it.[1]

– Perry Anderson

The rules must not be oriented toward the weak but toward the strong. That is a hard message. But it is an economic necessity.[2]

– Angela Merkel

I am sure we will get out of the economic crisis, although I do not agree with the way we'll do so. I am not so sure we will get out of the institutional crisis, however. This crisis rushes toward a dissolving anarchy.[3]

– Felipe González

The previous chapter outlined the global transition towards neoliberalism in the 1970s, noting how it was conducted on a national basis, producing different local adaptations of a common international regime. With their differences and similarities, these national varieties formed the socio-economic fault lines along which populist parties and movements developed from 2008 onwards. The onset of neoliberalism did not take place in one single, dramatic shift, but developed at a series of critical junctures in each case.

In Spain, the first critical juncture came in the late 1970s and early 1980s as the country, transitioning from dictatorship to democracy, embraced a compensatory version of neoliberalism. The second critical juncture was in the early 1990s, as the converging criteria for the Economic and Monetary Union (EMU) and euro membership locked in countercyclical economic management and outsourced monetary policy to the European Central Bank (ECB).

The resulting growth model was successful in refining the rougher edges of neoliberalism – thus its compensatory nature – and shoring up a decisive social bloc of support. After four decades of dictatorship, Spain enjoyed something like normality: it became yet another European polity with cartelised political parties, decreasing civic engagement, and a markedly anaemic associational culture, punctured by brief episodes of intense mobilisation.[4] But its economy had two fundamental weaknesses, derived from each critical juncture. The post-1982 growth model coexisted with structurally high levels of unemployment, which never dipped below 8 per cent of the workforce. At the same time, euro accession opened the floodgates to capital flows from core Eurozone countries into the Spanish economy. In this context, a massive real estate bubble – seemingly addressing the unemployment problem and giving the misleading impression that Spain was making the best use of foreign credit – developed with the connivance of the country's leading political parties.

The third critical juncture came in 2008-2013. First, the combined impact of the financial crash and the bursting of the real estate bubble highlighted the weakness of Spain's developmental model. In 2010, the European push for austerity measures forced Spanish policymakers to adopt a series of unpopular and counterproductive economic policies. From 2011 onwards, these two developments led to a crisis of representation. Spain's political elites witnessed their legitimacy erode at an unprecedented rate, in a climate of intense social contestation characterised by the development of widespread, spontaneous protests against austerity policies – that is, a Polanyian countermovement leading to a populist moment.

Embedded neoliberalism

In retrospect, the road to Spain's post-2008 purgatory seems paved with good intentions. Few democratisation processes have received as much praise as the country's 1975-82 transition, which witnessed the end of Francisco Franco's thirty-six-year dictatorship and the establishment of a constitutional monarchy through a collaborative process of reform between the old regime and the democratic opposition. This process crystallised in the 1978 constitution, frequently upheld as the seminal achievement of a political culture that had abandoned the vicious antagonism of the past in favour of 'consensus' among elites and between political parties. In their classic study, Juan Linz and Alfred Stepan hailed Spain's democratisation as a 'paradigmatic' example, worthy of study and emulation; a fellow transitionologist gushed that 'no other new democracy birthed by the global democratic revolution of the last three decades is more celebrated than Spain in the comparative literature on democratic transitions'.[5]

La transición unfolded on the basis of the opposition's inability to topple the Franco regime, coupled with many Francoists' realisation of the need to bring Spanish politics into line with those of the rest of Western Europe. A well-known observer of the process, Manuel Vázquez Montalbán, described this relationship as a 'correlation of weaknesses'.[6] While hagiography on the subject is common, the transition, which witnessed the murder of more than 600 Spaniards for political reasons in the decade following Franco's death, was more violent than Portugal's Carnation Revolution, which took place at roughly the same time. Furthermore, and as Robert Fishman has shown at length, the latter delivered greater levels of social and economic cohesion across a number of important indicators, producing a more inclusive culture of democratic practice.[7] In contrast to the emancipatory outburst brought by Portugal's revolution, the dominating sentiment in Spain throughout the transition, according to one of its leading participants, was fear.[8]

Economically, the country emerged from four decades of authoritarian rule in an ambiguous economic position. In 1959, the Franco dictatorship had jettisoned its autarchic economic model in favour of a developmental programme that led Spain's economy to grow at a pace second only to Japan's throughout the 1960s. To an extent this boom reflected Spain catching up with the rest of Western Europe – all the more so given the fact that the country had failed to experience a post-war economic recovery similar to France or Italy's, instead stagnating for the two decades that followed the civil war. While key policymakers within the dictatorship's technocrat faction saw France's *dirigisme* and state-dominated economy as an example to follow, their plans to emulate it were thwarted by the regime's unwillingness to strengthen its tax base by pressuring upper income brackets – under Franco, fiscal revenues never surpassed 22 per cent of GDP – as well as by the assassination of their leading patron, and the end of French indicative planning in 1973.[9]

By the mid 1970s this developmental model had run out of steam. Unemployment and inflation rose to double digits following the impact of the oil crises. Economic unrest went hand-in-hand with political uncertainty: Franco died in November 1975 and the first democratic elections, won by Francoist-turned-reformist Prime Minister Adolfo Suárez, were held in June 1977. The first attempt at stabilisation came in October of that year with the Moncloa pacts, reached between regime reformists (led by Suárez and economy minister Enrique Fuentes Quintana), the newly legalised Communist Party, and Comisiones Obreras (Workers' Commissions, or CCOO) (CCOO, the country's leading union, had witnessed spectacular, undercover growth during the late Franco years), and grudgingly supported by other opposition parties. The agreement committed the Spanish economy to 'mixed liberal measures, such as trade liberalisation, financial liberalisation, an orthodox stabilisation plan (currency devaluation, tight monetary policy, wage increases well below inflation rates), with more redistributionist measures, such as tax increases and increased welfare expenditures'.[10] While these measures averted an immediate crash, economic and political volatility persisted. As Suárez, who would face an – ultimately failed – coup d'état from Francoist hardliners in 1981, had presciently remarked,

> In other times the economic measures agreed upon by the cabinet would have been enough to drastically change the course of the economy. But now they have not been as efficient as one might have expected and this [is owing] to the impact of politics on our economy. So long as a country is haunted by unknown quantities of politics, the economy cannot be reactivated or stabilised.[11]

Such stabilisation did come in the early 1980s, as the post-Franco regime ossified into a bi-party system with an idiosyncratic political culture.[12] The mainstay of this edifice was the Spanish Socialist Workers' Party (PSOE). In 1982, the PSOE won the first of several landslide electoral victories, effectively bringing the transition to an end. The PSOE itself, however, emerged from the process a changed party. Pacts between regime and opposition elites necessitated the sidelining of protesters and the workers' movement, both of whom had initially been crucial to thwarting the dictatorship's hopes for continuity. With transition and its aftermath concentrating decision-making power in the hands of a few elites, and under the charismatic guidance of its young leader Felipe González and party whip Alfonso Guerra, the PSOE became profoundly centralised – an institution where, as Richard Gillespie notes in his landmark study, 'a handful of party bosses could sit down for a cup of coffee and chart the party's course for the next two years'.[13]

Under guidance from West German social democrats and the Spanish central bank's influential network of technocrats, the PSOE also moderated its macroeconomic agenda. Upon coming to power, González and his advisors restructured the Spanish economy around what Ban has termed an embedded neoliberal model: 'a neoliberalism ensconced within the measures that compensate citizens for the dislocating effects of the market'.[14] To this end, Spain's socialists oversaw the dismantling of loss-making industrial assets owned by the state and the transition towards a service-based economy through an orthodox stabilisation package. This strategy generated considerable tension with the PSOE's union arm, the UGT, leading to the latter's official break with the government following the 1988 general strike. But as Sebastián Royo has highlighted, party-union institutional links were configured so as to grant the former power over the latter. The UGT found itself in a position of weakness and its objections were, as Ban points out, 'no match for the combined forces of the [central bank heavyweight Luis Ángel] Rojo network and the Guerra party apparatus'.[15] As it broke its traditional ties to the labour movement and social movements – many of which withered away as their key leaders were drafted into the centre-left's ranks and became party loyalists – the PSOE under González effectively underwent a process of cartelisation, similar to those described in Chapter Three. In this way, Spain's socialists followed a slightly different evolution to the one Stephanie Mudge traces in *Leftism Reinvented*, whereby social democratic parties cycled through socialist, then Keynesian, then neoliberal reinventions over the course of the twentieth century. A classic socialist party until the civil war, the PSOE then came close to disappearing during the Franco dictatorship – when opposition to the regime was effectively led by the communists – and re-emerged in the late seventies as a neoliberal party *avant l'heure*.

The party, however, adopted a compensatory version of neoliberalism and did not allow its economic decision-making to be driven exclusively by market imperatives. While claiming that 'the best industrial policy is the one that doesn't exist', successive PSOE governments groomed 'national champions' in telecommunications, infrastructure, energy and banking.[16] Following Spain's 1986 accession to the European Economic Community, structural funds financed an ambitious national infrastructure programme, which over time consolidated the international competitiveness of Spanish construction and railway companies. The party also allocated funds to developing the welfare state, with considerable success in the field of healthcare – Spain's public healthcare system is repeatedly ranked among the world's best – as well as making significant progress in pensions and education.

Ultimately, the model's performance was mixed. In Ban's words, it provided 'rapid stabilisation, recovery, enhanced competitiveness, and internationalisation' of the Spanish economy at the expense of an 'implosion of large parts of Spain's industrial base and the highest unemployment rates among industrialised countries'.[17] Figure 4.1 highlights how high structural unemployment – which at one of its lowest points, at the height of the real estate bubble, still stood at 8.2 per cent of the workforce – became a defining feature of the Spanish economy from the 1980s onwards. Spain's developmental path stands in marked contrast to that of Portugal, where a radical democratisation process led to more inclusive labour market outcomes.[18] To external observers, however, the Spanish economy was the more sophisticated and appealing of the two Iberian countries. In the literature on European varieties of capitalism, Spain became, alongside Italy and France, an example of state-enhanced capitalism: a model halfway between the liberal economies of the Anglo-Saxon world and the coordinated economic management enforced by Germany and other northern European countries.[19]

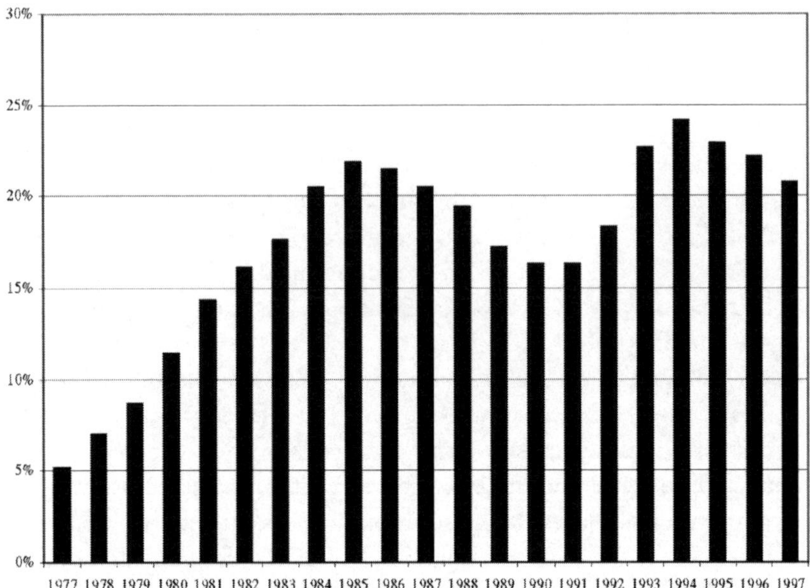

4.1: Annual rates of unemployment in Spain, 1977-1997. Source: Katrina Burgess, 'Unemployment and union strategies in Spain', *South European Society and Politics*, Vol. 4, No. 3, 1999.

A political changing of the guard, with the conservative People's Party (PP) succeeding the PSOE in 1996, brought adjustments at the edges of this economic model but no alterations to its fundamental course. José María Aznar (1996-2004) oversaw the privatisation of the state's telecoms, energy, infrastructure, and banking giants, consolidating an incestuous relationship between Spain's policy elites and the boardrooms of its leading firms – not an edifying partnership, but one that is prevalent across other West European countries.[20] The PP's tenure was characterised by economic continuity: the government developed a working relationship with the labour unions in its first term in office, during which Aznar positioned himself as a third-way centrist, in the spirit of Tony Blair and Gerhard Schröder.[21] A second term, now with an absolute majority in Parliament, witnessed a neoconservative turn in foreign policy and an increasingly confrontational relationship between the PP and Basque and Catalan nationalist parties, but no fundamental economic changes. Continuity at the top of the Economy Ministry, with only three ministers between 1985 and 2009, spoke to embedded neoliberalism's smooth sailing throughout this period. The PSOE and the PP had seemingly reached a consensus to maintain the existing macroeconomic model.

The 2000s also witnessed the creation of Spain's gigantic real estate bubble. By 2005, lending for construction companies was absorbing 29 per cent of GDP and Spain was developing a Dutch disease of sorts, with a real-estate, rather than oil, boom sapping the competitiveness of its economy. Education dropout rose rising rapidly as students moved to the construction industry.[22] The development was turbocharged by euro membership, which unleashed a flood of credit originating in the financial systems of core Eurozone countries. As Ban has pointed out, this boom 'concealed the inability of Spain's growth model to reduce high levels of unemployment, while locking a large part of the young males into low-productivity construction jobs.'[23] At the time, the Spanish authorities simply boasted that Spain was leading Europe in job creation. The responses that they got from Brussels often confirmed their optimism: Spain was maximising its competitive advantages –good weather, empty space, beautiful coastlines that could be turned into tourism assets– while maintaining fiscal discipline.

When the PSOE returned to power in 2004 some of its leading policymakers warned about the real estate boom, but the party eventually settled for a more complacent outlook.[24] Although the construction boom, fuelled by credit from the core Eurozone countries, generated a steep rise in private debt, Spain was running budget surpluses and abiding by the Maastricht criteria. A year before Lehman Brothers' collapse, Prime Minister José Luis Rodríguez Zapatero was celebrating Spain overtaking Italy in per capita GDP and joining what he called the global economy's 'Champions League'.[25] To please the left, the prime minister had an ambitious agenda on civil liberties, including the legalisation of gay marriage and the formation of gender-equal governments, as well as progressive economic policies, such as public allowances for families with disabled members.

'Once inside the EU, we have to follow German directives'

If the transition and the PSOE coming to power in the early 1980s marks the first critical juncture in Spain's recent economic history, the 1990s witnessed the second one, which consolidated the embedded neoliberal model. Spain's 1989 accession to the European Monetary System had already opened the door to the outsourcing of monetary policy to Germany's Bundesbank and the end of competitive devaluation as a policy tool in the face of recession. The 1992 Maastricht Treaty then reinforced this trend, committing its signatories to balanced budgets and low debt levels – a maximum deficit of 3 per cent of GDP, and public debt kept below 60 per cent of GDP. A year after the euro was adopted, and in a rare display of bipartisan consensus, the PP and the PSOE signed a commitment to balanced budgets. The implications of this process were already then reminiscent of Polanyi's writing on the gold standard. As Finance and Economy Minister Carlos Solchaga was told:

> Once inside the EU, we have to follow German directives on monetary and exchange rate policy. Any attempt to derail them would attract harsh sanctions from the market and a costly loss of credibility ... Believing you could act differently meant you did not understand the markets and lived in the past.[26]

If the development of neoliberalism proceeded mainly among national lines, the process of European integration, which has critically strengthened these dynamics in recent decades, merits a separate discussion and a brief digression from the Spanish case. Monetary union began to take shape following the 1970s and 1980s exchange rate crises in Europe, and accelerated with German reunification, which made other – especially French – European policymakers anxious to have Berlin firmly anchored within a united Europe. The drive for the single currency, then, coincided with the collapse of the Soviet Union and the high tide of neoliberalism in what economist Joseph Stiglitz has called 'the roaring nineties'. The decade witnessed the growing popularity of using central bank independence as a means of wresting monetary policy away from politicians, who supposedly faced time inconsistency problems (that is, they were permanently tempted to adjust the money supply to electoral rather than market cycles). Because the euro also took its founding inspiration from the Deutsche Mark – the only European currency to withstand instability and inflationary pressures throughout the 1970s – the ECB became the paragon of central bank independence, even more insulated from everyday, democratic politics than the Bundesbank, and with a narrow mandate to keep inflation below 2 per cent (the US Federal Reserve, in contrast, is entrusted with a dual mandate: promoting maximum employment and ensuring price stability). As Sheri Berman and Kathleen McNamara warned in a prescient article, this institutional architecture would have profound distributional effects:

> The extreme independence of the ECB is meant to reassure financial and business elites that price stability will trump other economic goals and that Europe's economic policy will be appropriately insulated from the demands of labour and other domestic interest groups. The decisions to free Europe's central bank from political control and to focus narrowly on fighting inflation, in other words, were not 'technical' or 'apolitical', as most advocates of independence argue. Rather, as with all difficult policy choices, they involve painful trade-offs that will benefit some more than others...the existing setup smoothens the bankers' dealings with one another at the expense of public trust. It will also exacerbate tensions between European monetary policy and national economic policies and cycles.[27]

Spain embraced this process uncritically, the only opposition to Maastricht coming from the communist-dominated coalition United Left (IU), which was nevertheless divided on the subject. Because the transition to democracy proceeded on the assumption that the dictatorship stood in the way of the country's aspirations to join 'Europe', and because Spanish public opinion combines low national self-regard with a generally positive view of the EU – an attitude enshrined in José Ortega y Gasset's famous dictum, 'Spain is the problem, Europe the solution' – the Spanish public tends to be supportive of European integration and, until the 2008 crisis, Spain was a strong example of the 'permissive consensus' regarding integration.[28] As a consequence, the notion that policymakers in

Brussels or Berlin might be more incompetent than those in Madrid barely resonates with most Spaniards.[29] This state of affairs was somewhat modified by the post-2010 push for austerity, as the EU's popularity witnessed an unprecedented downturn in Spanish public opinion, but has largely held.

It was also not immediately clear that the common currency's budgetary constraints would be strictly enforced. Throughout the early 2000s, Germany and France breached the Maastricht guidelines to address domestic economic considerations. Subsequently, however, this was understood as a clear policy failure that opened the door to fiscal indiscipline across the Eurozone periphery. Since that period, the Eurozone's macroeconomic policy has consisted of an increasingly loose monetary policy (especially following Mario Draghi's accession to the ECB presidency in 2011) and an increasingly tight fiscal policy, as national governments are bound not just by the Maastricht guidelines but by new layers of supervisory mechanisms, agreements, and sanctions, such as the 2011 Treaty on Stability, Coordination, and Governance.[30]

In the context of the 2010 push for austerity, and as economic historian Adam Tooze has documented, this framework enabled a massive bait and switch.[31] A troika composed of the ECB, the European Commission and the International Monetary Fund forced troubled peripheral economies (most notably Greece, Portugal, and Ireland) to prioritise debt reduction in order to cover the potential losses of banks in core Eurozone countries. Italy and Spain were also affected, with limited bailouts to their financial systems. Their exposure stemmed from reckless lending prior to 2008, when the convergence in Eurozone interest rates gave the misleading impression that investing in Greek and German sovereign bonds was equally safe. As part of the bait and switch, however, the notion that both lenders and borrowers should be held responsible when a loan falls through was conveniently ignored.

Also downplayed was the fact that core Eurozone banks, not peripheral economies, constituted the main systemic risk to the EU's financial architecture. Greece represents slightly over one per cent of the EU's total GDP.[32] Contrast this to Deutsche Bank, under considerable strain in 2012 – and still today – which had an asset footprint representing 80 per cent of Germany's GDP and a

40:1 leverage ratio, such that even a small downturn in its assets' valuation would have wreaked havoc with its balance sheet.[33] The Netherlands' ING had an asset footprint worth 211 per cent of the country's GDP, while the three largest French banks represented 316 per cent of their country's GDP. To give a sense of the problem's dimensions: on the eve of the 2008 crash, America's six largest banks had a *combined* asset footprint worth 61 per cent of US GDP. As Mark Blyth points out, the problem was not that European banks were, as in the US, 'too big to fail': they were simply too big to bail out.[34]

Demands for austerity came hand-in-hand with an essentialist narrative, in which southern EU countries were blamed for their allegedly counterproductive habits – a propensity to indulge in *fiestas*, *siestas*, and the general dissoluteness of Mediterranean lifestyles, in contrast to thrifty northern Europeans. Former Dutch Finance minister and Eurogroup President Jeroen Dijsselbloem, for example, famously remarked that 'as a social democrat, I attribute exceptional importance to solidarity. [But] you also have obligations. You cannot spend all the money on drinks and women and then ask for help.'[35] German Chancellor Angela Merkel, invariably upheld by mainstream analysts as the polar opposite of a populist, invoked the thriftiness of the 'Swabian housewife' who – unlike her indolent southern neighbours – never lived beyond her means. Such claim are false, of course – to this day, Spaniards on average spend 26 per cent more time at work than Germans – but they became a convenient trope to avoid blaming core European banks or examining the sustainability of Germany's repeated budget surpluses.[36]

Austerity failed to address the Eurozone's problems and proved counterproductive even on its own terms, as countries subjected to it have witnessed a build-up of their public debt.[37] This would have come as a predictable consequence to anyone who studied the lessons of the 1929 crash, as recessionary spending cuts effectively shrink national economies, thereby increasing debt-to-GDP ratios. But German elites have drawn questionable lessons from their country's economic history: namely, that it was hyperinflation that led to the rise of fascism.[38] As for the country's leading economists, to quote a *Financial Times* columnist, they 'fall roughly into two groups: those that have not read Keynes, and those that have not understood Keynes'.[39] Faced with an unprecedented economic crisis, and as soon as the 2008-09 Keynesian interlude was over, they began pressuring for austerity.

As Jonathan Hopkin has pointed out, the consequence of this push was to split the Eurozone between debtor – i.e., peripheral – and creditor – i.e., core – countries. It is no coincidence that, as he explains, the former (Spain, Portugal, Greece) have witnessed the rise of left populists seeking a more equitable outcome to the 2008 crisis and a mutualisation of Eurozone debts. Creditor countries, in contrast, initially witnessed a greater rise in radical-right populism, which opposes intra-European solidarity.[40] To this day the EU's macroeconomic problems remain unsolved, as Eurozone policymakers have failed to modify its fundamental architecture, and austerity – or, in the best-case scenario, fiscal inaction – has consolidated as the default policy response to new recessions.

While few economists still argue that austerity leads to economic growth in the short term, they can nevertheless justify its function beyond immediate fiscal consolidation – that is, repayment of the public sector's loans. According to this view, internal devaluation can improve a country's balance of payments and place it on the path to becoming an export-led economy, offering a viable development model in the future. Lowered wages make goods produced in the country become more competitive overseas, and therefore able to claim a bigger share of foreign markets. But this narrative is flawed on two accounts. First, it reverses the linearity of the reasoning behind export-led growth. Economies like Germany's have a structural bias toward wage moderation because they have powerful export sectors, but they did not develop the latter as a direct consequence of the former. It is not the case that Southern European economies can reconfigure and emulate this model in the space of a few years, and it is no surprise that attempts to do so through austerity policies have not yielded successful results.[41] Secondly, this strategy is only sustainable to the extent that it ignores the fact that any country's commercial surplus is another country's deficit: as the *Financial Times*' Martin Wolf once put it, if everybody followed in Germany's footsteps, the world would have to run a surplus against Mars.[42] The viability of such a strategy is all the more limited in the context of the European common market, an immense economic unit that conducts a much greater volume of trade within than beyond its borders.

Within the European left, this state of affairs has frequently led to the conclusion that the EU is a mere vehicle for German hegemony and neoliberalism or, at the very least, an institution that serves to hollow out national politics in the way that Mair foresaw.[43] Therefore, any political movement that seeks a more equitable society must frontally oppose it. There is ample evidence to sustain this interpretation but it is, nevertheless, an overly functionalist view that fails to take the power of ideas into serious consideration. As political economist Matthias Matthijs argues, the Eurozone's course of action from 2010 onwards was counterproductive even for the German government and Eurozone elites. It effectively transformed Greece's deficit problems into an existential crisis for the euro, which will remain a frail foundation for German hegemony in the absence of a banking and fiscal union and intra-European debt mutualisation.[44] In order to assess Germany's policy responses, then, one needs to understand the ideological framework that underpinned them, not simply its national interests or those of its ruling class – which are, in any case, not always objectively evident. Furthermore, it is not simply the case that the crisis was handled exclusively through a German – that is, 'ordoliberal' – ideological lens.[45] Oddny Helgadóttir has shown how key economic assumptions in the drive for austerity originated in Italy's Bocconi School, where Alberto Alesina developed the concept of expansionary austerity: the now-discredited notion that spending cuts in the middle of a recession can promote economic growth.[46]

A simply oppositional approach to the EU also fails to analyse the EU in time, miscasting its present state as the essence of the European integration project. But claiming that the EU is irredeemably flawed because it has furthered neoliberalism is rather like advocating for nation states to be dismantled, on the grounds that they have performed the same function since the late 1970s. In most left-Eurosceptic analyses, however, 'national sovereignty' (i.e., state power) is upheld as the key bulwark against EU-driven neoliberalism. The truth, of course, is that neither the EU nor individual states are explicitly designed for neoliberal management. As Wolfgang Streeck's review of European social policy makes clear, the EU, like its member states, has witnessed an involution from embedded liberalism and the promotion of far-reaching social schemes to a much less ambitious, market-conforming worldview.[47] Another left critic of the present EU, Perry Anderson, has highlighted, in his appraisal of Jean Monnet, how the integration process originally served to project, rather than to limit, state sovereignty, delivering a 'European rescue of the nation-state', in Alan Milward's formulation.[48]

Just as importantly, the prescriptions that flow from a standard left-Eurosceptic diagnosis are far from inspiring. In Spain, left Eurosceptics have argued for a policy of tacit alignment with radical-right populists in other EU countries, their assumption being that Matteo Salvini's Lega, for instance, instead of being a radical-right party with strong links to Italian business elites, is an anti-system force waging an unequal battle against Brussels (i.e., the 'main contradiction' that leftists must oppose).[49] But dropping out of the common currency and reintroducing the *peseta* is not a particularly appealing course of action for a medium-sized economy like Spain. It is also hard to conceive a juncture in which a breakup of the EU benefits leftists rather than the radical right, which remains far more adept at monopolising feelings of grievance and chauvinistic nationalism.

As historian Mark Mazower has pointed out, the origins of European federalism can be traced back to the Ventotene Manifesto and the anti-fascist resistance to Mussolini.[50] The left has a powerful claim on the European integration project, which it should seek to restore from its neoliberal drift, rather than reject. Regardless, it is clear that there is no easy or fully satisfactory 'eurocritical' middle road between the twin perils of austerity and Eurosceptic nationalism. To the extent that the EU remains driven by intergovernmental dynamics, attempting to change its federal institutions from a national standpoint, as Nicholas Moulder has argued, is the most viable course of action.[51] But the contradictions and limitations experienced by the country that embarked on this process most successfully in the aftermath of 2008, Portugal, serve as a warning that the process will be extremely challenging.

Crisis and austerity

Spain's underlying economic problems became evident after the 2008 crash – the third and final critical juncture in our study – but a close reading of the financial collapse suggested its roots stretched back to the early 1980s. The transition to democracy, the Spanish economy's modernisation through the PSOE's embedded neoliberalism, accession to the European Monetary Union, and the jobs bonanza brought by the real estate bubble had each been hailed as extraordinary achievements. But when Lehman Brothers crashed, the Spanish economy followed suit. As it did, the prestige of a longstanding socio-political model came into question.

The financial crisis brought a hard reckoning for Spain. Absent the distorting effects of the now quickly collapsing real estate bubble, Spain showed little convergence gain with respect to other Western European countries. Even in the golden years preceding the crisis, temporary work had been the norm for almost a third of the labour force.[52] The country's welfare state remained meagre by neighbouring standards, in part as a consequence of insufficient efforts to finance it: fiscal pressure was well below neighbouring standards (it currently stands at 34.5 per cent of GDP, against the Eurozone average of 41.5 per cent), and tax revenues further collapsed without the income derived from the real estate bubble. Per-capita income was 20 per cent below the OECD average: the same place it had been back in 1975.[53] Unemployment spiralled out of control, reaching a high-water mark of 26 per cent of the workforce in 2013, and twice as much for Spaniards under the age of 30.[54]

Initially, the Zapatero government responded to the shock with a stimulus programme larger than that of other OECD economies in relative terms. Besides providing liquidity for the restructuring of the ailing regional public banking system (*cajas*), the stimulus targeted investments in infrastructure and green energy, which it prioritised over tax breaks to stimulate consumption. Zapatero also replaced Finance Minister Pedro Solbes with the (less orthodox) Elena Salgado, while relying on advice from neo-Keynesian economists such as Paul Krugman and Joseph Stiglitz – who viewed the Spanish stimulus programme as more ambitious than Obama's in the US.[55] Taken together, these measures can be viewed as an attempt to reconfigure the economy away from the embedded neoliberal model that had dominated the past three decades. In Polanyi's terms, Zapatero's approach represented a mild but meaningful swing of the economic pendulum toward a framework more embedded in societal needs.

In 2010, however, the government undertook a 180-degree turn. Under international pressure – from the EU, the German government, the IMF, and the US – and concerned about the fragility of Spain's financial sector, which remained dependent on ECB liquidity, Zapatero adopted a package of austerity measures in May 2010.[56] Ban points out that the government was effectively forced into taking these measures, which contradicted its own programme:

> Spain's fiscal stimulus was terminated not by the reassertion of fiscal orthodoxy within the cabinet, but by external political and economic coercion enforced via financial channels ... resistance proved to be no match for the combined coercion deployed by the bond markets and the EU, which reached new heights in May 2010.[57]

In his memoirs, Zapatero himself details the extent to which this decision was driven by foreign pressure. The most intense example of this came from ECB president Jean-Claude Trichet, who took to writing personal letters demanding spending cuts to political leaders in the Eurozone periphery (his full letter to the Spanish prime minister is reproduced in Zapatero's book[58]). Another was US Vice President Joe Biden, who 'with a crudeness that I had never encountered said that the only way to get market confidence is to take decisions that make you suffer really hard ... that you are credible in a given set of circumstances if you subject your citizens to difficult tests and if unions openly reject your policies – in brief, if there are tears and suffering'.[59] According to one of Zapatero's advisers, the Spanish prime minister 'became convinced that if you give the blood of your own people, the markets will calm down'.[60]

The first round of austerity measures included wage freezes for the majority of public-sector employees, broad cuts in public spending, and specific restrictions on child and disability benefits, all of which was intended to save €10bn over the financial year.[61] In September 2011, the government approved a pro-market labour reform in response to pressure from business elites and in the hope of reducing unemployment. At the same time, and in what became the most powerful symbol of Zapatero's capitulation to international pressure, the PSOE and the PP joined forces in an overnight revision of the 1978 constitution, which enshrined the Maastricht fiscal guidelines and spending limits as state doctrine.[62] The gesture was symbolically shocking because it seemed to show that Spain's constitution, typically presented as a perfect product of a culture of political consensus that needs no modification, can in fact be altered at the behest of Brussels or financial markets, rather than Spanish citizens. (Here the contrast with Portugal is also revealing: that country's highest court ruled against specific austerity measures on the grounds that they contravened the spirit of solidarity enshrined in the constitution.)[63]

When the PP won an absolute majority shortly thereafter, it applied harsher austerity policies, slashing spending on education and healthcare – areas ruled out of bounds by the PSOE – by three and seven billion euros respectively.[64] Prime Minister Mariano Rajoy (2011-18) introduced yet another labour reform law that greatly weakened collective bargaining rights, and oversaw a bailout of the *cajas* and a subsequent privatisation of most of them, which ended up costing taxpayers forty-two billion euros that the Spanish central bank now views as irretrievable.[65] Taken together, the 2012 austerity package constituted the greatest reduction in Spain's welfare state in its three-decade existence, and effectively ended the embedded neoliberal model. This is not to say the country has developed a novel developmental path: as I will show, egregious inequality and unresolved challenges to social cohesion have become a permanent fixture of Spain's socio-economic landscape.

Rajoy's government viewed its economic reforms as saving Spain from the harsher conditions of a full EU-IMF bailout – €100bn was nevertheless provided, in June 2012, to assist the financial sector, paving the way for the country's economic recovery from 2015. In his final years in office, Rajoy oversaw an uptick in growth and job creation, with the economy growing above 3 per cent of GDP and unemployment eventually falling to 15 per cent.[66]

Spain's recovery is largely explained by external factors. The most important of these was Mario Draghi's tenure at the European Central Bank, which saw the bank adopt an activist monetary policy from mid 2012 onwards (jettisoning the monetarism of his predecessor, who in 2010 raised interest rates in the middle of a recession). Other windfalls include falling oil prices and an increase in tourism. Perhaps more importantly, growth picked up as the Rajoy government, faced with an adverse political scenario and the growing electoral threat of Podemos, ignored European directives and ditched austerity policies, adopting an expansionary budget in 2015-16.

Economic recovery has, however, left a majority of Spaniards behind, deepening the patterns of inequality that had already developed before 2008. While unemployment indicators improved, average income has taken a full decade (2007-17) to surpass its pre-crisis peak, and most income gains have been funnelled to the upper decile of the income distribution brackets, in particular to the top one per cent. According to the World Inequality Database, the top one per cent of earners in Spain experienced a 24 per cent growth in their income over the past decade, while the incomes of the bottom 90 per cent have stagnated, at two per cent growth. This trend seems related to the fact that 90 per cent of jobs created during the recovery are temporary, and working conditions have eroded substantially as a result of the 2011 and 2012 labour market reforms.[67] In the words of one mainstream economist, 'it is a recovery based on precarious jobs'.[68] Because of this, it should come as no surprise that apparently positive headline figures coexist with increases in wealth inequality, middle-class fears about downward social mobility, worsened child poverty and social inclusion indicators, and ongoing problems in the housing market. On housing, these can be traced to a spike in evictions after 2008 and a dramatic rise in rents following further deregulatory measures in 2013 – a development that has effectively left the Spanish housing market in the hands of venture funds like Blackstone and Cerberus. All this suggests that the Spanish growth model remains incapable of moving beyond its dependency on tourism and real estate, in spite of a much-publicised rise in exports.[69] For younger generations, securing a steady job that pays well enough to eventually afford the deposit and mortgage on a home – the traditional path to secure middle-class status – remains impossible as a result of rising real-estate prices and the precarious nature of most jobs created after the crisis.[70]

As Ignacio Sánchez-Cuenca has observed, Spain has been transformed along the fundamental variable of power. Power has become more concentrated across the financial sector (where the *cajas* were taken over by the larger Spanish banks, allowing these to consolidate their dominant position), the labour market (to the benefit of business and employer associations), administratively (the central state, on the pretext of pursuing balanced budgets, can now place fiscal constraints on municipalities) and territorially (with few urban enclaves, most notably Madrid, growing at a fast clip while rural areas become depopulated).[71] Taken together, the policy responses adopted by PSOE and PP policymakers under external pressure from 2010 onwards can be seen as a failure on their own terms. Austerity measures did not achieve their stated goal of reducing public debt and deficits, while they damaged growth prospects for the Spanish economy and caused lasting social damage to the less well off. They were widely unpopular and led to the electoral punishment of both political parties when they adopted them: the PSOE's vote share dropped from 43.6 per cent to 28.7 per cent between 2008 and 2011; the PP, which received 45 per cent in 2011, dropped to 28.7 per cent in 2015.[72]

Countermovement: 2011-2013

The impact and handling of the financial crisis created an unprecedented climate of social disaffection across the country. This effect is expressed in a time series produced by the Interior Ministry's Centre for Sociological Research, Spain's leading polling institute. Figure 4.2 charts public trust in politics between 1996 and 2020. There is a steep decline from 2008 onwards – at least in part a function of the failed policy responses to the economic crisis of both the PSOE and the PP. 2011 witnessed a slight decrease in mistrust as the PP took over, only to be followed by an even greater rise. (The chart also suggests a pattern of stabilisation from 2016, possibly due to the legitimising effect of the arrival of new political parties upon the old system.)

Figure 4.3 tells a similar story: trust in the entire government-opposition system collapsed between 2008 and 2011. After a brief rally following PP's electoral victory, trust fell even further, reaching an unprecedented low that was only corrected following the appearance of new political parties from 2014 onwards. This trend is in line with other studies on voting patterns during economic crises, which show a first round of elections punishing the incumbents and, if the crisis continues, disillusion with the entire party system becoming manifest.[73]

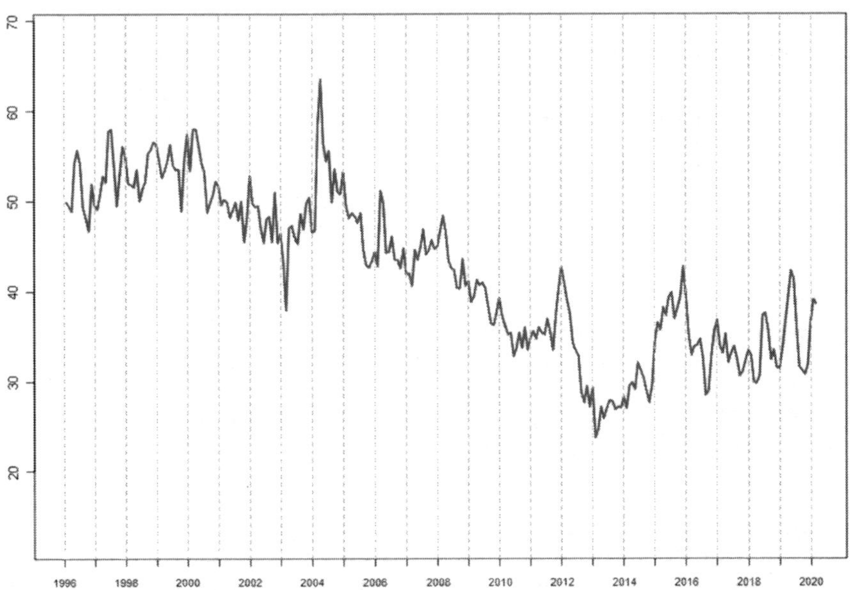

4.2: Spanish Public Attitudes Survey, Centre for Sociological Research. Political trust in Spain, 1996-2020. A steep collapse from 2008 followed by a fragile recovery from 2014. Source: http://www.cis.es/cis/opencms/ES/11_barometros/Indicadores_PI/documentos/serPol1.html

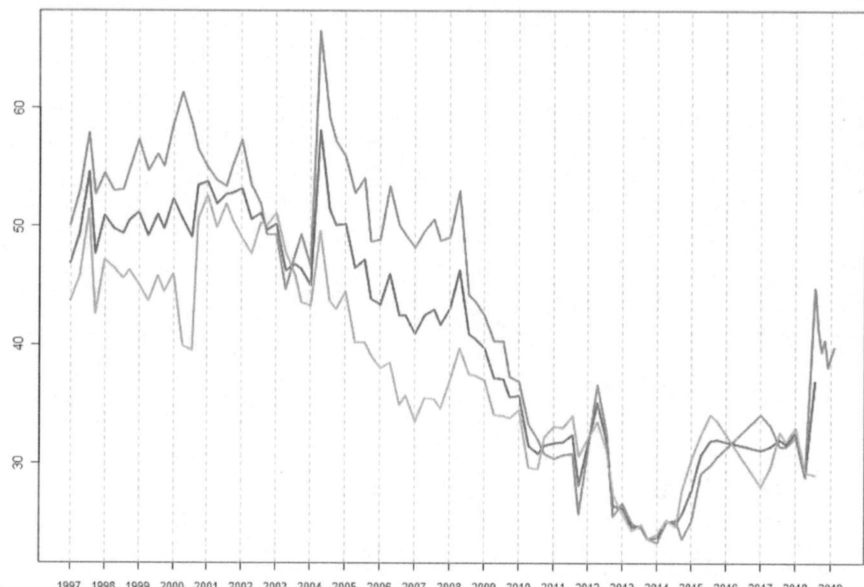

4.3. Spanish public attitudes survey, Centre for Sociological Research. Trust in the government-opposition system, 1997-2019. Black denotes trust in the overall system; dark grey, trust in the government, light grey, trust in the main opposition party. Source: http://www.cis.es/cis/opencms/ES/11_barometros/Indicadores_PI/gobierno.html

A complementary but more nuanced account of the impact of the crisis and its handling on Spain's party system is provided by Figure 4.4, which charts voting intentions in general elections between 1996 and 2020. This chart is especially revealing because it highlights that, at the peak of their standing during the real-estate bubble years, the PSOE and PP dyad represented a stable two-party system, with one of the two usually increasing its voter support at the expense of the other (mostly due to fluctuations in supporter mobilisation, rather than dramatic changes in voting patterns). This trend holds until the PP's electoral victory in late 2011. From 2012 onwards, the governing party's popularity begins to erode – in line with previous trends, but at a faster pace than usual – *while the opposition's does the same*: an unprecedented development. Furthermore, before 2014 this simultaneous dip takes places in the the absence of

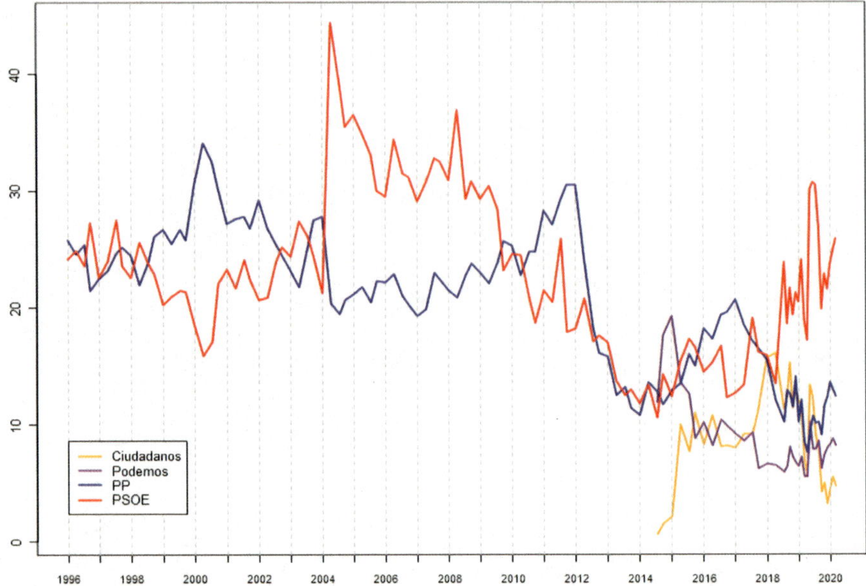

4.4: Spanish public attitudes survey, Centre for Sociological Research. Voting intention for the next general election, 1996-2020. Source: http://www.cis.es/ cis/opencms/ES/11_barometros/Indicadores_PI/documentos/B606

meaningful electoral competition from new challenger parties, suggesting that Spain was experiencing a crisis in democratic representation.

2011, then, is the year that witnessed a definitive break with established voting patterns and attitudes toward Spanish democracy. But this trend was not the result of the November elections. On 15 May 2011, a protest organised by students and civil-society associations gathered thousands of protesters across fifty different cities in Spain. The activists described themselves as 'homeless, jobless, and fearless', and demanded 'a dignified future'. When the demonstration in Madrid ended, several protesters decided to occupy the central square known as the Puerta del Sol, camping overnight. Within a week Sol had become a densely populated campsite. The 15 May movement (15-M), as it came to be known, was born spontaneously as similar sites mushroomed throughout Spain.

The 15-M was spontaneous, nonpartisan, and grassroots. While protesters were drawn from a variety of progressive activist circles, they were unanimous in their critique of Spain's established parties, which they referred to as 'PPSOE'. The movement's most popular slogan, which echoed widespread dissatisfaction with both parties, was 'they don't represent us'. Other popular slogans – 'we are not anti-system, the system is anti-us', 'we are not merchandise in the hands of politicians and bankers' – have a distinctly Polanyian ring to them. The *indignados* ('righteously angry'), as they became known, were demanding a radical democratisation of Spain's political and economic structures, not just a functioning jobs market. At the same time, and as César Rendueles and Jorge Sola have pointed out, the protesters were also conditioned by their social origins – a fact that would also affect Podemos' development:

> The social mobilisation of 15M ... has counted primarily on a certain social group: young middle class people with a university education whose expectations of social reproduction had been frustrated and who experienced more intensely the failed promise of meritocratic ideology. [In contrast], working-class youth and migrant populations were notably underrepresented both in the dynamics of the mobilisations, and in the rhetorics and images they projected.[74]

The *indignados* were committed to deliberative democracy and horizontalism – theirs was a 'rhizomatic revolution', in the words of a sympathetic observer.[75] In deliberative assemblies, in encampments and on digital platforms, they tried to engage as wide a public as possible. In so doing, they rejected the hierarchical leadership that they viewed as characteristic of Spain's party system. When the Sol camp was disbanded in the summer of 2011, the *indignados* faded from the front pages. The movement's retreat from the spotlight, however, did not lead to its disappearance, but to a reconfiguration within neighbourhoods and civil-society organisations.

The *indignados* were extremely popular. In June 2011, polls showed 81 per cent of Spanish citizens supporting them in their grievances; 90 per cent of the public followed the protesters in demanding that political parties reform and democratise their internal functioning. And while the 15-M garnered more sympathy from leftists than conservatives, 58 per cent of Spaniards believed the movement had no political or partisan bias. [76] In other words, in spite of its radical demands – or precisely because of them and the way in which they were framed – the 15-M was perceived as a refreshing and commonsense response to problems that Spain's political parties seemed incapable of addressing.

The 15-M would also contribute to popularising a repertoire of direct action and peaceful resistance within Spanish society, inspiring a dramatic surge in acts of civil disobedience between 2011 and 2014. At the same time, erstwhile *indignados* flocked to new protest groups that developed as austerity policies became entrenched. The most notable of these were the citizen 'tides' (*mareas*) that developed from 2012 onwards. Led by public-sector employees, they organised colour-coded protests against public spending cuts: green for education, orange for social services, and white for healthcare. The *mareas* garnered strong public support, manifested in several widely attended 'marches for dignity'. Spain's two leading trade unions, the UGT and the CCOO, eventually joined the wave of unrest, and 2012 became the first year in the history of Spanish democracy to witness two general strikes – a degree of social contestation with little precedent since the mass labour mobilisations of the 1970s.

Perhaps the most famous activist group in this period was the anti-eviction Platform for People Affected by Mortgages (PAH). The group was active from 2009 – before the appearance of the 15-M, which it also supported – but it became famous in 2012 as it organised sit-ins in the homes of families facing immediate foreclosures. As foreclosures had by then become a permanent feature of Spain's social landscape the PAH soon became a household name. In March 2013, the Platform submitted a citizen's initiative, signed by 1.5 million people, demanding a moratorium on evictions and a reform of the country's harsh mortgage laws. When the government rejected the initiative, the PAH initiated a campaign of sit-ins (*escraches*) outside the homes of legislators who supported the mortgage laws. The strategy provoked a backlash from right-wing pundits and politicians, but an overwhelming majority of Spanish citizens – 78 per cent, down from an original 89 per cent – continued to support the Platform's efforts.[77]

While it expressed profound social discontent and a comprehensive critique of Spanish democracy, the 15-M did not provoke a watershed shift to the left in institutional politics. In November 2011, the PSOE suffered its crushing defeat at the hands of the PP. The traditional left party in Parliament, the United Left, whose programme most resembled the demands of the 15-M, failed to benefit from either the movement's surge or the PSOE's collapse, obtaining less than seven per cent of the vote, four times less than the PSOE. Rajoy's PP won an absolute majority in Parliament and, as detailed above, reinforced the drive toward austerity. The governing party's mandate was weaker, however, than its parliamentary position suggested, as its victory was due to the PSOE's unprecedented electoral collapse, rather than to an increase in its own vote share. The PP remained embroiled in a series of decades-long, systemic corruption scandals affecting leading party figures and even Rajoy himself.

In what amounts to the only concession that the 15-M movement had taken place, austerity came hand in hand with a coercive social agenda. Between 2012 and 2015, the Rajoy government attempted to drastically curtail abortion rights – eventually abandoning the initiative in the face of public outcry – oversaw violent clashes between police and protesters, and approved a public-security law that reduced freedom of expression and was criticised by international media watchdogs and human-rights organisations.[78] As part of this, the country witnessed a slew of punitive rulings against radical left rappers and Twitter users on the grounds that they were conducting 'apologetics for terrorism' – a charge originally formulated during the fight against the Basque terrorist group ETA, which effectively disbanded in 2011. Among the most egregious episodes: a man was fined for carrying an ACAB ('all cops are bastards') sweatshirt; a woman was taken to court for wearing an ACAB ('all cats are beautiful') shirt; a trans woman faced a jail sentence for making jokes about the assassination of Franco's number-two man, Luis Carrero Blanco; one Facebook user was fined for taking pictures of an incorrectly parked police car; another, for calling local policemen 'shirkers' (*escaqueados*) in a private Facebook post.[79] Taken together, these absurd incidents may be viewed as symptoms of a process of democratic backsliding. As in the US, the disembedding process demanded a reconfiguration of the state's duties – from economic protection to coercion – rather than the state's withdrawal.[80]

At the peak of national discontent, in 2013, and in the context of the regional government of Catalonia taking active steps to secede from the rest of the country from 2012 onwards, former Prime Minister Felipe González warned that 'we shall find a way out of the economic crisis … but I'm not so sure we will come out of the political and institutional crisis. This crisis rushes towards a dissolving anarchy'.[81] Political scientist Simon Tormey spoke for many at the time when he labelled Spain a 'zombie democracy', stumbling around in its afterlife with little sense of legitimacy.[82] In early 2014, protests and riots in the neighbourhood of Gamonal in the town of Burgos showcased the explosive potential of a restive working class.[83] In Laclau's terminology, the 2008-2011 period had generated a multiplicity of demands that Spain's political institutions could no longer absorb. The post-Franco consensus was unwinding and the country had reached a tipping point. It was not until 2014, however, that a small group of activists and political scientists decided to take the initiative and seize this populist moment.

Notes

1. Perry Anderson, *The New Old World*, Verso: London, 2011, p19.
2. Quoted in Matthias Matthijs, 'Poweful rules governing the euro: The perverse logic of German economic ideas', *Journal of European Economic Policy*, Vol. 23, No. 6, January 2016, p375.
3. Vera Gutiérrez Calvo, 'Felipe González: "hay una crisis institucional que galopa hacia la anarquía"', *El País,* 10 April 2013.
4. César Rendueles and Jorge Sola, 'Strategic crossroads: the situation of the left in Spain', Rosa Luxemburg Stiftung, June 2019.
5. Juan J. Linz and Alfred C. Stepan, *Problems of Democratic Transition and Consolidation: Southern Europe, South America, and Post-communist Europe*, Johns Hopkins University Press, Baltimore, 1996; Omar G. Encarnación, 'The legacy of transitions: Pact-making and democratic consolidation in Spain', Estudio/Working Paper 2003/193, p3.
6. Pablo Elorduy, 'Ahora que Vázquez Montalbá está de moda', www.elsaltodiario.com, 25 August 2017.

7. For the most recent and complete account of this line of research, see Robert Fishman, *Democratic Practice: Origins of the Iberian Divide in Political Inclusion*, Oxford University Press: Oxford, 2019.

8. Juan Luis Cebrián, *La España que bosteza*, Taurus: Madrid, 1980, p9.

9. Miguel Ángel Noceda, '40 años de los Pactos de la Moncloa, el acuerdo que cambió España hace 40 año', *El País*, 21 October 2017; Cornel Ban, *Ruling Ideas: How Global Neoliberalism Goes Local*, Oxford University Press: Oxford, 2016.

10. Cornel Ban and Jorge Tamames, 'Political economy and the ghosts of the past: Revisiting the Spanish and Romanian transitions to democracy', *Historein*, Vol. 15, No. 1, 2015, p74.

11. Quoted in *ibid.*, p74.

12. On this subject, see Varios autores, *CT o la Cultura de la Transición: Crítica a 35 años de cultura española*, Debolsillo: Barcelona, 2012. On the cultural development of post-Franco democracy, see also Eduardo Maura, *Los 90. Euforia y miedo en la modernidad democrática española*, Madrid: Akal, 2018.

13. Richard Gillespie, *The Spanish Socialist Party: A History of Factionalism*, Oxford University Press: Oxford, 1989, p363.

14. Ban 2016, p33; see also Ban and Tamames 2015.

15. Ban 2016, p54; Sebastián Royo, *From Social Democracy to Neoliberalism: The Consequences of Party Hegemony in Spain, 1982-1996*, Saint Martin's Press: New York, 2000; on the UGT, see also Katrina Burgess, 'Unemployment and union strategies in Spain', *South European Society and Politics*, Vol. 4, No. 3, 1999, pp1-31.

16. Ban 2016; see also Pedro Schwartz, 'La mejor política industrial es...', *El País*, 15 July 1995.

17. Ban 2016, p35.

18. Fishman 2019.

19. Vivien A. Schmidt, 'Changes in comparative political economy: Taking labour out, bringing the state back in, putting the firm front and center', Boston University, June 2007.

20. Rubén Juste, *IBEX 35. Una historia herética del poder en España*, Capitán Swing: Madrid, 2017.

21. Joaquín Estefanía, 'La Tercera Vía como pensamiento único', *El País*, 25 July 1999.

22. Ban 2016, p63.

23. *Ibid.*, p64.

24. Author interview with Miguel Sebastián, June 2012.

25. 'Zapatero: 'El gobierno ha situado a España en la Champions League de las economías del mundo', https://cadenaser.com, 11 September 2007.

26. Carlos Solchaga's memoirs, quoted in Ban 2016, p55.

27. Sheri Berman and Kathleen McNamara, 'Bank on democracy', *Foreign Affairs*, Vol. 78, No. 2, March-April 1999, pp2-8.

28. Santos Juliá, 'España era el problema, Europa la solución', https://elpais.com/, 25 May 2014.

29. On this subject, see José Ignacio Torreblanca, *¿Quién gobierna en Europa? Reconstruir la democracia, recuperar a la ciudadanía*, Catarata: Madrid, 2014.

30. Mark Blyth and Matthias Matthijs, 'When is it rational to learn the wrong lessons? Technocratic authority, social learning, and euro fragility', *Perspectives on Politics*, Vol. 16, No. 1, pp110-126.

31. See Joaquín Estefanía, 'El mayor gato por liebre de la historia', *Política Exterior*, No. 191, September-October 2019.

32. 'Share of member states in EU GDP', https://ec.europa.eu/eurostat/web/main/home, 10 April 2017.

33. On this subject, see Blyth, *Austerity: The History of a Dangerous Idea*, Oxford University Press: New York, 2013; see also Blyth, 'The sovereign debt crisis that isn't: Or, how to turn a lending crisis into a spending crisis and pocket the spread', *American Consortium on European Union Studies*, January 2014, pp26-31.

34. *Ibid.*

35. Mehreen Khan and Paul McClean, 'Dijsselbloem under fire after saying Eurozone countries wasted money on "alcohol and women"', *Financial Times*, 21 March 2017

36. Gabriel Ubieto, 'Un español trabaja 26,1 per cent más de horas que un alemán', *El periodico*, 18 October 2018.

37. Blyth 2013; see also Martin Wolf, 'How austerity has failed', *New York Review of Books*, 11 July 2013

38. Blyth 2013.

39. Wolfgang Münchau, 'The wacky economics of Germany's parallel universe', *Financial Times*, 16 November 2014.

40. Jonathan Hopkin, 'División norte-sur en Europa', *Política Exterior*, No. 191, September-October 2019.

41. On this subject, see Sofia A. Perez and Manos Matsaganis, 'Export or perish: Can internal devaluation create enough good jobs in Southern Europe?' *South European Society and Politics*, Vol. 24, No. 2, pp259-85.

42. Martin Wolf, 'The challenges of managing our post-crisis world', *Financial Times*, 29 December 2009; see also Martin Wolf, 'Germany is a weight on the world', *Financial Times*, 5 November 2013.

43. Peter Mair, *Ruling the Void: The Hollowing out of Western Democracy*, Verso: London, 2013.

44. Matthijs 2016.

45. 'Ordoliberalism' is the dominant school of German economic thought, which stresses the state's role as the guarantor of free market competition – not through a hands-off, *laissez-faire* approach, but by actively setting and enforcing fair competition rules and regulations among economic actors. It is associated with the figure of Ludwig Erhard and Germany's post-war economic miracle, as well as the anti-inflationary policies of the Bundesbank. While ordoliberalism bears similarities to other liberal continental schools of economic thought – such as Italian *liberismo* – it is distinct from traditional liberalism or US libertarianism in that it acknowledges the state's importance as an economic actor. At the same time, it differs from more state-centric approaches, such as French *dirigisme*, which view the public sector as a force than can actively shape and plan economic development.

46. Oddny Helgadóttir, 'The Bocconi Boys go to Brussels: Italian economic ideas, professional networks and European austerity', *Journal of Economic Public Policy*, Vol. 23, No. 3, pp392-409.

47. Wolfgang Streeck, 'European social policy: Progressive regression', MPIfG Discussion Paper, November 2018.

48. Anderson 2011.

49. See Héctor Illueca, Manolo Monereo, and Julio Anguita, '¿Fascismo en Italia? Decreto Dignidad', www.cuartopoder.es, 5 September 2018.

50. Mark Mazower, *Governing the World: The History of an Idea*, Penguin, London, 2012.

51. Nicholas Moulder, 'The origins of European neoliberalism', *n+1*, 29 April 2019.

52. Fishman 2019; Ban 2016.

53. Ban 2016, p64.

54. *Ibid.*; Fishman, 'Anomalies of Spain's economy and economic policy-making', *Contributions to Political Economy* Vol. 31, Issue 1, June 2012, pp67-76.

55. Ban 2016, p190.

56. José Luis Rodríguez Zapatero, *El dilema: 600 días de vértigo*, Planeta: Barcelona, 2014.

57. Ban 2016, p200.

58. Zapatero 2014.

59. *Ibid.*, p200. See also Íñigo Aduriz, 'EEUU pidió a Zapatero "sufrimiento" para contentar a los mercados', www.publico.es/, 27 November 2013.

60. *Ibid.*

61. Fernando Garea, 'Zapatero da un vuelco a su estrategia con un recorte de sueldos públicos sin precedentes', *El País*, 13 May 2010.

62. Vera Gutiérrez Calvo and Ramón Muóz, 'Reforma exprés y sin referendumm', *El País*, 23 August 2011.

63. 'Corte de Portugal rechaza algunas medidas de austeridad, ratifica la mayoría', https://lta.reuters.com, 6 April 2013.

64. 'Sanidad tendrá un recorte de 7.000 millones y Educación de 3.000', www.elmundo.es, 9 April 2012; Garea, 'El gobierno anuncia el recorte de 10.000 millones de euros en Educación y Sanidad', *El País*, 9 April 2012.

65. J.S.G., 'El Banco de España da por perdidos 42.017 millones de euros (de momento) del rescate a los bancos', *El País,* 24 November 2018.

66. Tobias Buck, 'Spain job growth confirms recovery and boosts Rajoy', *Financial Time*s, 22 January 2015; see also Buck, 'New world of work: Political cost of Spain's recovery', *Financial Times*, 4 August 2015.

67. See Amory Gethin, Clara Martínez-Toledano, and Marco Morgan, 'Rising inequalities and political cleavages in Spain on the verge of new elections', World Inequality Database World Issue Brief, April 2019.

68. Quoted in Buck, January 2015.

69. 'Exclusión estructural e integración social', Fundación Foessa; see also Rebeca Arroyo, 'Blackstone hace caja en España con la venta de immuebles por 900 millones', expansion.com, 5 July 2019; 'Cerberus concluye la compra del 80 per cent del negocio inmobiliario del BBVA', elmundo.es, 15 October 2018.

70. On the subject of homeownership for young Spaniards, see María Sosa Troya and Noor Mahtani, 'Los jóvenes deben pagar el 94 per cent de su sueldo si quieren vivir solos de alquiler', *El País*, 17 December 2019. On the political economy of homeownership, see Gregory W. Fuller, Alison Johnston, and Aidan Regan, 'Housing prices and wealth inequality in Western Europe', *West European Politics*, Vol. 43, No. 2, 18 February 2019.

71. On this subject see Sergio del Molino, *La España vacía: viaje por un país que nunca fue,* Turner: Madrid, 2016.

72. Blyth and Matthijs 2017.

73. See Enrique Hernández and Hanspeter Kriesi, 'The electoral consequences of the financial and economic crisis in Europe', *European Journal of Political Research*, Vol. 55, No. 2, 2016, pp203-24.

74. Sola and Rendueles 2019, p31.

75. Manuel Castells, *Redes de indignación y esperanza,* Alianza: Madrid, 2015.

76. Garea, 'Apoyo a la indignación del 15-M', *El País*, 5 June 2011.

77. Garea, 'Mengua el fuerte apoyo inicial a los escraches, según Metroscopia', *El País*, 8 April 2013.

78. See for example 'Amnistía exige la reforma de la "ley mordaza, una amenaza real en España contra la libertad de expression e información"', *La Vanguardia*, 1 July 2019.

79. For a few examples, see A. T., 'Las ocho denuncias más sórdidas que deja la "ley mordaza" tras dos años en vigor', *Público*, 28 June 2017.

80. The escalation of the constitutional crisis in Catalonia, which the government addressed repressively, aggravated this process of democratic backsliding. Ignacio Sánchez-Cuenca, 'A vueltas con España (y su democracia)', ctxt.es, 2 April 2019.

81. Gutiérrez Calvo 2013.

82. Joao França, 'Simon Tormey: "En España hay una democracia zombie"', *El Diario*, 31 March 2013.

83. On this subject, see Marcos Erro García and José Medina Mateos, *Gamonal. La historia desde abajo*, Ediciones El Perdigón: Burgos, 2017.

CHAPTER FIVE

From New Deal to No Deal: America, 1977-2014

Nowhere has liberal philosophy failed so conspicuously as in its understanding of the problem of change. Fired by an emotional faith in spontaneity, the common-sense attitude toward change was discarded in favour of a mystical readiness to accept the social consequences of economic improvement, whatever they might be. The elementary truths of political science and state-craft were first discredited then forgotten. It should need no elaboration that a process of undirected change, the rate of which is deemed too fast, should be slowed down, if possible, so as to safeguard the welfare of the community.[1]

– Karl Polanyi

Government cannot solve our problems, it can't set our goals, it cannot define our vision. Government cannot eliminate poverty or provide a bountiful economy or reduce inflation or save our cities or cure illiteracy or provide energy.[2]

– Jimmy Carter

Change is upon us. We can do nothing about that. The pole stars that guided our affairs in the past years have disappeared.[3]

– Bill Clinton

On 17 July 2014, police approached a man at 202 Bay Street in New York's Staten Island borough and accused him of selling cigarettes illegally. When the man answered he was tired of getting harassed and was not even selling cigarettes, the policemen attempted to arrest him. The man refused to cooperate and one of the officers, Daniel Pantaleo, put him in a chokehold. The man's name was Eric Garner, and the last moments of his life were filmed by a bystander in a video that soon went viral:

> As he lay sideways on the ground, surrounded by four police, Garner for one brief moment thrust his right hand out. His fingers were all extended, his palm facing upward toward the sky. He appeared to be indicating surrender and reaching for open space at the same time.
>
> Then the outstretched hand twitched, as if in a spasm. Garner now coughed and for the first time gasped, 'I can't breathe.'
>
> One of the uniform cops saw his outstretched hand and grabbed it, hoping to throw cuffs around it.
>
> 'I can't breathe', Garner repeated. 'I can't breathe.'[4]

In his moving account of Garner's life, journalist Matt Taibbi describes his death as 'the killing that started a movement'.[5] Indeed, this movement, known as Black Lives Matter (BLM), made Garner's dying words into one of its most powerful slogans. But even if Eric Garner had not died, similarly gratuitous murders of black men – and sometimes women and even children – at the hands of US police would have sparked BLM. Before Garner's death, the fatal shooting of seventeen-year-old Trayvon Martin by George Zimmerman, whom a jury pronounced not guilty, had already made the persistence of structural racism in Obama's America painfully clear. After Garner's death, the killings of eighteen-year-old Michael Brown and twelve-year-old Tamir Rice by policemen threw salt on the wounds of black America, the former's leading to mass protests and riots in Ferguson, Missouri in 2014. In the final years of the Obama administration, BLM became an increasingly powerful and vocal movement, whose demands Democrats were forced to acknowledge and Republicans typically dismissed.

BLM was not the only movement that emerged in response to injustices in US society at a time when the Democratic Party, having overseen a nominal economic recovery from the 2008 crisis and led by a charismatic president, was drifting into complacency. This was a period when, for some, it seemed that – to quote the title of a 2014 book by political scientist Daniel Drezner – 'the system worked'.[6] Yet between 2011 and 2016, a growing array of progressive movements arose spontaneously, and achieved considerable reach and scope: from Occupy Wall Street in 2011 to the FightFor15 activists demanding a higher minimum wage, to the Standing Rock environmental protests and the women's mobilisation that has become a leading source of opposition to Donald Trump's presidency.[7] While their agendas and views do not always fully align, these movements share an overarching theme: all of them emerged in response to a disciplinarian and particularly brutal version of neoliberalism, which has run along and exacerbated the 'lines of weakness' in American society mentioned in Chapter Two: structural racism, nativism, and economic inequality, to name a few.[8] Trump himself is another reaction to this economic order, although he is set on recasting it in a more coercive direction, even while pretending to acknowledge the pain that 'globalists' have inflicted upon the country.

The US brand of neoliberalism is particularly important to understand for two reasons. The first is that it constitutes an extreme variant of this macroeconomic regime, generating even more inequality and sustained by greater levels of state coercion than embedded or compensatory versions like Spain's, even in the aftermath of the Eurozone's 2010 turn to austerity. The second is that it presents us with an image of what the future holds for other societies that fail to combat the drift toward increasingly market-centred governance.

As in the Spanish case, the transformation of US society took place at three critical junctures. The Carter-Reagan years witnessed the dismantling of the New Deal consensus and the emergence of neoliberalism in the US. In the 1990s, Bill Clinton's embrace of 'third way' politics and the Republican Party's increasing radicalisation forestalled the possibility of turning away from this course. The 2008 financial crisis and the Obama administration's first term constitute a third critical juncture, when the Democratic Party failed to transform the structure of the US economy when the circumstances aligned to make it possible. The rumbling from these tectonic plates grew louder in the run-up to the 2016 elections, when insurgent candidates from the right and left challenged the

Republican and Democratic establishment and Trump's brand of populism ultimately proved victorious.

The Reagan revolution?

A good departure point for understanding the changes that have afflicted US society over the past forty years is Jacob S. Hacker and Paul Pierson's *Winner-Take-All Politics*.[9] Published more than a decade ago, the book captures the extent of America's pro-market drift. A decades-long offensive of the country's rich against the working and middle classes – the class war that, according to billionaire Warren Buffett, his side keeps winning – has made the US an extraordinarily unequal society.[10] Between 1979 and the outbreak of the financial crisis, 36 per cent of household income gains were captured by the top one per cent of American earners, while only 13.5 per cent went to the bottom 60 per cent. Inequality appears even greater when viewed in terms of distribution: the top 0.1 per cent captured 20 per cent of those income gains, while from 2001 to 2006, 53 per cent of income gains were enjoyed by the top one per cent. If capital gains are included in the equation, the percentage of national income earned by the top one per cent has increased from roughly 9 per cent in 1974 to 23.5 per cent in 2007. Executive pay for CEOs, which in 1965 averaged twenty-four times the wages of their lowest-paid workers, was 300 times higher than the wages of their lowest paid in 2007.[11]

Unsurprisingly, this tendency benefits very few people. The inflection point at which Americans become better off under neoliberalism is located somewhere between the ninetieth and ninety-fifth percentiles of income distribution, meaning that roughly only one in fifteen has seen their fortunes rise over this period.[12] Comparisons with the era of embedded liberalism also cast a striking light: between the Depression and 1980, the bottom 90 per cent of American earners captured 70 per cent of income gains – that is to say, the top 10 per cent earned less of the total economic pie than just the top one per cent did in 2007.[13] The 2008 crash brought a sudden reversal of these trends, but in this respect it was a blip on the screen: inequality continued to increase as soon as the economy stabilised.

Hacker and Pierson suggest that the US has witnessed a 'transformation of American government over the last generation, a transformation that has fundamentally changed what the government does, and whom it does it for'. In their apt expression, the social contract has moved from the New Deal to 'no deal'.[14] America is an increasingly precarious society, frayed by massive inequality and kept in line by an autocratic, as well as racially driven, conception of law and order. The country's prison rates, above 700 per 100,000 citizens, are by far the highest in the world; its prison population, currently almost 2.3 million, is almost 50 per cent larger in absolute terms than that of China – an authoritarian country with more than four times America's population.[15]

Who is responsible for this state of affairs? Many accounts, mainstream and on the left, cite Ronald Reagan as the architect of the new socio-economic order. But as Hacker and Pierson, and indeed my own review of Thatcherism above argue, this lets off the hook both the politicians who paved the ground for the move to the markets in the late 1970s, and those who radicalised the agenda in the 1990s.

Consider the presidents who preceded Reagan. Richard Nixon, also a Republican, came to power expecting to apply austerity measures and ended up overseeing the largest expansion of public spending since the New Deal: a host of public regulations, government programmes and federal agencies were established on his watch, making him the last president to uphold and strengthen the New Deal consensus (on almost all other fronts his legacy is infamous, with good reason). Contrast this with Jimmy Carter, who defeated Nixon's successor Gerald Ford in the aftermath of the Watergate scandal and had a solid Democrat majority to work with in Congress. Instead of managing to build on Nixon's efforts, Carter's administration suffered a series of legislative defeats: on tax reform, the creation of a new consumer protection agency, and an ambitious labour bill that had the full backing of US unions. Upon the latter's defeat, United Auto Workers leader Douglas Fraser resigned from the administration's Labour Management Group with a prescient letter:

I believe leaders of the business community, with few exceptions, have chosen to wage a one-sided class war ... against working people ... and even many in the middle class of our society. The leaders of industry, commerce and finance in the United States have broken and discarded the fragile, unwritten compact previously existing during a past period of growth and progress ... At virtually every level, I discern a demand by business for docile government and unrestrained corporate individualism ... our tax laws are a scandal, yet corporate America wants even wider inequities.[16]

The Carter administration didn't just submit to business pressure. As Thomas Frank has observed in *Listen, Liberal*, his 2016 indictment of America's centre left, the Democrats initiated their own turn to the markets well in advance of Reagan. Frank traces the abandonment of the New Deal consensus to the 1968 McGovern-Fraser Commission, which he views as leading the party away from its alliance with the working class and off in search of middle-class electorates concerned with 'post-material' issues, rather than economic justice.[17] The turn became explicit during Carter's presidency, which following its early defeats oversaw a deregulatory and liberalising agenda, including an initial round of tax cuts in 1978 that reduced taxes on capital gains from 48 per cent to 28 per cent. As the chapter's opening quote suggests, Carter himself apparently came to believe the liberal creed. Few captured the Democratic Party's newfound faith in market logics so clearly as Carter adviser Alfred Kahn, who in 1981 remarked that:

I'd love the Teamsters to be worse off. I'd love the automobile workers to be worse off. You may say that's inhumane; I'm putting it rather baldly but I want to eliminate a situation in which certain protected workers in industries insulated from competition can increase their wages much more rapidly than the average without regard to their merit to what a free market would do, and in so doing exploit other workers.[18]

What accounts for the striking divergence between Nixon and Carter's economic agendas? Not each president's personal views or the makeup of their respective electoral coalitions. Instead, Hacker and Pierson analyse what they call 'politics as organised combat' –

to an extent, the equivalent on an institutional level of the agonism that Mouffe describes from the standpoint of political theory. Following a string of legislative defeats in the early and mid 1970s, American business organised a monumental effort to influence US legislators. The rise of lobbyists and lobbying firms and networks in this period highlight the extent to which this effort was carried forward. In 1968 there were 100 corporations with public offices in Washington, DC; by 1978, the number had risen to 500. Firms with registered lobbyists in DC, totalling 175 in 1968, had mushroomed to 2,500 by 1982. Corporate Political Action Committees (PACs – vehicles that funnel private money into elections) went from 300 in 1976 to 1,200 in 1980; while unions' spending in electoral races went up by 2.5 during this period, it increased fivefold for corporate PACs.[19] Generous campaign funding for sympathetic politicians – precisely at a time when the rise of televised coverage was making elections more expensive – went hand in hand with an ideological effort to question the fundamental tenets of embedded liberalism, undertaken through reinvigorated conservative think tanks such as the American Enterprise Institute and the Heritage Foundation (the latter founded in 1973). In the context of stagflation and the 1970s 'malaise', as Carter put it in a notoriously pessimistic speech, these arguments secured an increasingly strong foothold in American public debate. And because the Republican Party, traditionally the representative of American business, was in a better position to funnel this agenda, it soon gained a massive organisational edge over the Democratic Party.

Reagan accelerated this dynamic, with lobbying efforts now centred on dictating the agenda rather than simply blocking progressive legislation. As in Thatcher's case, however, it would be simplistic to view his political project as simply a tool for America's ruling class. Reagan's seminal piece of legislation, the 1981 Economic Recovery Tax Act (ERTA), was the largest tax cut in US economic history and 'the most central blow to state capacity that the American state has experienced', according to sociologist Monica Prasad. Besides cutting top marginal tax rates from 70 per cent to 50 per cent and slashing other individual and business rates, it also inaugurated an era of decreasing fiscal pressure on America's top income earners and wealthiest individuals. This is not because it was unprecedented – as already noted, Carter had taken a similar decision in 1978, as had the Kennedy and Johnson administrations before him – but because, under the guidance of Republican activist and former American football player Jack Kemp, the policy became a skilfully crafted piece of propaganda, projecting an image of individual freedom and free enterprise that proved seductive to a majority of the US electorate. Prasad provides an alternative – or perhaps complementary – account to those of Hacker and Pierson, and Marxist authors such as David Harvey, highlighting the extent to which the tax cuts were popular among working-class constituencies (she mentions, for example, how Kemp got an audience from America's largest union, the AFL-CIO, on its feet in one of his anti-tax speeches) and not fully supported by big business, which wanted lower corporate taxation but opposed individual tax cuts.[20]

It is also not the case that the Republican Party came to embody plutocratic interests while the Democrats were left with a weakened working class. To this day, both parties mobilise diverse coalitions that crosscut class lines. Through its strategy for retaking the South from Democrats through barely disguised race-baiting – the 'Southern strategy' pioneered by Nixon, improved by Reagan, and a staple of conservative rhetoric thereafter – the Republicans effectively secured electoral support from poor white evangelicals. Conversely, Democrats have spent decades grooming the kind of urban, upwardly mobile professionals – doctors, lawyers, engineers, tech workers – who previously constituted the centre right's electoral backbone.[21] As noted above, Stuart Hall's Gramscian reading of Thatcherism remains more useful to understanding Reagan's project than does viewing it simply as a vehicle for the interests of the US ruling class.

Nevertheless, this realignment left the centre left in a position of weakness. Under the embedded liberal framework it was Republicans who, as the party of fiscal discipline, were forced to take unpopular measures in order to pay for the Democrats' fiscal activism – a dynamic that turned the centre right, in Newt Gingrich's words, into 'the tax collector for the welfare state'. Furthermore, the embedded liberal framework generated its own inertia (or 'drift', in Hacker and Pierson's terminology). Inflation, for example, effectively increased marginal tax rates as salaries rose – a phenomenon known as 'bracket creep', which the ERTA cut short by indexing taxes to inflation. Reagan's simultaneous embrace of tax cuts and public deficits, however, turned the tables on this relationship. Under his new, 'starve the beast' theory, it was Republicans who would begin piling up public debt by approving fiscally unsustainable tax cuts, while Democrats were left to square the budget – not by raising taxes again, which they now deemed political suicide, but by slashing public spending, usually on social programmes.[22]

Economic and political transformation also dramatically weakened US labour unions – possibly the only institutions with the capacity and willingness to act as a counterweight to business lobbies. Between 1970 and 2010 the proportion of American workers affiliated to unions went down from one in three to one in nine, and from 25 per cent to 7 per cent of the private sector's workforce – meaning that the number of union members is now higher in the public than in the private sector. There are several reasons behind de-unionisation, the main ones being the dislocation of production chains and the offshoring of manufacturing jobs in the context of globalisation; the enforcement of intransigent anti-union legislation in state legislatures; and the general transition, across Western economies, to the services sector, where regulation and organisation are harder to establish than in a Fordist production chain. To make matters worse, the weakening of unions generates a vicious circle: the smaller unions become, the more narrow their focus on ensuring a series of standards are upheld in increasingly localised sectors of the economy. This makes it easier for pro-market politicians to dismiss them as mere interest groups, narrowly concerned with a small slice of the labour force and missing the bigger picture.[23]

In their heyday, in fact, unions were the precise opposite. They were the leading actors in the Democratic Party's electoral coalition, which they supported with volunteers, votes, and funds. Their role often transcended labour relations: in the context of the civil-rights movement, labour not only struggled to fight racism within its ranks, but also played a critical part in supporting the passage of the 1969 Civil Rights Act.[24] Finally, unions offered an avenue for workers to be socialised into clear political choices that upheld their social and economic interests. This last point is especially important, as it highlights the increasing de-structuration of societies that has taken place under neoliberalism. Similarly to José Fernández-Albertos' observations on the 'politically precarious', Hacker and Pierson point out that:

> To be more than bystanders in American politics wondering whom to shoot, voters need strong organizational mooring and consistent cues to recognize and respond to changes in public policy. Yet, on economic matters, this mooring and these cues have eroded just as they have become more crucial. This erosion hasn't just made it harder for voters to know whom to shoot. It has also dramatically undermined voter's confidence in government and politicians, especially their sense that elected officials are looking out for their interests.[25]

The dynamic also exemplifies the 'double withdrawal' that Peter Mair warned about. As politicians desert their voters, organised citizens retreat from politics, making it easier for political elites to remain unaccountable.

In theory, while unions are much diminished, today there is a complementary set of progressive advocacy groups pressing politicians on a broad array of civil-rights issues. But these organisations – take, for example, Emily's List, which focuses on electing women candidates but often prioritises those with centrist credentials – are smaller, DC-based outfits centred on lobbying or funnelling money from wealthy progressive donors to specific candidates. To be clear, I am not seeking to establish a rigid distinction between economic and civil rights, or claim a zero-sum relationship between 'material' and 'identitarian' demands. The point is that NGOs and advocacy groups are in no position to match the structural force that unions once boasted, much less go toe-to-toe with their right-wing counterparts, well-oiled machines that run on generous funding from a host of conservative billionaires such as Sheldon Adelson and the Koch family. This has become especially true in the aftermath of the Supreme Court's 2010 ruling on Citizens United v. Federal Election Commission, a landmark case that resulted in further deregulation of campaign finance laws and made it substantively easier for billionaires and corporate lobbies (as well as unions and advocacy groups, in theory, though in practice their financial clout is by no means comparable) to fund the electoral campaigns of pliable candidates.

Defenders of the status quo seeking to retain a varnish of progressivism – that is, supporters of the Democratic Party establishment – often presume that advances on social issues achieved in recent decades somehow mitigate neoliberalism's flaws, or at the very least justify a sanguine attitude toward existing economic arrangements. Aren't rapid advancements in LGBT rights, for example, something to be desired? Don't mainstream politicians like Obama and Hillary Clinton deserve to be cut some slack? Shouldn't our criticism take into account the fact that the former is black and the latter a woman? For the most part, these objections are, as a famous physicist once observed of sloppy scientific arguments, 'not even wrong'. Advances in the recognition of LGBT rights should be supported, celebrated, and never taken for granted. But, quite clearly, these result from the effort and mobilisation of LGBT activists themselves, not some inherent and hidden virtue in the neoliberal policy package, or the invisible hand of the market. Obama and Clinton have indeed been subject to racism and sexism, but, I would aver, that fact is neither related to, nor does it automatically excuse them for, some of the ways that they have chosen to exercise their political power.

The question, then, is: why has there been an attempt to justify neoliberalism from an allegedly progressive standpoint? In order to understand this, it is necessary to analyse the Democratic Party's full acceptance of the neoliberal paradigm under Bill Clinton's presidency.

New Democrats

If Carter opened the door to the transition toward a disembedded economy and Reagan took a great leap forward, it was during Bill Clinton's presidency that the turn to the markets was finally consolidated. To an extent this was to do with the nature and achievements of his administration. At the same time, changes in the character of both the Democratic and Republican parties, and the international context following the Soviet Union's breakup – the era of Francis Fukuyama's famous 'end of history' thesis, in which liberal democracy and deregulated capitalism were apparently fated to rule supreme – furthered the process.[26]

Following a string of defeats during the Reagan and George H. W. Bush presidencies and their loss in the 1994 midterms, when the Republican Party achieved full control of House of Representatives for the first time in forty years, Democrats had to adapt to a new, unfavourable environment. They did this by emulating Republicans and developing similar ties with lobbies and interest groups. Like the PSOE in Spain, the party therefore underwent a process of cartelisation and embarked on its neoliberal reinvention, severing its close ties to the labour movement – and, to an extent, minority communities – and cultivating wealthy donors. The financial sector became one of its new major sources of support because, under embedded liberalism, it had remained relatively weak actor, and as such was initially viewed as a relatively innocuous interest group.[27]

As these organisational changes took place, party elites had also began to shift ideologically. After every electoral defeat, the Democratic Leadership Council (DLC) – an internal lobby group led by moderate Democrats – would invariably insist that the party needed to shift rightwards if it expected to become electorally competitive. The 'New Democrats', as the DLC operatives called themselves, eventually found their paladin in Bill Clinton, a young and ambitious governor from a Southern state who briefly chaired the DLC in the early 1990s. As is well known, Clinton's signal achievement, acknowledged by both his critics and admirers, was his rejection of the New Deal's legacy in his journey to become 'an authentic New Democrat, ready to break with old liberalism, even at a personal cost'.[28] The greater cost, it should be said, was borne by a majority of the US population. Clinton's landmark accomplishments – the 1992 signature of NAFTA, Wall Street deregulation, the 1994 crime bill, and the 1996 welfare reform act – paved the way for the 2008 crisis and the establishment of a populist moment in American politics.

These four measures are worth discussing briefly, as they collectively illustrate the contradictory and utopian nature that Polanyi ascribed to liberalism. NAFTA and Wall Street deregulation were unambiguously aimed at extending the reach of the market. Neither policy's reputation has withstood the test of time, if public opinion is an acceptable benchmark: in 2016, both the Bernie Sanders and Trump campaigns expressed a rejection of free trade deals, forcing even Hillary Clinton to recalibrate her commercial policy. Financial deregulation and the repeal of the Glass-Steagall Act – which kept commercial and investment banking separate – are now widely acknowledged to have actively contributed to the 2008 crash. Welfare reform – which involved restricting welfare's coverage in scope and time, adding work requirements for beneficiaries, and delegating its delivery to state governments – was liberalising in content, but moralising and disciplinarian in spirit. On the pretext of upholding an ethic of 'personal responsibility', it stigmatised minority communities – especially black Americans – implicitly criticising them for dependence on welfare (itself a term insidiously associated with passivity and assistance, rather than with fundamental rights with which citizens are endowed).[29]

The crime bill, finally, strengthened a prison-industrial complex state that is responsible for record incarceration rates and the world's largest prison population. As Fred Block notes, throughout this period 'there has been not been any actual contraction in the size and scope of governmental activity', but rather 'a vast expansion of the population of the mostly black and brown people subjected to the control of the state through the criminal justice system'.[30] Not coincidentally, over-criminalisation has affected precisely those sectors of society that could not easily benefit from Clinton's leap into the globalised economy, for which a very particular culture of 'merit' and 'personal responsibility', as well as advanced labour-market skills, was deemed indispensable. While Spain's compensatory neoliberalism resorted to the integration of young, non-skilled workers into a low-productivity construction sector via an unsustainable real-estate boom, the US's disciplinary neoliberalism opted for over-criminalising the same demographic that would be likely to perform these tasks in that country: young, under-educated, black and brown men. This is not to say that racism does not produce a dynamic of its own, often irrespective of class, but to highlight the links between the US's political economy and its punitive prison system.

In fact, it is striking to observe how each successive move toward the markets in the US has been accompanied by a simultaneous deployment of the state's coercive capacity. The 'war on drugs' during Reagan's administration, Clinton's 1992 crime bill, and the post-9/11 securitisation enforced by George W. Bush all served the additional purpose of containing social turbulence introduced by each move toward the markets. As Figure 5.1 makes clear, the state's gradual retreat from the arena of welfare provision has been almost mirrored by increases in its coercive capacity. To use Georges Dumézil's metaphor of Indo-European deities, the utopian nature of market economy demanded at every step that Mitra – the nurturing, protective embodiment of sovereignty – give way to the raw coercive power of Varuna.[31] And this is precisely what Polanyi had in mind when he characterised the self-regulating market as a 'stark utopia'.

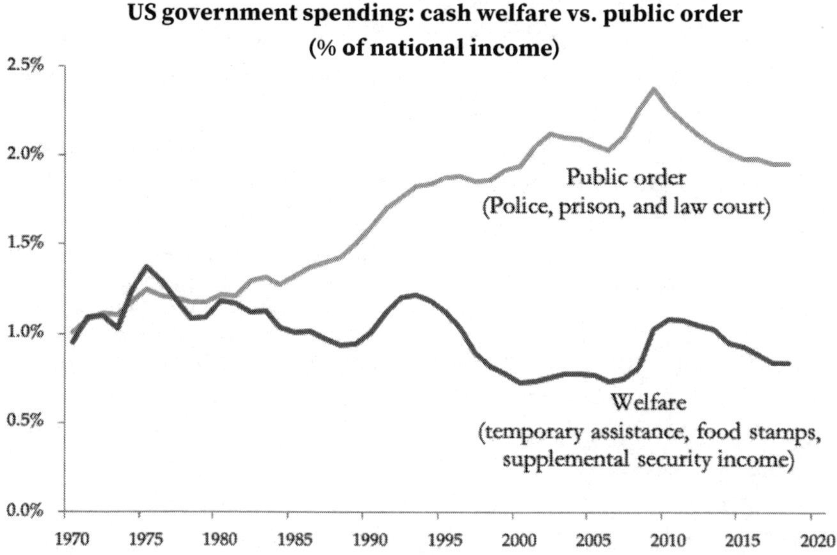

5.1: Mitra and Varuna in America: Cuts to public spending on welfare have gone hand-in-hand with increased spending on securitisation. Source: https://twitter.com/gabriel_zucman/status/1267482595228397574

Did the Democratic Party's move toward the centre at least inaugurate an era of placid bipartisan consensus? A period of stable governance under a centrist coalition, confident in America's unipolar moment after the USSR's collapse? Not at all. In the 1990s, the Republican Party continued to radicalise its social and economic agenda. The party of Reagan – already greatly different from that of Eisenhower – gave way to the party of Newt Gingrich and Grover Norquist, the libertarian, anti-tax activist who famously claimed to want to shrink the government to its pre-World War Two size by making it so small that 'I can drag it into the bathroom and drown it in the bathtub'.[32] Norquist's advocacy group, Americans for Tax Reform, became an extraordinarily effective tool to force moderate Republicans into pledging never to raise taxes during their mandates – and run primaries against those who didn't. This position became popularised following Bush's 1992 electoral defeat, widely perceived as a result of his decision to break a pledge not to raise taxes.[33] Equally important was Stephen Moore's Club for Growth, which among other things lobbied legislators for a flat tax. In the words of a Republican member of the House, 'when you have 100 per cent of Republicans voting for the [George W.] Bush tax cuts, you know that they are looking over their shoulder and not wanting to have Steve Moore recruiting candidates in their district'.[34] Gingrich summarised this drive for aggressive tax cuts and the dismantling of social services as 'Reaganism at warp speed'.[35] As Speaker of the House following the 1994 midterm elections, Gingrich was in a strong position to press his agenda on Clinton. Fortunately for the country, the increasingly radicalised dynamic in which the Republican Party was caught, coupled with the breaking of the Monica Lewinsky scandal, got in the way of the two politicians establishing a 'grand bargain' on social security, which would in all likelihood have involved part-privatisation and spending cuts.[36]

From the failed 1998 impeachment onwards, Republicans have been the main driver of social polarisation in America, largely due to their repeated lurches to the right. The Democratic Party has followed them partially and half-heartedly – thereby increasing the ideological distances between the two parties, even as the political centre of American politics has kept gravitating rightwards. It was only from 2011 onwards, with the emergence of new progressive social movements, that this dynamic was reversed and spaces for left politics began to open, even within the ranks of the Democratic Party – often to the chagrin of its elites.

Fortress liberalism

For these movements to emerge, however, it was necessary that the Democratic Party fail one last and definitive time at offering an inspiring socio-economic project. During Barack Obama's first term, it became clear to leftists and progressives that uncritical acceptance of politics-as-usual was a dead end if they expected systemic change. The monumental gap between the urgency of transforming the US economy in the aftermath of the 2008 crisis, the means at Obama's disposal, and the massive expectations his campaign deliberately stoked on the one hand; and the administration's actual accomplishments on the other, served as a painful indictment of the Democratic Party. Indeed, the question to ask of Democrats during the Obama years is, as Thomas Frank puts it, 'how they failed when the conditions for success were perfect'.[37] As we will see, it might be argued that they did not fail at all, but rather addressed the crisis in a manner consistent with their worldview.[38]

To understand why Obama's first term constitutes the third critical juncture in the transformation of US society towards the populist moment, it is worth remembering the circumstances under which his victory took place. In the fall of 2008, President Bush's popularity had fallen to unprecedented lows, largely as a result of the ongoing war in Iraq and the 2008 financial meltdown (and, earlier, his disastrous handling of Hurricane Katrina). These were no minor policy mistakes, but monumental failures grounded in the administration's guiding ideological tenets (which, incidentally, were those of the Republican Party from the Reagan years onwards). Neoconservative foreign policy had proved murderous and incompetent, while deregulation and financialisation had led to the 2008 crisis and exposed neoliberalism as an unsustainable economic paradigm. The crisis demanded immediate state intervention in financial markets and an overnight discarding of *laissez-faire* economics. Even Alan Greenspan – the once highly respected, 'free marketeering' head of the Federal Reserve between 1987 and 2006 – admitted during a Senate hearing that his ideology had failed him, blinding him to the risks posed by self-regulating markets.[39] His successor, Ben Bernanke, was hardly better placed: a scholar of the Great Depression, he had spent the years leading up to the crisis extolling the virtues of the 'great moderation' brought about by neoliberal macroeconomic stability.[40]

Against this backdrop, Obama won a landslide victory: 53 per cent of the popular vote (ten million votes ahead of his rival), an expanded majority in the House of Representatives, and a supermajority in the Senate (60 out of 100 seats, which prevented the Republicans from derailing legislation through filibusters). He did so on the back of an inspiring campaign filled with soaring, ambitious – if sometimes vague – rhetoric. Indeed, the closing lines of his nomination speech took a distinctly messianic tone:

> The journey will be difficult. The road will be long. I face this challenge with profound humility, and knowledge of my own limitations. But I also face it with limitless faith in the capacity of the American people. Because if we are willing to work for it, and fight for it, and believe in it, then I am absolutely certain that generations from now, we will be able to look back and tell our children that this was the moment when we began to provide care for the sick and good jobs to the jobless; this was the moment when the rise of the oceans began to slow and our planet began to heal; this was the moment when we ended a war and secured our nation and restored our image as the last, best hope on Earth. This was the moment – this was the time – when we came together to remake this great nation so that it may always reflect our very best selves, and our highest ideals.

The fact that Obama was America's first black president increased expectations of a transformative mandate. The institutional power he had won on 4 November 2008 made such transformation imaginable. To top it off, the Obama campaign had developed an unprecedented internet and ground mobilisation effort, Obama for America. At the end of 2009, the structure – renamed Organize for America – boasted two million volunteers, four million donors, and a fifteen-million email database of supporters: it was an impressive social movement, geared to keep fighting for a progressive agenda.[41] As Obama took power in January 2009, the US seemed ready for a paradigm shift.

What happened then? Not much. To the extent that, as the saying goes, personnel is policy, Obama made his priorities clear from the moment he put together a government of Clinton administration veterans. Larry Summers – Secretary of the Treasury in 1999-2001 – was appointed to head the National Economic Council. His old position in the Clinton administration went to New York Federal Reserve chairman Timothy Geithner, who would focus a considerable portion of his efforts on shielding the financial sector from what he called 'Old Testament justice' (that is, accountability), and who went on to run a Wall-Street based private equity firm once his mandate was over.[42] Attorney General Eric Holder would adopt a similarly lenient line, refusing to prosecute often-blatant malpractice among Wall Street CEOs responsible for the worst recession in the US since 1929.[43] The rest of the team was equally uninspiring, with Robert Gates retaining his position from the late Bush years at the helm of the Pentagon, Hillary Clinton at the Department of State, and the vice presidency going to Joe Biden: the quintessential moderate Democrat, with a track record of tepidness toward desegregation, supporting financial deregulation in his capacity as Delaware senator, and arguing for cuts in social spending.

The most revealing appointment, however, was that of Rahm Emanuel as Chief of Staff. A New Democrat with a knack for private fundraising and yelling expletives, Emanuel had made his name as chair of the Democratic Congressional Campaign Committee (DCCC) in 2005-07 (that is, in the period when Nancy Pelosi wrested control of Congress from the Republican Party). His maxim for conducting campaigns was a perfect illustration of both the Democratic Party's cartelisation and its simultaneous pro-market drift: 'The first third of your campaign is money, money, money. The second is money, money, and press. And the last third is votes, press, and money.'[44] As it happened, Emanuel's predilection for conservative primary candidates ('strong' on defence, capable of accessing generous private funding, concerned about fiscal deficits, and immune to leftist flights of fancy) was not always a recipe for success: as journalist Ryan Grimm has pointed out, many of the candidates supported by the DCCC ended up underperforming in districts that could have elected Democrats with more progressive profiles. After running the White House, Emanuel would go on to became mayor of Chicago, where his tenure was marred by recurrent police brutality scandals that he failed to tackle seriously.[45]

What were the accomplishments of this 'team of rivals', as it was termed because its members had competing professional aspirations, rather than diverse ideological viewpoints? Circumstances surely demanded that Obama's first 100 days resemble those of FDR, unleashing an uncompromising programme of 'shock therapy', as the right is prone to administer against its rivals when in power.[46] Instead, the administration dithered. Its initial fiscal stimulus (the February 2009 American Reinvestment and Recovery Act) began to be watered down not by the Republican Party but by Democrats: both in the House – where Emanuel's 2006 candidates proved eager to show their credentials as deficit hawks – and inside the White House. Christina Romer, at the time chair of the Council of Economic Advisors, proposed a $1.8 trillion fiscal stimulus that was immediately scaled down to roughly $800 billion by Summers, Geithner, and Emanuel on political rather than economic grounds: as the administration's leading pollster David Axelrod was fond of repeating, Americans appeared to be very concerned about the deficit.[47] The administration then wasted precious time attempting – and ultimately failing – to bring moderate Republicans on board with its healthcare reform. Providing healthcare for 24 million Americans through a Heritage Foundation-inspired plan that left another 28 million uninsured was the administration's greatest achievement in domestic policy.[48]

Because US policymakers did not apply austerity policies with the same zeal as EU elites did, there is a tendency for European onlookers to view their treatment of the 2008 crisis as markedly more competent, especially from the standpoint of monetary policy. This is unambiguously true on a macroeconomic level. The Federal Reserve's activism under Ben Bernanke during the first years of the crisis stands in stark contrast to the ECB, which under Jean-Claude Trichet raised interest rates in the middle of a recession. The US federal government at no point operated under the recessionary paradigm that gripped Eurozone elites, much less bought into the

Bocconi School's expansionary austerity theses that informed much of the latter's response to the crisis.

If we analyse the 2008 crisis in terms of its societal impact, however, we find that the US presents a similar picture to that of the Eurozone periphery. For one thing, America lacks the shock absorbers of Western European welfare states. The Obama administration, whose attempts to deliver social improvement invariably relied on market mechanisms – as was the case with both the 2010 healthcare law and the administration's technocratic approach to education – at no point attempted to use its initial supermajority to undertake a widespread reform programme in the spirit of the New Deal. After losing the House of Representatives to the Republican Party in 2010, the Democrats ended up overseeing a series of social spending cuts – first via budgetary compromises and, once the opposition refused to collaborate, through the sequester mechanism, which automatically enforces cuts to federal spending in the absence of political compromise. These decisions confirmed the Democratic Party's reinvention as a party of urban professional classes who, together with millennials, women, and ethnic minorities, constituted Obama's electoral coalition. The first of these groups acts as the hegemonic actor within this coalition, much in the way that labour did under embedded liberalism, but shaping a different set of policy preferences.[49]

As a result, the picture that emerges of the societal cost of the financial crisis in the US is somewhat similar to that of Spain. As the crisis hit, evictions, impoverishment and unemployment generated profound social dislocation across the country. An increase in suicides and deaths related to opioids, heroin, and alcohol addiction led to unprecedented increases in mortality rates among poor white Americans, which Nobel-winning economist Angus Deaton and Anne Case have likened to the AIDS epidemic that ravaged the country throughout the 1980s.[50] Against the complacent belief that Barack Obama's election might somehow miraculously exorcise the spectre of racism from the US, black communities remained afflicted by economic stagnation, police brutality, and mass incarceration. Undocumented immigrants experienced unprecedented numbers of deportations and recurrent workplace exploitation.[51] The clearest example of the cumulative impact of decades of disciplinary neoliberalism became the town of Flint, Michigan. As the auto industry's manufacturing jobs moved overseas, its residents were subjected to joblessness, impoverishment, and bankruptcy. A technical board of unelected economists then took over the city's management and, in a drive to cut public expenditure, ended up polluting its water supply with deadly levels of lead. In his 2014 book *The Divide*, Matt Taibbi has argued forcefully that these problems, apparently isolated from each other, share the common nexus of a society torn apart by increasing economic and social inequality.[52]

This societal crisis unfolded on the watch of an administration headed by a charismatic orator who campaigned on rousing promises, but turned to market-friendly policies when each election was over. Obama's campaign rhetoric – his call for hope and change in 2008, his 2012 imitation of a class warrior intent on crushing the 'cartoon plutocrat' Mitt Romney – contrasted with the reality of a White House that kept 82 per cent of Bush's tax cuts, called for the federal government's 'belt-tightening' in the middle of a recession, allowed Organize for America to wither away while it privileged failed bipartisan agreements, and lobbied for aggressive free-trade deals across the world.[53] At a time when finance capitalism seemed exhausted as a viable economic model, the administration's achievements were Hippocratic, aimed at avoiding further harm, rather than on presenting an alternative, inspiring vision of society.[54] The president who came to office promising to stop the oceans' rise ended his days with a different set of fluvial metaphors, musing that a government resembles a cruise ship:

> Sometimes your job is just to make stuff work. Sometimes the task of government is to make incremental improvements or try to steer the ocean liner two degrees north or south so that, ten years from now, suddenly we're in a very different place than we were. At the moment, people may feel like we need a fifty-degree turn; we don't need a two-degree turn. And you say, 'Well, if I turn fifty degrees, the whole ship turns'.[55]

Equally bewildering for anyone who took Obama's campaign rhetoric seriously was his passion for bipartisan consensus once in the White House. Although this inclination preceded his run for office, his ongoing commitment to it might be viewed as eccentric after January 2010, when the Republican Senate leadership, faced with an economic crisis unlike any in recent memory, affirmed that its main political priority was to ensure that Obama was not re-elected.[56] The administration's disposition reflected not just the president's character but the Democratic Party's transformation since the end of embedded liberalism. If Clinton and Gingrich had attempted to reach a 'grand bargain' on social-security privatisation, it was only natural for Obama to 'reach across the aisle' and seek compromise with Republicans.

Symptomatic of the Democratic Party's neoliberal drift was its timidity in actively pressing for a progressive agenda. As historian Matt Karp notes, this passivity was anchored in the belief that the hegemony of conservative ideas has been the defining feature of American politics since Ronald Reagan's time. Thus, 'opposition is not to be dislodged, let alone defeated. At best, it is to be resisted from within the walls of the Democratic Party fortress known as the White House.'[57] What this means is that Democrats from 2010 focused on placating a Republican Party that was invested in derailing the entire administration. This position of moderation in the face of radicalised adversaries put them at a constant disadvantage: as a Republican Senator observed, 'throwing grenades is easier than catching them'.[58] While it may be tempting to conclude, as Hacker and Pierson do, that the administration did its best in the face of powerful adversaries (lobbies, big business, conservative news media, the Tea Party movement, Republicans), a more plausible assessment is that Obama never considered embracing a transformative agenda, and was happy to play defence for the majority of his mandate.[59] Predictably, fortress liberalism was to become a self-fulfilling prophecy: between 2008 and 2016, the Democrats lost the House of Representatives and more than 900 state legislature seats, effectively making the White House their last stronghold.[60]

Beyond its walls, the natives were restless. In 2009, backlash against the financial bailouts, coupled with racist rejection of a black president and generous funding from conservative donors, led to the appearance of the Tea Party movement. By 2011, discontent had spread across the political spectrum with the appearance of Occupy

Wall Street. The socialist left was slowly gaining traction, with the appearance and success of outlets such as *Jacobin* magazine, which rejected overly theoretical jargon in a clear attempt to make its brand of socialism accessible to a growing number of Americans.[61] The Black Lives Matter movement began rallying across the country, dominating the news cycle and drawing attention to the persistence of police brutality and mass incarceration.[62] The struggle to raise the minimum wage to fifteen dollars an hour achieved a series of previously unimaginable victories at state and local levels.[63]

On specific occasions these progressive movements cooperated with each other, fighting for common goals.[64] As 2016 approached, the task of the Bernie Sanders presidential campaign would be to weld these varied expressions of social resistance into a collective project, with the veteran leftist senator as a unifier of different but commonly rooted demands.

Notes

1. Polanyi, *The Great Transformation: The Political and Economic Origins of Our Time*, Beacon Press: Boston, MA, 2001 [1944], p35.
2. Jimmy Carter, 1978 State of the Union Address, www.jimmycarterlibrary.gov/assets/documents/speeches/su78jec.phtml.
3. Remarks to the Asia-Pacific Economic Counsel, 1993, 'Public Papers of the Presidents of the United States, William J. Clinton', Book II, Federal Register Publications, p2014.
4. Matt Taibbi, *I Can't Breathe: A Killing on Bay Street*, Spiegel & Grau: New York, 2017, p120.
5. *Ibid.*
6. Daniel Drezner, *The System Worked: How the World Stopped Another Great Depression*, Oxford University Press: Oxford, 2014.
7. Lara Putnam and Theda Skocpol, 'Women are rebuilding the Democratic Party from the ground up', *The New Republic*, 21 August 2018.
8. See Taibbi, *The Divide: American Injustice in the Age of the Wealth Gap*, Penguin Random House: New York, 2014.
9. Jacob S. Hacker and Paul Pierson, *Winner-Take-All Politics: How Washington Made the Rich Richer – And Turned its Back on the Middle Class*, Simon & Schuster: New York, 2010.
10. Ben Stein, 'In class warfare, guess which side is winning', *New York Times*, 26 November 2006.

11. *Ibid.*

12. *Ibid.* Also keep in mind that income is generally more evenly distributed than wealth, which has only become more hyper-concentrated in recent decades.

13. These figures come from Piketty and Saez's research, quoted in Thomas Frank, *Listen Liberal: Or, Whatever Happened to the Party of the People?* Picador: New York, 2016.

14. *Ibid.*, p7.

15. Adam Liptak, 'US prison populiation dwarfs that of other nations', *New York Times*, 23 April 2018.

16. Hacker and Pierson 2010, pp131-2.

17. Frank 2016.

18. Quoted in Frank 2016.

19. Hacker and Pierson 2010, p121.

20. Monica Prasad, 'The popular origin of neoliberalism in the Reagan tax cut of 1981', *Journal of Policy History*, Vol. 24, No. 3, July 2012, pp351-83.

21. On this subject, see Gabriel Winant, 'Professional-managerial chasm', *n+1*, 10 October 2019.

22. See Corey Robin, '"We're going to tax their ass off!"', https://coreyrobin.com/, 30 August 2012.

23. See Hacker and Pierson 2010.

24. *Ibid.*, p139. It's worth noting that while unions were the dominant actor in the Democratic Party at the time, the US has never had a 'labour party' in the tradition of European social democracy.

25. Hacker and Pierson 2010, p110.

26. Francis Fukuyama, 'The end of history?', *National Interest*, No. 16 (Summer 1989), pp 3-18.

27. On this subject, see Eric Helleiner, *States and the Reemergence of Global Finance: From Bretton Woods to the 1990s*, Cornell University Press: Ithaca, NY, 2015.

28. John Harris, quoted in Frank 2016, p95. Within the Clinton administration, policymakers guided by a neoliberal ethic soon displaced the few heterodox voices, such as Secretary of Labour Robert Reich. See Stephanie L. Mudge, *Leftism Reinvented: Western Parties from Socialism to Neoliberalism*, Harvard University Press: Cambridge, MA, 2018, pp287-303.

29. An example of this trend is *The New Republic's* now-infamous 1996 front cover, 'Day of reckoning', which featured a black mother smoking while her young son drinks milk from a feeding bottle.

30. Fred Block and Margaret R. Somers, 'Karl Polanyi in an age of uncertainty', *Contemporary Sociology*, Vol. 46, No. 4, June 2017, p387.

31. Georges Dumezil, *Mitra-Varuna: An Essay on Two Indo-European Representations of Sovereignty*, MIT Press: Cambridge, MA, 1990.

32. See for example Jeff Spross, 'The GOP plot to drown Medicaid in the bathtub', https://theweek.com, 9 March 2017.

33. Hacker and Pierson 2010.

34. *Ibid.*, p210.

35. *Ibid.*, p212.

36. Frank 2016.

37. *Ibid.*, p6.

38. For an excellent dissection of said worldview, see Robin, 'The Obamanauts', *Dissent*, Fall 2019.

39. Edmund L. Andrews, 'Greenspan concedes error on regulation', *New York Times*, 23 October 2008.

40. See for example 'Remarks by Governor Ben S. Bernanke at the meeting of the Eastern Economic Association, Washington DC', www.federalreserve.gov, 20 February 2004.

41. Hacker and Pierson, p259.

42. Timothy Geithner, *Stress Test: Reflections on Financial Crises*, Crown Publishing: New York, 2014.

43. Taibbi, 'Eric Holder, Wall Street double agent come in from the cold', *Rolling Stone*, 8 July 2015.

44. Ryan Grimm, *We've Got People: From Jesse Jackson to AOC, the End of Big Money and the Rise of a Movement*, Strong Arm Press: Washington, DC, 2019.

45. Brentin Mock, 'How Rahm Emanuel blew it on police reform', www.citylab.com, 7 September 2018.

46. Naomi Klein, *The Shock Doctrine: The Rise of Disaster Capitalism*, Random House Canada: Toronto, 2007.

47. Grimm 2019.

48. See Robin 2019; on the shortcomings of healthcare reform, see the discussion of the Congressional Budget Office's estimates in Matt Bruenig, 'Opponents of single payer are moral monsters on par with AHCA proponents', https://medium.com, 18 March 2017.

49. Frank 2016. For a nuanced discussion of the 'professional-managerial class' in left circles, see Winant 2019.

50. Anne Case and Angus Deaton, 'Mortality and morbidity in the 21st century', www.brookings.edu/, 23 March 2017.

51. See, for example, Ana Gonzalez-Barrera and Jens Manuel Krogstad, 'US immigrant deportations declined in 2014, but remain near record high', www.pewresearch.org, 29 June 2016.

52. Taibbi 2014.

53. The description of Romney as a 'cartoon plutocrat' is Jan-Werner

Müller's. Jan-Werner Müller, 'Capitalism in one family', *London Review of Books*, Vol. 38, No. 23, December 2016, p10. Chye-Ching Huang, 'Budget deal makes permanent 82 percent of President Bush's tax cuts', www.cbpp.org, 3 January 2013.

54. On Obama as a Hippocratic president, see Tamames, 'El presidente hipocrático', politicaexterior.com, 15 March 2016. On the shortcomings of healthcare reform, see the discussion of the Congressional Budget Office's estimates in Bruenig, 2017.

55. Adam Gopnik, 'Liberal-in-Chief', *New Yorker*, 23 May 2016.

56. Andy Barr, 'The GOP's no-compromise pledge', politico.com, 28 October 2010.

57. Matt Karp, 'Against fortress liberalism', *Jacobin*, 18 April 2016.

58. Carl Huse and Adam Nagourney, 'Senate GOP leader finds weapon in unity', *New York Times, 16 March 2010.*

59. Hacker and Pierson 2010.

60. *Ibid.*

61. See Bhaskar Sunkara, 'The *Jacobin* project', *New Left Review* 90, January-February 2015.

62. On the Black Lives Matter movement, see Keeanga-Yamahtta Taylor, *From Black Lives Matter to Black Liberation*, Haymarket: Chicago, IL, 2016.

63. Chris Kirkham and Samantha Masunga, 'Why the success of the $15 minimum wage movement has surprised its founders', *LA Times*, 11 November 2015.

64. Brendan McQuade, 'A united front', *Jacobin*, 2 September 2015.

III
Landslides

CHAPTER SIX

Storming Heaven: Podemos at Spain's Populist Moment

The only starting point for a realistic left today is a lucid registration of historical defeat. [1]

Perry Anderson

The enemy wants us small, using a language that nobody understands; it wants us minoritarian, sheltered in our traditional symbols. It is delighted because it knows that, this way, we do not represent a threat ... However, when you gather hundreds, thousands of people – when suddenly what you say convinces the majority, even those who voted for them, then they start feeling fear. And that's simply called politics. [2]

Pablo Iglesias

The most productive actions take place at the frontiers, or at the limit; the great revolutions happen where the instruction sheets say it is impossible. [3]

Íñigo Errejón

The European Parliament elections of 25 May 2014 delivered a result unprecedented in the history of Spanish democracy. For the first time since the consolidation of its two-party system in 1982, votes for the centre-right People's Party (PP) and the centre-left Spanish Socialist Workers' Party (PSOE) fell below 50 per cent of the total votes cast. United Left (IU), Spain's traditional left coalition, dominated by the Spanish Communist Party, raised its vote share to 10 per cent. Smaller centrist and progressive parties also made noticeable electoral gains. [4]

The greatest surprise that night, however, was the success of a virtually unknown movement launched only a few months earlier. Led by a ponytailed political science professor called Pablo Iglesias, and running on a collectively drafted anti-austerity manifesto – signature proposals included auditing Spain's public debt, renationalising strategic sectors of the economy, establishing an indefinite moratorium on evictions, and providing a universal basic income – Podemos won 1.2 million votes: 8 per cent of the total share, corresponding to five seats in the European Parliament.[5] These results were almost five times better than polls had predicted.[6] At the post-election rally, however, Iglesias urged his supporters to avoid complacency:

> Tomorrow there will still be six million unemployed, and families will keep being evicted in our country. Tomorrow hospitals will keep being privatised, people will keep working in shameful conditions, young people will have to exile themselves, a quarter of our citizens will still live in conditions of poverty, migrant workers will still be treated like animals, there will still be bankers in impunity and corrupt bankers getting rides in official state cars.[7]

In mid 2014, Podemos was still an unidentified political object. Its electoral platform, while not presented in leftist language, went well beyond an appeal to smoothen the rough edges of neoliberalism, sketching a paradigm change in which economic goals were subordinated to social needs, and the Eurozone's austerity drive was corrected in favour of intra-European solidarity.[8] Its most visible leader was Iglesias: a former communist who now refused to identify as either leftist or right wing. While it often appeared as an organic outgrowth of the 15-M movement, expressing its goals in a language similar to that of the *indignados,* an observer pointedly described it as a 'laboratory party', designed under closely controlled conditions.[9] Indeed, Podemos' populist style coexisted with the existence of a resolute leadership team made up of political science and philosophy professors from Madrid's Universidad Complutense: Iglesias himself, his number two Íñigo Errejón, Juan Carlos Monedero, Carolina Bescansa, and Luis Alegre. Like its voting base, the founding group was remarkably young, with Iglesias thirty-five years old and Errejón thirty.

Political elites' initial response to the party's appearance was dismissive. Asked to explain Podemos' unexpected surge, the PP's longstanding campaign guru shrugged it off as an eccentric blip. 'All the nerds end up hovering around Madrid', he quipped in reference to the movement's strong showing in the Spanish capital.[10] One year later, the nerds had dislodged his party from the municipality of Madrid, and went on to govern Spain's second, third, and fifth largest cities as well. To return to our opening metaphors, Spanish political elites thought they faced a tornado. Normality might perhaps resume when this sudden blast of wind exhausted itself. But Spain's established parties had failed to apprehend the severity of the crisis that gripped the country from 2008 onwards, much less imagine its potential political impact. In 2014 a landslide took place, and the ground began to collapse under their feet.

Between 2014 and 2016, Podemos came close to overtaking the PSOE as the leading progressive party and reconfiguring Spain's politics. Ultimately, however, it fell short of this goal. From 2017 onwards, facing internal divisions and a complex political juncture, in which the Catalan regional government's bid for independence loomed large, the party stagnated electorally, and then began to shed support. The downward trend consolidated in 2019, when Podemos fell markedly behind the PSOE in the April and November general elections and the May regional and municipal elections. At the end of the year, however, the party's fortunes lurched back upward, as it joined the PSOE as a junior coalition party in the first left coalition government since the Second Spanish Republic in the mid 1930s. Taken together, Podemos's six-year rollercoaster offers a useful case study for examining the conditions and choices that influence the fortunes of emergent left populist parties.

'An ethics of victory'

As Chapter Four highlighted, structural conditions in Spain in the 2010s suggested that an electoral upset of the sort Podemos created in 2014 was not inconceivable. The 15-M and anti-austerity mobilisations had offered an interpretation of the country's crisis as the result of a failed political and economic model, and laid out progressive solutions to it. In early 2014, however, there was nothing to suggest that any political party would articulate them in a way that resonated with the public. But Iglesias and his collaborators had been laying the groundwork for their operation and Podemos' subsequent rise between 2011 and 2013. In order to explain how the party's breakthrough came about, and how it was able to capitalise on its strong initial showing, we must review the Universidad Complutense group's guiding strategic assumptions and its elaboration of a successful populist discourse.

Podemos' founding team came from different leftist traditions. Iglesias had been a long-time member of the Communist Party. The same was true of Juan Carlos Monedero, although he briefly joined the PSOE in the 1980s. While also a long-time left activist, Íñigo Errejón came from a Marxist libertarian background, had written his PhD thesis on Bolivia's Movement for Socialism, and was strongly influenced by Mouffe and Laclau's writing on populism. All of them, however, shared two important influences and a guiding assumption that flowed from their combination.[11]

The first influence was the work of Antonio Gramsci, the Italian communist thinker whose theory of hegemony, formulated during his imprisonment by Mussolini during the interwar years, is essential to understanding Podemos' rise. Gramsci explained the failure of the 1918 revolutions across Europe through a distinction between political and civil society, defining the former as the domain of the state, which imposes domination, and the second as the terrain of the intellectual, who 'manufactures consent' in order to build hegemony. He defined the latter as 'the capacity to convince social majorities of the narratives that justify and explain political order'.[12] Simply stated, hegemony refers to a set of assumptions enshrined as the 'common sense' of the day, which reflect the interests of a ruling group that, in addition to exercising political power, believes in itself as a ruling class and is similarly believed in by other, subaltern classes.[13] A corollary to Gramsci's insights is that, in Western democracies, socio-cultural change must precede and accompany political transformations – or, as right-wing propagandist Andrew Breitbart once put it, 'politics is downstream from culture'.[14]

Iglesias explained Podemos' strategic underpinnings in a 2015 *New Left Review* article. Spain's 2008 financial crisis and the 2010 turn to austerity, he explained, had generated a crisis of representation (or, to put it in Gramscian terms, an organic crisis) characterised by 'the exhaustion of the social and political model developed after the death of Franco in 1975'.[15] The clearest example of this state of affairs had been the emergence of the *indignados*. The 15-M movement, followed by the citizen tides (*mareas*), had also given hands-on activist experience to a young generation of future Podemos members. And while Podemos did not imagine itself to be the same thing as the 15-M, it did represent a political expression of Spain's crisis of representation in which, as Errejón put it, 'those in power still rule, but they no longer convince'.[16] To Iglesias' initial frustration, IU (the traditional left bloc in Parliament) had proved incapable of capitalising on the 15-M movement, overlooking its young, dynamic party members and sometimes viewing protesters with open scepticism – it was not uncommon for older leftists to complain that they had been outraged 'for decades now', that the *indignados* were newcomers and dilettantes or they belonged to an 'aspirational middle class' and were therefore useless for the purposes of transformative politics.[17] Spain's representation crisis, then, overlapped with a crisis of its 'really existing left'.[18] As shown in Chapter Four, public opinion largely tracked with Iglesias and Errejón's view of the situation.

Accordingly, Iglesias and his team set out to construct a counter-hegemonic communication project in the years prior to 2014. They began with *La Tuerka* ('The Screw'), a TV series in which Iglesias and his friends explained 'the ideas of the left in a language geared toward the common sense of the social majority'.[19] With the team promoting the show through social networks, *La Tuerka* gained visibility between 2010 and 2013. From 2013 onwards, Iglesias began appearing frequently on TV talk shows, many of them hosted by small, right-wing channels, where a host of reactionary pundits took turns attempting to lampoon his views. As César Rendueles and Jorge Sola have noted, this strategy went against the grain of dominant communication theories:

> The prevailing idea among the Spanish left was that conventional media was either inaccessible or technologically

obsolete, and therefore the most favourable battlefield was that of social networks. Iglesias disagreed. In Spain, political consensus is built via traditional media: about 60 per cent of the population favours television as their source of political information.[20]

Iglesias combined this approach with Laclau and Mouffe's insights on the importance of establishing an agonistic rhetoric and the need for populist projects to develop 'equivalential links' between different popular demands. The goal was to become a figurehead for those who had suffered from the economic crisis:

What we said allowed these victims – subaltern layers, above all the impoverished middle classes – to identify themselves as such and to visualise, through the form of a new 'us', the 'them' of their adversaries: the old elites. The TV phenomenon of 'the ponytailed professor' might be defined as the most effective occupation of that space ... Step by step, an unconventional left-wing talk-show guest became a reference-point for the socio-political discontent caused by the crisis ... The main goal of the [2014] campaign was to explain that 'the guy with the ponytail' on TV was taking part in the election.[21]

In the summer of 2013, Podemos' future leaders decided it was time to run candidates in elections. After being rebuffed by IU, with whom most of them had previously collaborated, they decided to launch a separate project, partnering with the Anti-capitalist Left, a Trotskyist party with a small presence in Madrid and a few other urban enclaves.[22] By then, Iglesias's media profile had turned him into a household name across Spain. Realising that only 5 per cent of voters knew about Podemos but roughly 50 per cent of Spaniards knew who he was, his team took the decision to print Iglesias' face instead of the party logo on the voting ballot.[23] Critics on the left derided what they viewed as a borderline *caudillista* tactic – that is, personalistic and authoritarian – but had to acknowledge its success when Podemos' electoral performance exceeded expectations. In the words of political scientist José Ignacio Torreblanca:

Podemos is a political party that began as a television studio; that is, in a format that says everything about the kind of society we live in and about its leaders' enormous capacity to anticipate events. Podemos created itself through television, and then television created Podemos. The conclusion, for Pablo Iglesias, is concise and meaningful: 'TV is to contemporary politics as gunpowder was to warfare.' This is not a trivial quote ... gunpowder rendered fortified castles useless, forcing armies to deploy across the territory, occupy it, defend it, and conquer it, in the process becoming much more vulnerable.[24]

The party was not simply a (traditional) media phenomenon – it was more than that, and it also used social networks with great skill and success – but the above quotation highlights how hyper-mediatised it was from its inception. Once their electoral performance had raised their profile further, Podemos leaders multiplied their appearances on the debate shows of mainstream TV channels such as *La Sexta*, making audience ratings soar and ensuring a regular platform for their political views that drew a mass audience.

Along with Gramsci's theory of hegemony, Podemos' founders were also influenced by the experience and practice of the Latin American 'pink tide' leftist governments that swept to power in the late 1990s and early 2000s. This second influence gave the party a distinctive character. As Boaventura de Sousa Santos notes, Podemos was 'the end result of a learning process that originated in the South'.[25] Much of the party's leaders' political experience came from Latin America, where they had worked as political consultants for leftist governments in Ecuador, Venezuela, and Bolivia. As Germán Cano, a member of the party's original leadership, remarked, 'Latin America has been a laboratory that has shown us that it's possible to build a majoritarian political will without adhering to the horizon they've told us is inevitable'.[26] While the region was a relatively novel source of inspiration for the European left, the circumstances surrounding Podemos' rise had an immediate precedent in Latin America. As Naomi Klein has pointed out in her famous study of 'disaster capitalism', Augusto Pinochet's Chile had been a test case for authoritarian neoliberalism.[27] Latin America's 1982 debt crisis was followed by a decade of austerity imposed from abroad. The rise of a new left there was linked to the effects of aggressive neoliberal policies, the political and economic bankruptcy of the governments applying them, and the absence of viable political alternatives from either the social-democratic or the communist left. One important difference is that Spain, unlike most Latin American societies, lacked a strong tradition of populism. Another one was that Spain in the 2010s was not in the midst of a state crisis, as several Latin American countries were in the 1990s.[28] While poverty and immiseration were rising, Spain retained social cohesion and functioning public services – more so, one could argue, than the US as it weathered the 2008 crisis.

Nevertheless, the country was facing a crisis with no viable political alternatives on the left. For Podemos' leaders, it was essential to acknowledge this problem, which they viewed as rooted in the Communist Party's melancholic attachment to a particular symbolic repertoire (red flags, Marxist jargon, the Second Spanish Republic, grievances dating back to the transition to democracy) that had ceased to have any resonance in contemporary Spanish politics. Their criticism was not aimed at the content of the symbols themselves, but rather at their uselessness as vehicles for reaching a wider public. A succession of historical defeats had made the left unable to lay claim to common sense, even when a majority of people might in fact agree with what it stood for:

> Most people are against capitalism, and they don't know it. Most people defend feminism and they haven't read Judith Butler or Simone de Beauvoir. When you see a father doing the dishes or playing with his daughter, or a grandfather teaching his grandkid that toys must be shared – there is more social transformation in those acts than in all the red flags you can bring to a demonstration. And if we fail to understand that those things can serve as unifiers, they will keep laughing at us.[29]

It was this urge to avoid the left's past mistakes that led the party to craft an unorthodox communication strategy. Recognising that the left-right axis is one that Spain's political, economic, and media elites are comfortable with – in part because it provides a ready-made framework through which to marginalise parties as 'extremist' – Podemos established a different axis of opposition, that would endow it with transversal appeal. Instead of mobilising the left versus the right, or progressives against conservatives, Iglesias spoke in the name of 'the people' (*la gente*) and against *la casta* ('the caste'), meaning Spain's political and economic elites. Unlike Trump's excoriations of 'the establishment', however, this framing did not pander to xenophobia or an exclusionary agenda. It was an agonistic, rather than an antagonistic, frontier.

Parties of the Spanish left were critical of the strategy, which they (correctly) perceived as alien to the country's political traditions and associated with excessive moderation. Why hide Podemos' leftist roots or talk about 'the establishment', instead of denouncing capitalism? Such criticism only intensified when Iglesias announced the party's ambition to occupy 'the centrality' of Spain's 'political chessboard', signalling Podemos' desire to appeal to a 'social majority' and become the hegemonic actor in the country's party system.[30] For IU and occasionally the PSOE, this rhetoric constituted an unforgivable abandonment of the left's traditions. Iglesias responded to criticism by doubling down on this newly established frontier: 'power doesn't fear the left, it fears the people'.[31]

A greater heresy was yet to come. On 31 January 2015, Iglesias addressed an audience of between 100,000 and 300,000 followers in Madrid's Puerta del Sol – the site of the *indignados'* original encampment.[32] Breaking a taboo of sorts among the Spanish left, Iglesias engaged in a discursive attempt to wrest Spanish patriotism from the hands of the PP. Instead of couching patriotism in the exclusionary terms of right-wing nationalism, Iglesias' appeal to *la patria* – 'the motherland', a term that is as frequent in Latin American political discourse as it is rare in Spain's – extolled Spain's tradition of resistance and idealism, from Don Quixote to the May 1808 uprising and subsequent resistance against Napoleonic troops, while excoriating the PP's hollow nationalism, damning it as a party whose leaders 'wave Spanish flags but place their money in Swiss bank accounts'.[33] Errejón has stressed the importance of this rally in the party's history, defining it as:

> a quantum leap in the sort of affections and subjectivity being created. It was no longer about people saying 'no' to

things, rejecting anti-popular and damaging measures against people's interests; it was fundamentally about people saying 'yes'. Saying 'yes' with a kind of hope, of affection, that comes with the shared passion of feeling that together we can make a difference ... That plebeian energy, of common people saying: 'this time it might be, this time we might win'.[34]

Eventually, Podemos would come to be perceived as a left-wing party.[35] In 2014 and 2015, however, this neither-one-nor-the-other strategy worked effectively. At the time of Iglesias' Sol rally the one-year-old party was riding high, with polls placing it ahead of both the PP and the PSOE. As Figure 6.1 shows, Podemos at the end of 2014 was taking 24.7 per cent of its voters from the PP and another quarter from former socialists, according to a poll conducted by the digital newspaper *El Diario*. Admittedly, polls such as this only provide a snapshot of a quickly changing electoral landscape. Podemos' demographic base was, in fact, similar to those of other left parties: young, urban, and drawing support mainly from culture-sector

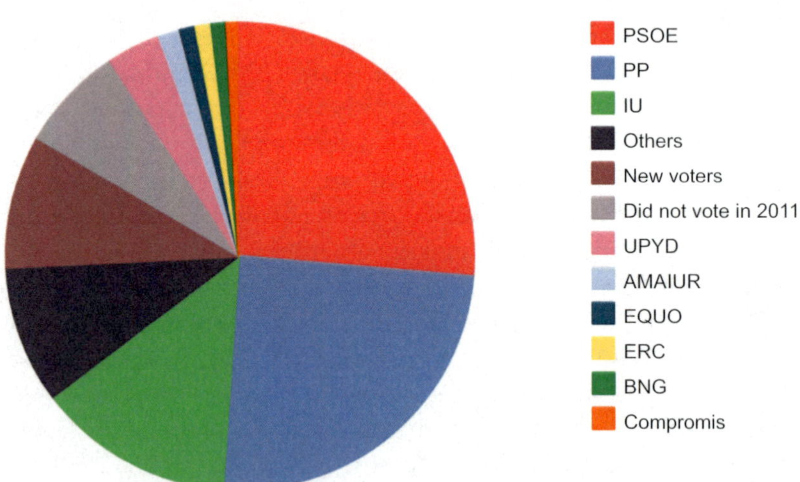

6.1: Provenance of Podemos voters, late 2014: More than half had previously supported Spain's two main parties, the centre-right PP and the centre-left PSOE. Source: https://www.eldiario.es/politica/ENCUESTA-cuarta-Podemos-procede-PP_0_326868090.html

professionals, while making inroads into precarious workers.[36] Younger Spaniards flocked to the party in considerable numbers, but rural and working-class constituencies retained the PP and the PSOE as their favoured options, respectively.[37] Nevertheless, Podemos' growth in this period shows the extent to which an innovative discourse could harness Spain's populist moment.

Another approach the party took to expanding its appeal beyond the classic – and relatively small – voting base of the Spanish left was its stated commitment to participatory democracy. From its inception in January 2014, Podemos promised to offer 'a participatory method open to all', instead of a traditional party hierarchy.[38] This commitment to fluidity and horizontalism was embodied in the party's grassroots associations, the *círculos* (circles), which were responsible for writing the party's first election manifesto. These allowed Podemos to present itself as an appealing alternative to the stifling bureaucracy common to Spain's established parties, tapping into a transversal electorate disillusioned with traditional politics. Doing this enabled the party to unleash the 15-M's potential in the field of electoral politics: no small feat considering many *indignados'* scepticism toward representative democracy and Spanish party politics.

Taken together, these tactical and strategic choices signalled a qualitative contrast with the rest of the Spanish left: Podemos' goal was to win. The party unambiguously stated that it would not content itself with a small share of the vote that consigned it to being a disposable crutch at the PSOE's left hand, as IU had been in the past.[39] From its inception, Podemos staked a claim to become the driving force in the process of democratic renewal and change in Spain. This commitment infused the party with an 'ethics of victory', in the words of former Podemos MP Pablo Bustinduy: a will to power that made it distinct from other non-social-democratic parties of the European left.[40] 'We were not born to play a minor role', Iglesias announced to the party's foundational congress. Borrowing a page from Marx's writing on the Paris Commune, he called on his followers to think boldly and act in consequence: 'heaven is not taken by consensus, it is taken by storm'.[41]

Challenges and contradictions

Spain's established parties were not going to wait passively for the newcomers to eject them. A week after the May 2014 elections, King Juan Carlos, whose public approval ratings had collapsed following a succession of personal scandals, abdicated in favour of his more popular son, Felipe. Generational renewal also visited the PSOE's leadership, with secretary general Alfredo Pérez-Rubalcaba, a veteran of the González and Zapatero governments, resigning shortly thereafter. The winner of the socialist primaries was Pedro Sánchez, a 42-year-old MP who would now be tasked with stopping the haemorrhage of the party's young voters toward Podemos. Only the PP seemed impervious to the changing times, elevating one of its most abrasive members – notorious for denying the existence of climate change, mocking victims of the Franco dictatorship and having once attempted to punch Rubalcaba – to the position of parliamentary spokesperson.[42]

In the following months, Podemos would also run into challenges that complicated its original strategy. The first was the nature of its leadership. In the Complutense team's view, the window of opportunity opened by the 2008 crisis would not stay open indefinitely. Accordingly, they trained their sights on the general elections scheduled to take place in late 2015. Podemos had twenty-four months to go from nothing to wielding power or, at the very least, overtaking the PSOE – a party that Iglesias viewed as torn between its function as a pillar of Spain's post-1978 regime (a logic that would compel it to band with the PP to stop Podemos) and its imperatives as a competitive centre-left party (which would pull the socialists away from coalition with the PP).[43] In between, Podemos would also stand in regional and municipal elections, scheduled for May 2015. Their strategy in this time came to be known as the 'onslaught' or blitzkrieg – a series of fast-paced operations designed to shock, awe, and ultimately overcome Spain's party system in the space of two years.

An offensive operation of this nature required a tight chain of command. Podemos would have to shed the 15-M's horizontalism and become a 'swift and powerful armoured vehicle', in the words of its leaders.[44] At the party's first congress, held in Madrid's Vistalegre arena in October 2014, which officially constituted it as a political party, the founding team designed what Errejón termed an 'electoral war machine' – a disciplined party with a steeply vertical structure with the Complutense team at its helm. This model, which was submitted to all Podemos members for approval at the congress, received 80 per cent of the vote, defeating the Anti-capitalist Left's counter-proposal, which called for a less hierarchical organisation.[45] The process illustrated one of the party's initial – and recurrent – challenges: how to combine grassroots mobilisation and a degree of intra-party democracy that was more developed than that of any other large Spanish political party, with a highly centralised leadership style – a 'friendly Leninism', in Juan Carlos Monedero's striking phrase.[46] Errejón argued that the party's 'war machine' would give way to a 'popular moment' once the December 2015 general election was over – the assumption being that Podemos would somehow modify its minimalist, top-down structure, more appropriate to an electoral campaign than a political party, once it was in power. The feeling of improvisation was captured in another of Errejón's phrases: the party would have to 'run and tie its shoelaces' at the same time.[47]

A second challenge was getting the right balance between attacking the old order and offering a credible alternative to it. This meant combining a thorough questioning of the existing system with a 'constitutive' drive.[48] While a brilliant polemicist who could channel the animosity that millions of voters felt toward the status quo, Iglesias had also established a reputation for controversial remarks, including praising the guillotine as 'the mother of democracy'.[49] Over time, and in the context of an unprecedentedly intense campaign of media hostility, Iglesias became an increasingly polarising figure. At stake was an issue that transcended the person of the party's leader: Podemos had to harness the 15-M's anti-systemic outrage – embodied in slogans like *no nos representan* – while projecting an alternative model of society in the imagination of its potential voters. Philosopher José Luis Villacañas has theorised this in terms of the transition from a 'populist' to a 'republican' moment in politics. This would mean the combative style that harnessed outrage giving way to a more constructive approach, which framed the party and its leaders as guarantors of a fairer, alternative social order. In Villacañas's words, 'Podemos would have to fight against everyone and against itself'.[50]

A third issue that would challenge the party's construction of 'the people' was the national question. Spain's territorial organisation is asymmetric, with different regions exercising different degrees of self-government. For historical reasons – most notably the Franco dictatorship's virulent nationalism – symbols of national unity have little purchase among leftists, or in regions with separatist nationalist movements, such as Catalonia and the Basque Country. In response, Spanish national identity has often defined itself through denial and repression of Basque and Catalan identities – which often project negative and essentialist views of Spanish identity in return.[51] While Spanish conservatives have come to accept Catalan and Basque regional autonomy as a fait accompli, they show hostility towards demands for greater self-government, punctuated by spells of collaboration with each region's right-wing nationalist parties. The left, on the other hand, finds the entire subject profoundly uncomfortable, traditionally opting either to avoid the subject, or to support demands for further devolution.

In this context, the Catalan right's pivot from a regionalist to a pro-independence stance in 2012 – conveniently redirecting pressure from the *indignados* movement, which had become especially contentious in Barcelona and had been dealt with brutally – galvanised regional nationalists while generating a profound sense of grievance among both Catalans who opposed independence and in the rest of Spain. Catalan society itself is divided on the subject of independence, with just over half of the population preferring to remain in Spain. The Spanish left's stance on this project is inherently uneasy. On the one hand, it wishes to avoid a punitive resolution of the impasse between the Catalan administration and Madrid, and often defends Catalan secessionists from a civil-rights standpoint. At the same time, the pro-independence agenda is more popular among wealthier Catalans, many of who oppose the region's fiscal transfers to poorer regions of Spain.[52] The Spanish right, by simply rejecting demands for independence and repressing them when they become impossible to ignore, finds itself in a more coherent – if, of course, ultimately untenable – position. To return to our earthquake metaphor, this conflict's increased salience became a line of weakness along which the nationalist right – both Catalan and Spanish – was able to develop itself, while the left languished.

As we saw, in early 2015 Podemos began to try and break the PP's symbolic monopoly on Spanish patriotism, presenting itself as a genuinely patriotic force, in contrast to those 'who wave the Spanish flag but keep their bank accounts in Switzerland'.[53] But it combined this discourse with a decentralising agenda, which included recognising Spain as a plurinational country and addressing the Catalan impasse through a negotiated referendum for self-determination. This position found little resonance with the rest of Spain's national parties, which for the most part have approached the question as a legal rather than a political problem, claiming that a referendum on self-determination would be non-negotiable because the constitution does not permit such referenda – a 'legalistic Catch-22', in the words of one foreign journalist.[54] As a result of its centralising agenda, the PP has virtually disappeared in Catalonia. It therefore uses its hard line against the independence movement as a recruiting tool across the rest of Spain, turning the Catalan question into a stick with which to beat Podemos. The PSOE and the centre-right Ciudadanos (aka Cs) joined in this effort, the former a little less enthusiastically.

Support for a referendum did not translate into smooth relations with the Catalan independence movement either. In Catalonia and other regions with nationalist traditions, such as Galicia and the Basque Country, Podemos painstakingly worked to build electoral platforms that integrated local concerns and demands for regional autonomy with the agenda of a party whose scope is national. The resulting alliances (*confluencias*) were different in each of Spain's historic nationalities and granted considerable independence to local leaders. Initially, this approach turned Podemos into the most voted-for party in general elections in both Catalonia and the Basque Country. But from 2017 onwards, as we will see, it became a liability across the rest of the country, just as voters in those two regions flocked back to the PSOE and left Basque and Catalan parties.

There were other challenges, too. Podemos was increasingly disadvantaged by developments in Spain's media landscape. The country's debt-ridden media conglomerates are heavily reliant on public financing, as well as support from the banking sector in the aftermath of the 2008 crisis.[55] RTVE, the country's once-prestigious public broadcasting channel, was in the mid 2010s run by a former member of the PP and prone to biased coverage.[56] A 2015 public security law, criticised by international media watchdogs, sharply curtailed freedom of expression, with instances of journalists being fined for such infractions as taking unauthorised pictures of police officers.[57] Spain at this time also developed a 'fake news' industry, opaquely financed and contributing to the spread of propaganda against both Podemos and pro-independence Catalan politicians. In contrast to the US, where misinformation campaigns are viewed as having helped Trump in his populist crusade against 'the establishment', in Spain members of the then-governing party occasionally relied upon these outlets. Key media misinformation campaigns (both in 'fake news' outlets and traditional newspapers) took place with the connivance and active cooperation of the Interior Ministry and politicised members of the security services.[58]

It should come as no surprise, then, that Iglesias faced unprecedented media hostility from late 2014 onwards, when it became clear that Podemos was attempting to beat the PP and PSOE, rather than content itself with a marginal share of the vote. These conditions, combined with a series of ill-judged outbursts of frustration on Iglesias' part, led to recurrent clashes between the party and some of the country's leading media outlets.[59] 'Everything burns under a magnifying glass', the writer Isaac Rosa observed of the effect of the media's gaze on Podemos.[60] The party responded by focusing on the press's hostility, sometimes in self-pitying ways. For a party as focused on discursive manoeuvres and with such a media-driven approach to politics, this development presented obvious problems. The industry that had given Podemos its profile in the first place soon developed an adversarial relationship with it that amplified every other problem faced by the party.

One such problem was the party leadership's past activities in Latin America. In early 2015 Spain's finance minister, in a shocking breach of confidentiality, leaked Monedero's tax returns.[61] It transpired that he had earned a considerable amount of money as a political consultant for Hugo Chávez's government while employed by a think tank co-managed by other Podemos leaders, including Iglesias. Monedero had declared this income in a manner that allowed him to pay a smaller rate than a straightforward reading of the tax code demanded. The scandal should have ended with his resignation in late April, but it blew a hole in the party's narrative. With its discourse about the corruption of *la casta*'s and revolving doors between politics and business, Podemos had set a high standard it now seemed incapable of abiding by. The PP consistently equated the tax mismanagement of one Podemos member with its own intricate and pervasive graft network, spreading the notion that all parties were equally sullied by corruption. Several media outlets promoted the theory that Podemos' financing came from the Venezuelan government – a charge that was repeatedly rebutted in Spanish courts, but ended up convincing up to 50 per cent of Spaniards.[62] Venezuela's ongoing travails, as well as those of its hapless president, have been repeatedly used to attack Podemos, often showing comical levels of opportunism on the part of its attackers.[63]

From early 2015 onwards, Greece became another source of external pressure. The victory of fellow left populists Syriza in Greece's January elections appeared to open the door to a renegotiation of the Eurozone's public debt and a reversal of the pro-austerity agenda that had dominated the Eurozone since 2010. Podemos viewed Alexis Tsipras and his party as key allies, and believed the 2015-17 electoral cycle in the Eurozone's southern countries – Greece, Spain, and Portugal; perhaps Italy and France as well – might set the stage for a challenge of the ruling austerity paradigm. They were not alone in this assessment, as shown by Tsipras' own view that Podemos' growing strength would steel European negotiators to adopt a hard line, on the assumption that concessions made to Greece would boost Podemos' standing in Spain.[64] Unsurprisingly, therefore, the two governments who took the hardest line against Athens in Eurogroup meetings were those of Lisbon and Madrid. The populations of Portugal and Spain would benefit from an overhaul of austerity policies across the Eurozone, but neither country's government wanted Syriza to be able to claim credit for such a change.[65] Following the outcome of the 2015 referendum in Greece on the terms of the bailout package proposed by the 'European troika',[66] in which the Greek people overwhelmingly voted 'no' to the deal, Greece was coerced into adopting an even more stringent bailout package. In Spain, rival political parties and leading media outlets simplified the entire experience into a morality tale: this is what happens when populists win.[67] The narrative that was built around the Greek crisis was particularly hard for Podemos to overcome, for the reasons outlined in Chapter Four: Spain today lacks the constituency for a left Eurosceptic party, so adopting an anti-EU position was never an option for Podemos.

As the party coped with these obstacles, it soon had to deal with a larger domestic challenge to its foundational strategy. Podemos had blasted a hole in Spain's two-party system. Then, in 2015, Ciudadanos (Citizens, or Cs), a market-friendly, anti-Catalan independence party formed in Barcelona nine years before, eased itself into the space Podemos had opened up. Led by Albert Rivera, a young, telegenic Catalan who relied on a sleek but somewhat bland message of anti-corruption reforms, the party presented itself as a 'safe' version of Podemos, appropriating its discourse against the PP and PSOE while maintaining an ideological ambiguity that allowed it to catch voters right, left, and centre.[68] (The party, which never showed strong ideological commitments, gravitated rightwards from 2017 onwards; in 2019, the radical-right party Vox emerged with strength and brought about its near-disappearance.) While Cs fell short of surpassing Podemos, its transformation from a Catalan into a national party effectively broke the monopoly on voters seeking change, curtailing Podemos' growth. To an extent its success, as IU secretary-general Alberto Garzón pointed out, could be viewed as a side effect of the hyper-discursive style adopted by Podemos. If the point was to fight corrupt politicians and improve 'the people's' lot, why take the risk of voting for a potentially radical party like Podemos? Cs in this respect came to fulfil the desires of the head of Catalonia's second-largest bank, who had publicly mused on the need for a 'right-wing Podemos'.[69]

The 2015 and 2016 elections

The period between early 2014 and late 2016 saw an electoral blizzard in Spain: elections to the European Parliament, two general elections, regional and municipal elections, and elections in Andalusia, Catalonia, Galicia, and the Basque Country. I will focus on three key dates.

The first is 24 May 2015. Podemos's leadership struggled with the question of whether to field candidates in the municipal and regional elections at all. Their main focus was the general election, and the party was still in the process of organising its party structures. An intermediate position was reached: they decided to run candidates in regional (*autonomías*) elections, while joining grassroots coalitions at a municipal level. These coalitions, which drew together IU and a wide range of civil-society activists and organisations, won the mayoralties of Spain's three largest cities: Madrid, Barcelona, Valencia, as well as Zaragoza, Cádiz, A Coruña, and Santiago. Podemos' state-level campaigns were not as successful, and the party often ended supporting the PSOE in order to end the PP's near monopoly of regional governments. The mayoral results, however, allowed Podemos to present a compelling narrative for the general election: as in the transition to democracy, larger cities were the first to open up to a process of emancipatory change.[70] The task would be to run these municipalities in an efficient and inspiring way, and hold them as proof that, beyond running successful campaigns, Podemos was ready to govern.

The cases of Spain's two largest cities were especially significant. In Madrid, Manuela Carmena, a seventy-one-year-old former Communist judge ended the PP's more than two-decade-long grip on the city. With 15 per cent of the vote, the PSOE was reduced to half the size of Carmena's coalition, and supported her bid for mayor. In Barcelona the victor was Ada Colau, the renowned former leader of the anti-eviction platform PAH.[71] Both women boasted an impressive independent trajectory, and neither fully identified as a member of Podemos. But their call to govern in a gentle and inclusive manner served to soften the image of the party, which was thus no longer exclusively associated with the founding group's unrelenting and predominantly masculine style.

20 December 2015, Podemos's first general election, was 'the moment for which we were born', as Podemos leaders liked to say. But the party was bracing for defeat as it entered the campaign. Cs, buoyed by its strong showing in Catalonia's September snap elections, seemed ready to overtake Podemos and perhaps the PSOE as well. The unwillingness of Podemos and IU leaders to form a coalition – the first because they viewed the Communist Party's tactics and rhetoric with

disdain, the second because they viewed Podemos as unacceptably reformist – meant that the left would not present a united front. To make matters worse, terrorist attacks in Paris' the month before threatened to impose a hard security frame on an election that had, until then, discursively hinged on the need for change.

Podemos managed to overcome these obstacles. Presenting itself as the underdog and the election as a comeback (*remontada*), it managed to re-energise the party's base. Iglesias' vigorous debate performances helped sway an unprecedented number of undecided voters. The party's campaign ads and social media strategists, traditionally a step ahead of those of other parties, came up with effective viral content that projected an iconoclastic and cheerful style: in one clip, candidates appeared as characters in the trailer for *Star Wars: The Force Awakens*; at rallies, candidates would take the stage to the tune of *Ghostbusters*; one of the main campaign ads was set to the tune of Eminem's 'Lose Yourself'.

The elections delivered a hung parliament (Figure 6.2). The PP came in first, but lost 3.5 million votes in its worst electoral result since 1989. Podemos and Cs' entry had turned Spain's bi-party system

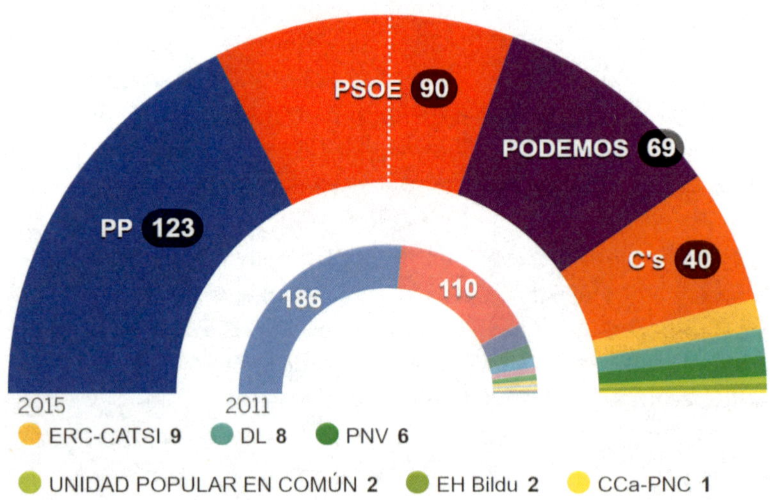

6.2: From bi-party rule to a hung parliament. The 2011-2015 (smaller semi-circle) and 2015-16 legislatures. Source: https://resultados.elpais.com/elecciones/2015/generales/congreso/

into a multiparty one, with the PP and PSOE's total share of seats shrinking by almost a third. Podemos and its regional allies came in a narrow third with more than five million votes. The PSOE were 1.5 percentage points and 21 parliamentary seats ahead, thanks to the rural bias in Spain's electoral system, but the party had fallen below its 2011 showing, previously a record low. It was displaced by Podemos in Spain's major cities and among voters beneath the age of 55, and lost its historical claim to be the left's main representative in Spain, as the sum of Podemos and IU votes exceeded its own. Cs, which the polls had projected as fighting for the second position, came a distant fourth.

These results, while exceptional for a new party like Podemos, amounted to what Errejón termed a 'catastrophic draw'.[72] Neither a Podemos-PSOE nor a PP-Cs coalition would have enough seats to form a government without the support of Catalan and Basque parties. Thus Podemos leaders made a bold offer to the PSOE: a coalition government, in which Podemos would hold key ministries such as Defence, Economy, and Foreign Affairs, as well as the vice presidency for Iglesias. Sánchez baulked at this, perceiving the offer as an attempt to deepen the splits within his own party. As he subsequently acknowledged, Sánchez was under pressure from media and party elites – mainly former Prime Minister González and the PSOE in Andalusia, the region with the strongest local party – to establish red lines that would effectively veto Podemos and the Catalan parties as negotiating partners.[73] The PSOE turned instead to the right, reaching an agreement with Cs, and pressuring Podemos to support it. Podemos' refusal to do so foreclosed the opportunity to form a government that would dislodge the PP's Rajoy, who throughout this time was preparing for a second round of elections, in which he hoped an exasperated electorate would punish the progressive parties.

The second round of elections was held on 26 June 2016. Podemos approached the date in a state of euphoria, as it had finally decided – against the objections of part of its leadership, most notably Errejón – to form a coalition with IU. According to most polls Unidas Podemos (UP), as the alliance was to be called, would become Spain's second-largest parliamentary force, capable of leading a coalition government with the PSOE. This time, however, Podemos' leaders made a major miscalculation. As the PP had surmised, voters were demoralised by the seven gruelling months that had failed to deliver an alternative to Rajoy. UP obtained a million votes fewer than Podemos and IU had won separately in 2015. The PSOE set a new record low, but once again took second place by 1.5 percentage points. The PP emerged greatly reinforced, eventually forming a government thanks to support from Cs and the PSOE's abstention – a dramatic decision on the latter's part that involved the abrupt ousting of Sánchez and the installation of a 'technical directorate', under guidance from the party's conservative elites. This decision paved the way for what journalist Enric Juliana called a national alliance between Spain's two largest parties ('hard parliamentary opposition during the daytime, strategic convergence at night'), which lasted until Sánchez's return as party leader in mid 2017.[74] Podemos had effectively forced the PSOE's contradictions to the point where it tacitly supported its until-then political rival, but for Podemos, the result was a pyrrhic victory at best.

Mishandled crises: Podemos's second party congress and Catalonia

Worse than falling short of expectations in 2015-16 was the way Podemos dealt with its first major setback. 'Failure is too strong a word, but it is probably the most appropriate for a party fixated with the rhetoric of "winners" and "losers", and which from the beginning insisted it was born to "win"', remarked a critic of the Complutense team's disciplined, top-down model for the party that had been adopted at its first congress at Vistalegre in 2014.[75] Differing interpretations of the crisis split the founding group apart and divided Iglesias and Errejón. Monedero accused Errejón of running an excessively moderate campaign that blunted Podemos' anti-system appeal and demobilised its base.[76] For Errejón and his followers, however, it was the coalition with IU that had dispelled Podemos's transversal appeal and seen the party fall back into the leftist clichés and rhetoric it was supposed to have avoided all along. Constant media scrutiny, combined with his own oscillation between harshly criticising *la casta* and courting the PSOE, damaged Iglesias' public image, leading observers to wonder if he had become a liability for the party. These problems, papered over as long as victory seemed to be in sight, now emerged with virulence.

This angry debate largely missed the point. Rather than too-moderate rhetoric or Iglesias' polarising public profile, what had doomed the campaign from the start were a variety of flawed premises. Podemos' leadership relied too heavily on Interior Ministry polling for its understanding of voting patterns. Neglecting to conduct its own surveys, it launched a campaign based on the assumption that it was poised within striking distance of the PP.[77] But its main ·errors came later – namely, in the seven months between the two rounds of elections, during which it seemingly focused more on exacerbating the PSOE's internal contradictions than on trying to dislodge the PP from power.

Indeed, the relationship with the PSOE splintered the party as the second congress approached. Iglesias, pivoting toward the Anti-capitalist Left and surrounded by an entourage of former communists unsympathetic to Podemos's original populist hypothesis, pressed for a strategy of open confrontation with the socialists that, in his view, would stay true to Podemos' anti-establishment roots. Errejón retained the support of most of the party's original operatives, and stressed that a more conciliatory approach would ultimately benefit Podemos. One onlooker at Vistalegre II, as the congress was called, drew an apt parallel with the US drama *The Wire*, Errejón playing the subtler Stringer Bell to the party leader's unapologetic Avon Barksdale.[78] At stake was whether the party's strength stemmed from its capacity to seduce voters, or its power to make the powerful afraid, and whether it should prioritise addressing discontent in the country's streets or developing policy work inside its political institutions. These choices were presented as binaries, and debated publicly in sectarian, unintelligent terms – a disappointing display from a party that had, until then, displayed outstanding communication skills.

As internal tensions spiralled out of control, it became clear that the Vistalegre I 'war machine', successful in ensuring rapid electoral growth, had generated an internal culture that was could not manage defeat and dissent.[79] At the second Vistalegre, Iglesias managed to push through his vision for the party, winning slightly above 50 per cent of delegates' votes for his proposal for the party's next steps, versus 33 per cent for Errejón's.[80] But a contest fought in these terms was always going to produce more heat than light.

The relationship with the PSOE continued to haunt Podemos. No sooner had the dust settled on Vistalegre II than PSOE members, ignoring the demands of the party elite, re-elected Sánchez by an overwhelming margin, rejecting the more conservative, Hillary-esque candidate supported by the party establishment and the directorate that had supported the PP. Previously an ordinary third-way centrist known for his good looks and a somewhat comical tendency to seem out of his depth, Sánchez now presented himself as a firebrand, blasting the PSOE's old guard for blocking the possibility of a left coalition government, and supporting policies previously advocated by Podemos. While his conversion was mostly for show, Sánchez's victory against his party apparatus and its powerful media supporters in May 2017 gave him a compelling outsider narrative. Polls registered an immediate rise in his party's popularity and Podemos was forced to soften the unforgiving stance toward the PSOE it had embraced under Iglesias's direction at Vistalegre II.

A few months later, a constitutional crisis derived from the Catalan government's – largely performative – attempt to unilaterally secede from Spain reoriented national politics in a reactionary direction.[81] In October 2017, Sánchez heeded King Felipe's speech calling for firm opposition to the pro-independence drive – a breach of the monarchy's political neutrality – and abandoned his progressive rebranding, rallying behind the Rajoy government. The PP dealt with the crisis in an autocratic and counterproductive way: attempting but failing to repress the pro-independence referendum, then briefly suspending Catalan self-government and calling for regional elections that delivered an almost identical result to the previous ones. Iglesias responded by excoriating the king and the parties supporting the government, now referred to by Podemos as the 'monarchic bloc' – a staple term from the old left's rhetorical playbook, which Podemos leaders had once disdained to use. He then proposed a referendum on the monarchy in late 2018, an idea that was swiftly shelved following a failed public rollout of the campaign.

Podemos's adoption of a patriotic discourse, which once had promised much, lost traction at this point. Opposed to both unilateral secession and the suppression of Catalan self-government, all while calling for a legal referendum, Podemos struggled to get a handle on the media narrative and its own contradictions. The party's position was further weakened by its Catalan subsidiary, which often ended mirroring the pro-independence camp's rhetoric (and, on certain occasions, defecting to its ranks), in spite of the fact that a majority of the party's voting base opposes independence. To Catalan nationalists, Podemos' position was nevertheless deemed remote and unhelpful in the face of oppression. For Spanish nationalists, the party's position constituted an unacceptable concession to secessionism. Podemos, for its part, claimed to be paying the price for its role as the political force bridging the unionist-secessionist divide in a time of growing polarisation – an indulgent reading of events, understandable after its first electoral upset in the region but not after underperforming consistently.

For the most part, such hesitancy betrayed the party's lack of confidence in its own constitutional vision, in which Catalonia remains within a more federalised, plurinational Spain, if necessary after an independence referendum in which independence is voted down. No doubt, this is an ambitious proposal, involving supermajorities and referendums whose outcome cannot, of course, be certain. But it remains more desirable and pragmatic than endless suppression of Catalan nationalism or unilateral separation. In the meantime, however, the Catalan crisis allowed Cs to make inroads among working-class voters opposed to independence.[82]

Spain's territorial tensions should be viewed as a line of weakness that reactionary populists can develop and exploit, much like racism in the US, immigration in Italy, Islamophobia in France, and Brexit in the UK. If in 2011 the 15-M managed to open a progressive line of weakness, delivering a critique of the status quo that geared Spanish society toward emancipatory change, the 2017 constitutional crisis empowered an increasingly chauvinistic right in both Catalonia and the rest of Spain. This crisis also fuelled the rise of Vox, Spain's first large radical-right party, which simply notched up Cs and the PP's hyperbolic rhetoric in the context of the Catalan crisis, calling for an abolition of regional governments across Spain and adding in the time-honoured repertoire of grievances against 'globalists', feminists, Muslims, LGBT activists, and refugees.

Power returns to power?

Today, Podemos finds itself in a mixed position. In mid 2018, the party provided critical support for a no-confidence vote against Rajoy led by Sánchez. The PSOE was weak in Parliament, and needed Podemos's support to govern. Spanish progressives were briefly euphoric as Sánchez appointed a majority-female cabinet, welcomed refugees crossing the Mediterranean and announced the exhumation of Franco's corpse from the fascist-era Valley of the Fallen. Podemos took a leading role in drafting the government's budget proposal, which included an unprecedented 22 per cent increase in the minimum wage as well as the reversal of key public spending cuts, financed through higher taxes on the wealthy. While limited in scope, the budget represented an earnest attempt to begin reversing the damage inflicted by eight years of austerity.[83]

Uncompromising opposition from the right, however, coupled with Sánchez's own lack of conviction, led him to turn his back on this initial impulse and vacillate in a political no-man's land. In this context, the decision of the pro-independence Catalan parties to vote against the PSOE-Podemos budget made a call for early elections inevitable. With Sánchez successfully presenting himself as the sole alternative to a hard-right coalition, the PSOE became Spain's biggest party in April 2019, garnering 28 per cent of the vote.[84] UP, the Podemos-IU coalition, won half the number of votes the PSOE did: one third less than in 2016, and thirty fewer parliamentary seats. Municipal, regional, and European elections in May made UP's position even more precarious. Errejón announced that he was joining forces with Madrid's mayor to create a separate electoral platform. The departure of other leading figures – some of them until recently aligned with Iglesias – further highlighted the party leader's isolation. Ultimately, Madrid fell to a right-wing alliance of the PP, Cs, and Vox. Podemos lost control of most of the cities it had gained in 2015 – the main exceptions being Barcelona and Cádiz, run by mayors who are de facto independent of Podemos – and saw its regional presence dramatically diminished. Following the failure of the PSOE and Podemos to form a coalition government that summer, a second round of national elections (the fourth in the space of four years), undertaken amid public protests and riots in Catalonia, witnessed Vox climb to third place, with 15 per cent of the vote – slightly below the sum of UP and Errejón's new grouping, which performed well below expectations. While a concerning result, one immediate consequence of Vox's rise was to compel the PSOE's leadership to abandon its reluctance about a left coalition and accept Podemos' presence in the national government, which it had until then actively discouraged.

With the PSOE near full strength and Podemos at an all-time low, the stage is set for a return to Spanish politics-as-usual. 'Spain has concluded the most convulsive political cycle of its democratic history [by] reinstituting the regime', journalist Antonio Maestre writes. 'Power has returned to power.'[85] Normalisation, however, may turn out to be an advantageous condition for the left. It remains to be seen how effectively Podemos can leverage its small governmental presence and whether doing so allows both parties to chart a course of action that goes beyond simple resistance to the radical right. There is reason for optimism if the joint governing programme is followed through. While uncomfortably ambitious for the PSOE, excessively moderate for Podemos, and beholden to the European Union's oversight, this programme holds the promise to transition away from the economic dogmas that have guided Spain's policymaking for most of its recent history.[86] The government is nevertheless fragile, as it still depends on support from Catalan nationalists.

The end of Spain's populist moment expresses itself in the changing style of the parties it birthed. UP has come to resemble the traditional left parties Iglesias once criticised. Errejón heads a green party with an amicable rather than agonistic rhetoric. If between 2014 and 2016 Spain's political establishment trembled at Podemos' advance, the main story from 2017 onwards has been the resilience of the established political structures and cleavages. The PSOE has not only survived the landslide, but also reemerged as the country's leading political force. Unlike other social democratic parties, reliant on culture-sector professionals as their key electoral base (thus becoming what Thomas Piketty terms a 'Brahmin left', highly educated but unmoored from poorer voters), Spanish socialists still command support from unskilled, precarious, and unskilled workers.[87] To an extent, this state of affairs owes much to Sánchez's 2017 comeback, when he harnessed Podemos' anti-establishment discourse and directed it not only against the Rajoy government but also against his own party's elites. In order to remain appealing, however, his rhetoric will have to be matched by ambitious policies. Whether Sánchez is willing to take that step remains to be seen.

In retrospect, the resilience of the left-right axis as a locus of political competition is as surprising as the PSOE's recovery. Electoral volatility in Spain did not bring about a realignment of right and left voters, who have for the most part switched within the same bloc (see Figure 6.3). (The outlier year in this respect is 2011, when disaffection caused by the economic crisis and the PSOE's embrace of austerity led to lower turnout rates among progressives.) This is

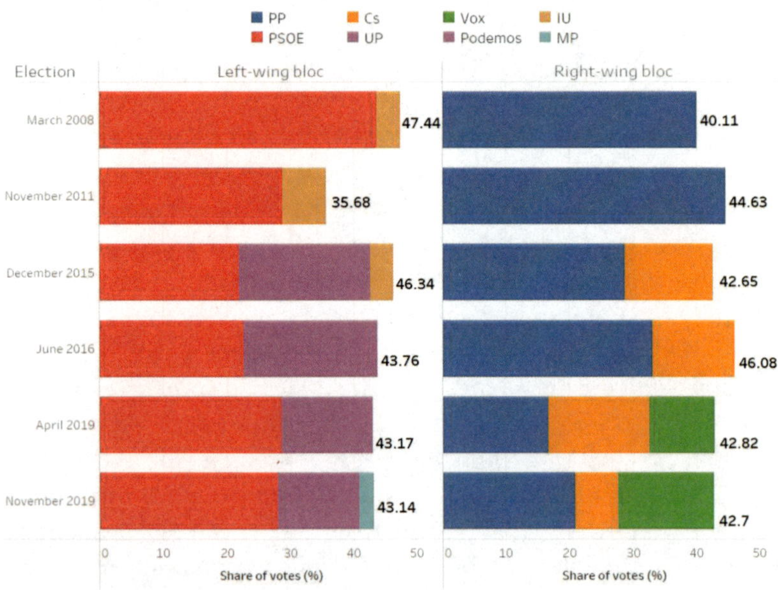

6.3: Electoral volatility and simultaneous left-right stability in Spain, 2008-2019. The total number of left votes (votes for PSOE, IU, Podemos, and Errejón's Más País) remained roughly equal, as did that of the right-wing parties (PP, Ciudadanos, Vox). Source: https://twitter.com/LuisCornagoB/status/1198227402465447936

not to say that Podemos' populist rhetoric failed to achieve its goals, as it clearly reached and mobilised voters well beyond the confines of the traditional left. Even after its 2019 woes, it retains a higher share of the vote than the Communist Party or IU ever acquired. What it means, however, is that voters did perceive Podemos as fundamentally a left party – although one that was qualitatively different from both the PSOE and IU.

What went wrong for Podemos? To an extent, the question is misleading. Podemos' post-2017 travails seem disheartening when seen from the distorting vantage point of 2014 and 2015, when the party raised immense expectations. There was never a clear path to victory for the party to follow, but a series of junctures it set out to leverage – initially with striking success, from 2016 onwards with decreasing fortunes. Equally important, the structural conditions and problems that led to its appearance remain in place. Joblessness, austerity policies, and economic inequality remain the order of the day. Neoliberal labour market reforms have led to the appearance of the working poor in the precarious service sectors. The country remains attached to a real estate-based growth model, now fuelled by gentrification and tourism rather than a mortgage bubble. A more appropriate question, then, is what can we learn from Podemos' swift rise and collapse? This question demands a larger reflection on the merits of populist strategies in advanced capitalist democracies, which I will offer in the closing chapter.

Notes

1. Perry Anderson, 'Renewals', *New Left Review*, 1, January-February 2000, p16.
2. Pablo Iglesias, 'The issue of the working class', youtube.com, 24 August 2014.
3. Íñigo Errejón and Chantal Mouffe, *Podemos: In the Name of the People*, Lawrence & Wishart: London, 2016, p18.
4. For the election results, see 'Elecciones europeas 2014', elpais.com, 26 May 2014.
5. *Ibid.*
6. M.K., 'El recién nacido Podemos se convierte en la sorpresa del CIS con un escaño', elpais.com, 9 May 2014.

7. Iglesias, *Disputar la democracia. Política para tiempos de crisis*, Akal, Madrid, 2014.

8. While Podemos's first manifesto was a rough sketch, subsequent ones would develop these commitments, proposing an expansion of the welfare state, a 30 per cent increase in the minimum wage, the reversal of the 2010 and 2012 labour market reforms, and free, universal pre-kindergarten childcare, among other measures. Most of the above would be financed through increases in taxation for wealthier Spaniards, closing tax loopholes and taking stricter measures against tax evasion in tax havens. Regional and municipal programmes also proposed public ownership of key utilities, such as water and electricity. For the 2014 manifesto, see 'Programa electoral de Podemos para las Europeas 2014', eldiario.es, 9 May 2014; for the 2016 manifesto, see Aitor Rivero, 'Podemos convierte su programa en un catálogo de Ikea para aumentar su difusión', eldiario.es, 8 June 2016; for 2019, see 'DOCUMENTO | Podemos presenta su programa electoral', eldiario.es, 5 April 2019.

9. 'Ignacio Escolar: "Podemos es un partido muy pensado, como de laboratorio"', libertaddigital.com, 17 September 2014.

10. 'Arriola sobre Podemos: "Todos los frikis acaban planeando sobre Madrid"', eldiario.es, 27 May 2014.

11. Errejón, 'La lucha por la hegemonía durante el primer gobierno del MAS en Bolivia (2006-2009): un análisis discursivo', Universidad Complutense de Madrid, 2012.

12. Quintin Hoare and Geoffrey Nowell Smith (eds), *Antonio Gramsci: Selections from the Prison Notebooks*, International: New York, 1971, pp206-75.

13. Eric Hobsbawm, *How to Change the World: Reflections on Marx and Marxism*, Yale University Press: New Haven, CT, 2011, p83; on the subject of Gramsci, see also Jorge Tamames, 'Retornos de Gramsci', https://elpais.com/,13 March 2020.

14. See Hugh Linehan, 'Extreme politics stoking the fire of the culture wars', *Irish Times*, 29 June 2019.

15. Iglesias, 'Understanding Podemos', *New Left Review* 93, May-June 2015; see also Iglesias, 'Spain on edge', *New Left Review* 93, May-June 2015.

16. *Ibid.*

17. *Ibid.*

18. *Ibid.*

19. César Rendueles and Jorge Sola, 'Podemos and the Paradigm Shift', *Jacobin*, 13 April 2015.

20. *Ibid.*

21. Iglesias 2015a.

22. *Ibid.* Podemos also learned from the example of AGE, a leftist Galician coalition that in 2012 managed to win 14 per cent of the vote in that region's elections. See Enric Juliana, 'Todo comenzó con los irmandiños', lavanguardia.com, 27 October 2014.

23. Iglesias 2015a.

24. José Ignacio Torreblanca, *Asaltar los cielos: Podemos o la política después de la crisis*, Debate: Madrid, 2015, p107.

25. Boaventura de Sousa Santos, 'The Podemos wave', telesurenglish. net, 12 June 2014.

26. Bécquer Seguín, 'Podemos's Latin American roots', *Jacobin*, 27 March 2015.

27. On this subject, see Naomi Klein, *The Shock Doctrine: The Rise of Disaster Capitalism*, Random House Canada: Toronto, 2007.

28. Iglesias 2015a.

29. Iglesias 2014.

30. Francesco Manetto, 'Pablo Iglesias apela a la mayoría para ocupar "la centralidad del tablero"', elpais.com, 18 October 2014.

31. Olga Rodríguez, 'Pablo Iglesias: "El poder no teme a laizquierda, sino a la gente"', eldiario.es, 25 June 2016.

32. On the speech and its meaning, see José Ignacio Torreblanca, 'Podemos arrebata el nacionalismo al PP', elpais.com, 2 February 2015.

33. *Ibid.*

34. Errejón and Mouffe 2016, pp63-4.

35. See V. G. C., 'Sólo uno de cada diez votantes de Podemos se considera demócrata', elpais.com, 10 June 2016.

36. On this subject see Alberto Garzón Espinosa, '¿A quién vota la clase trabajadora en España?', lau.org, 8 August 2019.

37. *Ibid.*

38. Seguín 2015.

39. For an instance of the IU's electoral stagnation, see François Ralle Andreoli, 'El "camarada" Meyer y la unidad popular', ctxt.es, 16 December 2015.

40. Interview with author, 12 June 2017.

41. Manetto 2014.

42. Esteban Ordóñez, 'Rafael Hernando, el hombre que nos permite vivir', ctxt.es, 13 June 2017.

43. Iglesias 2015a.

44. The description is found in Errejón's team's motion to the Vistalegre II congress: 'Desplegar las Velas: un Podemos para gobernar', p6.

45. Aitor Rivero, 'Podemos confía en Pablo Iglesias: su modelo obtiene el 80,7 per cent de los votos', eldiario.es, 27 October 2014.

46. Antonio Elorza 'Leninismo amable', *El País*, 3 July 2015.

47. 'Errejón, tras las elecciones generales: Podemos tiene que "ir mutando de maquinaria de guerra a movimiento popular", eldiario. es, 24 July 2015; see also Manetto, 'Correr y atarse los cordones', elpais.com, 19 March 2016.

48. As Giorgio Agamben puts it, 'Whereas constituent power seeks to resume and reform the law, destituent power seeks to render it inoperable'. Quoted in Errejón and Mouffe 2016, p51.

49. Iglesias, 'La guillotina es la madre de la democracia', youtube.com, 27 January 2013.

50. José Luis Villacañas, *El lento aprendizaje de Podemos*, Catarata: Madrid, 2017, p148.

51. On this subject see Carmen González Enríquez, 'El declive de la identidad nacional española', realinstitutoelcano.org, 29 June 2016; see also Tamames, 'The roots of Spanish rage', *Jacobin*, 11 November 2017; Tamames, 'Spain against itself', *Jacobin*, 12 June 2018.

52. Guillem Vidal, '¿"La pela es la pela"? Renta, clase social y secesionismo', http://agendapublica.elpais.com, 22 December 2019.

53. For a sample of this discourse, see 'Pablo Iglesias: "A mí no me veréis darme un abrazo ni con Rajoy ni con Mas"', elespañol.com, 22 December 2014.

54. Gideon Rachman, 'Spain, Britain, and the forbidden fruits of independence', *Financial Times*, 15 October 2012.

55. Raphael Minder, 'Spain's new media are squeezed by government and debt', *New York Times*, 5 November 2015.

56. Jaime Olmo, 'Los periodistas de TVE contabilizan 48 casos de manipulación o censura en los últimos tres meses', infolibre.es, 16 January 2017.

57. 'Spanish journalist fired under controversial "gag law"', *The Guardian*, 8 April 2016.

58. See Jordi Évole, *Salvados: La máquina del fango*, atresplayer.com.

59. See, for example, Santiago Alba Rico, 'El error de Pablo Iglesias', publico.es, 22 April 2016; see also Andrés Gil, 'El desayuno de Podemos, la libertad de prensa y los espacios restringidos', eldiario. es, 21 June 2017.

60. Isaac Rosa, 'Todo arde bajo la lupa', eldiario.es, 29 January 2015.

61. Pedro Águeda, 'Montoro se libra de un proceso penal porque Hacienda no dio con él antes de la regularización del pago', eldiario.es, 30 July 2917. Leaking Monedero's tax returns was viewed by many inside the Finance Ministry as a blatant politicisation of the institution. See Jesús Sérvulo González, 'Malestar en Hacienda con Montoro por el uso político de datos fiscales', *El País*, 2 October 2015.

62. *Ibid.*

63. See, for example, 'El zasca "demoledor" de Pablo Bustinduy al PP por usar a Venezuela como "constante cortina de humo,"', www.lasexta.com, 10 May 2017.

64. Iglesias 2015b.

65. *Ibid.*

66. The European Commission, the European Central Bank, and the International Monetary Fund.

67. 'El PP recuerda que Podemos tiene como referente al griego Syriza', elpais.com, 19 December 2014.

68. Isaac Rosa, 'Ciudadanos: ¿Un Podemos sin lo malo de Podemos?', eldiario.es, 2 February 2017.

69. 'Josep Oliu quiere proponer "una especie de Podemos de derechas"', elperiodico.com, 25 June 2015.

70. Ignacio Jurado, '¿El cambio empieza por las ciudades?', eldiario.es, 14 June 2015.

71. For an excellent account of Colau's campaign in Barcelona, see Pau Faus' documentary *Alcaldessa* (2016).

72. Manetto, 'Errejón: "unas nuevas elecciones no son deseables ni necesarias"', elpais.com, 7 February 2016.

73. See the Jodri Évole interview in 'Salvados: Entrevista a Pedro Sánchez', atresplayer.com.

74. Enric Juliana, 'Alianza nacional', lavanguardia.com, 26 October 2016.

75. Emmanuel Rodríguez, 'Por qué ha fracasado Podemos', ctxt.es, 27 June 2017.

76. Fernando León's 2016 documentary *Política: manual de instrucciones* presents a good overview of these divisions, as well as the tensions generated during Vistalegre I.

77. Carlos Elordi, 'La ilusión es ya otra cosa', eldiario.es, 1 July 2016.

78. Josep María Antentas, 'Podemos: Avon Barksdale se impuso a Stringer Bell', vientosur.info, 14 February 2017.

79. In the weeks leading up to Vistalegre II, the country's major media outlets sided stridently with Errejón, in the apparent belief that he constituted the 'moderate' alternative to Iglesias. In a display of siege mentality, the latter's entourage presented the *errejonista* faction as an internal enemy, explicitly working to destroy Podemos from within. On this subject, see Carlos Fernández Liria, 'Abrazos, pero sin mentiras', cuartopoder.es, 7 February 2017; Santiago Alba Rico, 'Los que no Podemos', cuartopoder.es, 31 December 2016.

80. 'Así han quedado los resultados de Vistalegre 2', eldiario.es, 2 December 2017

81. On this subject, see Ignacio Sánchez-Cuenca, *La confusión nacional. La democracia española ante la crisis catalana,* Catarata: Madrid, 2018.

82. Pol Pareja, 'El voto urbano catapulta a Ciudadanos hasta el primer puesto', eldiario.es, 21 December 2017.

83. For a summary, see 'Las 20 medidas clave del acuerdo de Presupuestos entre Gobierno y Podemos', elperiodico.com, 10 November 2018.

84. On the PSOE's electoral strategy, see Àngel Ferrero, 'Pedro Sánchez Katehon', elsaltodiario.com, 18 February 2019.

85. Antonio Maestre, 'La rueda sigue girando', lasexta.com, 27 May 2019.

86. On this subject, see Tamames, 'La fuerza tranquila', politicaexterior.com, 14 January 2020.

87. Jan Rovny, 'The "Brahmin left" vs the "Merchant right": A comment on Thomas Piketty's new book', https://blogs.lse.ac.uk, 16 September 2019.

CHAPTER SEVEN

Bernie Sanders' Political Revolution

I knew what the message would be; no consultant, no pollster had to tell me. It was the message I had been delivering my entire life. We had to listen to and express to the public the real pain of the people: the working families of our country, the elderly, the children, the sick, the poor, and the young ... We had to forcefully take on the arrogance and greed of the ruling class, a small group of powerful people who wanted it all. [1]

– Bernie Sanders

The first third of your campaign is money, money, and money. The second is money, money, and press. And the last third is votes, press, and money.[2]

– Rahm Emanuel

They've got money, we've got people.[3]

– Alexandria Ocasio-Cortez

One year and one day after Podemos' electoral debut, on 26 May 2015, Bernie Sanders took the stage in the Waterfront Park at Burlington, Vermont, to announce his candidacy for the 2016 presidential election. In front of 5,000 attendees, the socialist senator called for a 'political revolution' to implement universal healthcare, a breakup of Wall Street's largest banks, free public college tuition, a $15/hour minimum wage, an ambitious campaign of finance reform, and a less interventionist foreign policy. At the heart of his campaign was the fight against wealth and income inequality, 'the great moral, economic, and political issue of our time'.[4] In order to fulfil these goals a standard presidential run would not suffice,

Sanders said: 'we're going to build a movement of millions of Americans who are prepared to stand up and fight back'.[5] The campaign, therefore, was 'not about Bernie Sanders', 'not about Hillary Clinton', and 'not about [then-Republican frontrunner and hapless Donald Trump rival] Jeb Bush', but 'about the needs of the American people, and the ideas and proposals that effectively address those needs'.[6]

Taken together, these pledges positioned Sanders as the most progressive candidate in the upcoming Democratic Party primaries. *The Atlantic*, however, was more amused than impressed by the campaign's 'typically atypical' inauguration: 'Sanders has been making noise about a 2016 campaign since last year', the magazine pointed out, 'but until recently it was hard to tell whether he'd be an all-talk tease like John Bolton and Donald Trump, a slightly-more-youthful version of the liberal rock-thrower Mike Gravel, or something more serious'.[7] Henceforth, the challenge for Americans would be 'to imagine – without laughing – a self-described socialist sporting a thick Brooklyn accent and a shock of Doc Brown hair in the Oval Office'.[8]

The passage is representative of the mainstream press's initial reaction to the Sanders campaign. In retrospect, it also reads as a sample of the tired horse-race coverage that would be upended by 'an all-talk tease' on 8 November 2016. At the time, however, it was hard to anticipate a septuagenarian socialist from a small rural state posing a threat to Hillary Clinton's chances. A CNN/ORC poll released in early June gave Sanders 10 per cent of the primary votes: twice as much as in April and well ahead of soon-resigning hopefuls Martin O'Malley, Lincoln Chaffe, and Jim Webb, but a full fifty points behind the Democratic frontrunner.[9] Sanders himself did not take his candidacy all that seriously: before the Burlington event, he had officially announced that he was running in a five-minute speech during a Senate lunch break. He would go on to run an insurgent campaign with a bare bones operation.

Sanders did not endorse Clinton until 12 July 2016, two weeks before the Democratic National Convention was held in Philadelphia. By then, his campaign had gathered thirteen million votes, won primaries in twenty-two states, and received support from 1,846 pledged delegates – 46 per cent of the total.[10] True to

Sanders' repeated slogan that 'this is not about me; it's about us', it also developed an impressive network of volunteers and an online operation on a par with that of Barack Obama's 2008 campaign. If these numbers were unexpected for what was originally assumed to be a fringe protest candidate, the campaign's fundraising prowess was even more staggering: with eight million contributions from 2.5 million Americans, Sanders raised 232 million dollars, mostly from micro-donations.[11] Even more surprising for a candidate that was not viewed as electable or 'presidential', Sanders consistently outperformed Clinton in polls pitting him against Trump, by then the Republican nominee.[12]

Socialism we can believe in?

As we saw above, the populist countermovement was accelerated after the 2008 crisis. By 2014, US political institutions faced an accumulation of demands – from the Black Lives Matter protests, the Fight for 15 minimum-wage demands, and many others – that could barely be absorbed in a compartmentalised manner. The Sanders campaign's task would be to weld these varied expressions of social discontent into a collective project, with the senator as a unifier of different, but commonly rooted, popular demands.

Several elements in the Sanders campaign made it appealing to audiences alienated by traditional electoral politics. The most obvious was perhaps the candidate's blunt, unapologetic embrace of 'democratic socialism', a term that, while unremarkable in Western Europe, still comes across as radical in the US. None of the progressive democrats that Sanders cites as partial models for his campaign – Howard Dean, Jesse Jackson, and Dennis Kucinich – had run as socialists. All of them were defeated by candidates to their right before Sanders was. They did, however, provide useful guidance for the Sanders campaign. As journalist Ryan Grimm points out and Sanders has also acknowledged, Jackson's presidential runs in 1984 and 1988 and his 'rainbow coalition' pointed a way forward for progressive democrats, creating a grassroots-driven, multiracial coalition addressing the needs of middle- and working-class Americans at a time when the party seemed intent on swerving to the right. Dean pioneered online grassroots organisation in his 2004 presidential campaign, which never recovered from an incident at the Iowa caucuses, in which he yelled too loudly and/or awkwardly for the press' liking and was lampooned systematically as a result – a reminder of the gatekeeping power that US media wielded until 2016.[13]

Sanders's use of the label 'socialist' provided a critical element of transgression at a time of growing social frustration with the status quo. It was particularly useful for connecting with younger Americans. As a variety of polls have shown in recent years, a growing share of millennials and Gen Z-ers have a negative view of capitalism – a predictable result of coming of age during the 2008 financial crisis, associating e free market with precarious jobs and lowered life expectations, and not having lived through the Cold War.[14] Discussing what democratic socialism actually meant for the candidate and what this says about his conception of politics is therefore essential to contextualising his appeal.

Sanders addressed this question in a November 2015 speech at Georgetown University. Elsewhere Sanders has claimed to find Eugene Debs, the early twentieth-century union leader and candidate for the Socialist Party of America, an inspiring example.[15] At Georgetown, however, he stuck to a deliberately tame version of socialism, rejecting the notion that 'government should take over the grocery store down the street or own the means of production'.[16] He also connected his understanding of socialism to two better-known figures. The first was Franklin Delano Roosevelt, whose New Deal and Second Bill of Rights, which states that 'true individual freedom cannot exist without economic security and independence', Sanders viewed as particularly meaningful.[17] The second was Martin Luther King Jr, who famously declared that 'this country has socialism for the rich, rugged individualism for the poor'.[18] Roosevelt was not a socialist; King became one only towards the end of his life. The use of such references, however, serves to ground Sanders' outlook in a distinctively American tradition, and present 'democratic socialism' as a commonsensical project. After all, institutions such as Medicare and social security, rarely acknowledged as 'socialist', remain immensely popular among US voters.[19] Furthermore, the latter stages of King's life, when he worked to unify the demands of poor white Americans and the civil rights movement with opposition to the Vietnam War, offer a powerful example of the kind of movement Sanders sought to build. The senator, who as a student at the University of Chicago in the 1960s was active in the city's anti-segregation movement, found King's radical turn particularly inspiring:

> Against very strong opposition from his financial backers and 'liberal' supporters, King spoke out against the war in Vietnam. … King, taking on the entire establishment, plunged ahead into uncharted territory and media hostility. He demanded that the issues of poverty and income and wealth inequality be addressed. He refused to be just a great black civil rights leader. Instead, he became a great American leader who was black.[20]

Another key figure that Sanders repeatedly praised throughout his 2016 campaign – and one who is especially important for understanding the nature of his project – is Pope Francis. Claiming to have been 'very much helped and guided' by the head of the Catholic Church, Sanders even took time out from the all-important New York primaries to attend a Vatican seminar on the need to create a 'moral economy'.[21] In the senator's words,

> Pope Francis was distinguishing himself as one of the great moral and religious leaders not only of our time, but of modern history … His focus on the 'dispossessed' – the poor, the elderly, and the unemployed, who were being cast aside by country after country – was awakening the conscience of the entire planet. His call for a 'moral economy', an economy that addressed the needs of ordinary people and not just capitalist profiteers, was also inspiring to millions.[22]

This connection – and its relation to our Polanyian frame – is worth exploring briefly. The Pope and Sanders share a stated concern with the interplay between morality and the economy – a subject that was the topic of Sanders' September 2015 speech at Liberty University, where he attempted to reach out to conservative Christians by stressing the moral dimension of poverty and immiseration, in spite of differences on civil rights issues.[23] It is a concern that also courses through Polanyi's work (*The Great Transformation*, incidentally, was written at Vermont's Bennington College during Sanders's childhood). As historians Patrick Iber and Mike Konczal have pointed out, 'the vast majority of Sanders's supporters ... are, probably, without knowing, secret followers of Karl Polanyi'.[24] Iber and Konczal suggest that Sanders's framing of issues such as healthcare and education as basic rights not only changed the nature of policy debates, but was also 'at odds with the kind of politics that the leadership of the Democratic Party has offered more or less since Carter and the narrow policy "wonk" focus that tends to dominate coverage'.[25] Several thinkers on the left have also highlighted the similarities between Francis' world-view and Polanyi's. Brazilian liberation theologian Leonardo Boff has noted a 'perceptible affinity' between them, while Michael Burawoy links their vision of political economy to the work of Thomas Piketty.[26] At *The Atlantic*, Heather Horn has also made the case – as Iber and Konczal have of Sanders – that Polanyi is Francis' guiding political economist. As she points out, the Pope's charge that inequality results from 'ideologies which defend the absolute autonomy of the marketplace and financial speculation' has a distinctively Polanyian ring to it. In recent years Francis has in fact become something of a problem for the radical right in Europe and the US, because it cannot link its exclusionary agenda to the Catholic Church as long as that church remains headed by a Pope who excoriates economic inequality and stands up for the rights of migrants and workers.[27]

Gearing up for the 2020 campaign in the summer of 2019, Sanders again sought to define what he meant by being a democratic socialist, this time at George Washington University. The speech, like the previous one, drew heavily on Roosevelt as a source of inspiration. What was new since 2015 was the emphasis not just on fighting 'oligarchy' but also on 'authoritarianism' – linking Trump to a host of authoritarian politicians including Rodrigo Duterte, Vladimir Putin, Xi Jinping, Mohammed bin Salman, and Jair Bolsonaro. The speech catalogues those who oppose oligarchy and authoritarianism, and points to their common opposition to the top one per cent:

They are the teachers taking to the streets to make certain that schools are adequately funded and that their students get a quality education. They are workers at Disney, Amazon, Walmart and the fast food industry standing up and fighting for a living wage of at least $15 an hour and the right to have a union. They are young people taking on the fossil fuel industry and demanding policies that transform our energy system and protect our planet from the ravages of climate change. They are women who refuse to give control of their bodies to local, state and federal politicians. They are people of colour and their allies demanding an end to systemic racism and massive racial inequities that exist throughout our society. They are immigrants and their allies fighting to end the demonisation of undocumented people and for comprehensive immigration reform.

When we talk about oligarchy, let us be clear about what we mean. Right now, in the United States of America, three families control more wealth than the bottom half of our country, some 160 million Americans. The top one per cent own more wealth than the bottom 92 per cent and 49 per cent of all new income generated today goes to the top one per cent. In fact, income and wealth inequality today in the United States is greater than at any time since the 1920s.[28]

In making the case for democratic socialism, Sanders attacks the 'corporate socialism' that coddles Wall Street, large pharmaceutical companies, the Walton family (which owns Walmart) and others, for example Trump himself:

If you are the Trump family, you got $885 million worth of tax breaks and subsidies for your family's housing empire that is built on racial discrimination. When Trump screams socialism, all of his hypocrisy will not be lost on the American people. Americans will know that he is attacking all that we take for granted: from Social Security to Medicare to veterans' health care to roads and bridges to public schools to national parks to clean water and clean air. When Trump attacks socialism, I am reminded of what Dr Martin Luther King, Jr said, 'This country has socialism for the rich, rugged individualism for the poor.'

And that is the difference between Donald Trump and me. He believes in corporate socialism for the rich and powerful. I believe in a democratic socialism that works for the working families of this country. What I believe is that the American people deserve freedom – true freedom. Freedom is an often-used word but it's time we took a hard look at what that word actually means. Ask yourself: what does it actually mean to be free?[29]

The results of Sanders explicitly running as a socialist are mixed. Undoubtedly, it has helped popularise and destigmatise the term, which is useful for pushing political debates in the US in a more progressive direction. By the campaign's own account, however, the use of the term 'socialist' also put off some older Americans who remember the Cold War.[30] While the decision to use the word endowed Sanders's campaigns with an anti-systemic component that partly explains their appeal, it was the establishment of a horizontal frontier – between the 'us' of the American people and the 'them' of the one per cent – that proved key to Sanders' rise.

Between antagonism and 'a politics without frontiers'

As Trump's ascent polarised the 2016 Republican primaries – and, eventually, the presidential election itself – the contrasting tones set by his campaign, Sanders's, and Clinton's constitute text-book examples of the differences that Chantal Mouffe identifies between antagonism, agonism, and 'a politics without frontiers', which relies on the upholding of a fictitious social consensus.[31] To understand these differences it is worth comparing the Trump and Clinton campaigns briefly, before analysing Sanders' at length.

The polarising nature of Trump's candidacy requires the least discussion. With its appeals to xenophobic nativism, its denunciation of a corrupt establishment and media, its demonisation of immigrants and Muslims, and its incitement of violence against protesters, it relied on a Schmittian 'friend-enemy' distinction from the beginning. Trump's conception of 'the people' is exclusionary and not very subtly based on race. His 2016 campaign used every device within reach, frequently resorting to lies and misinformation to stigmatise his rivals and political opponents.[32] Mouffe's warning regarding the 'explosion of antagonisms that can tear up the very basis of civility' if the existence of societal conflict is never acknowledged seems especially apposite.[33] Trump's movement struck at the American body politic in a literal as well as figurative sense, with hate crimes – recurrently dismissed as inconsequential – rising consistently throughout his campaign and presidency.[34] A violent antagonism of this sort represents a threat to civil liberties and pluralism and is ultimately incompatible with liberal democracy.

Faced with this tide of aggressive nativism, Clinton's campaign responded with the opposite approach. As its own staffers acknowledged, and in stark contrast to Sanders and Trump, their candidate never settled on an idea to run on. Jonathan Allen and Amie Parnes, in their account of Clinton's disastrous campaign, make an observation that is at once astonishing and unsurprising: 'all of the jockeying might have been all right, but for one problem that confounded everyone inside the campaign and outside of it. Hillary had been running for president for almost a decade and she still didn't have a rationale'.[35] It was simply *her turn*, as the journalist Doug Henwood remarked in a scathing review of her political trajectory.[36]

Once the primaries were over – and, with them, the need to defeat the party's left flank – Clinton opted for messaging designed to conceal the existence of profound social divisions, rather than channel them into a progressive project. But 'America is already great' came across as a complacent counter-slogan, viable only if one ignored the socio-economic trends that had catapulted Trump and Sanders to prominence in the first place. The campaign's short-lived portrayal of Trump as 'Dangerous Donald' revealed an equally troubling failure of the imagination, the Democrats reduced to mimicking their rival. This may have to do with the fact that – as Republican operatives remarked – the Democratic National Convention, with its defence of 'family values', emotive emphasis on safeguarding US national security, and a speech extolling the Democrats' record on business by New York's billionaire (and former Republican) ex-mayor Michael Bloomberg (who was himself to briefly stand in the Democratic primaries four years later) seemed intent on appropriating the Republican Party's totems.[37] Senator

Chuck Schumer captured the thrust of this ultimately disastrous strategy when he played down Trump's appeal among working-class whites across the Midwest's Rust Belt, claiming that 'for every blue-collar Democrat we lose in western Pennsylvania, we will pick up two moderate Republicans in the suburbs in Philadelphia, and you can repeat that in Ohio and Illinois and Wisconsin'.[38] To the extent that Clinton adopted a confrontational attitude, it was to refer to half of Trump's supporters as 'deplorables' at a New York fundraiser – inept wording that further weakened her campaign and for which she was forced to apologise.

Democrats also centred their 2016 messaging on the candidates' respective temperaments. As a Wesleyan University study discovered (Figure 7.1), the Clinton campaign devoted far less campaign time to debating policy – and, consequently, much more to personality – than did any of its recent predecessors.[39] 'Tomorrow', the campaign's closing ad, is a good example. It features Clinton sitting and addressing Americans as the camera draws closer to her face. While 'values' are vaguely discussed, not a single policy is mentioned

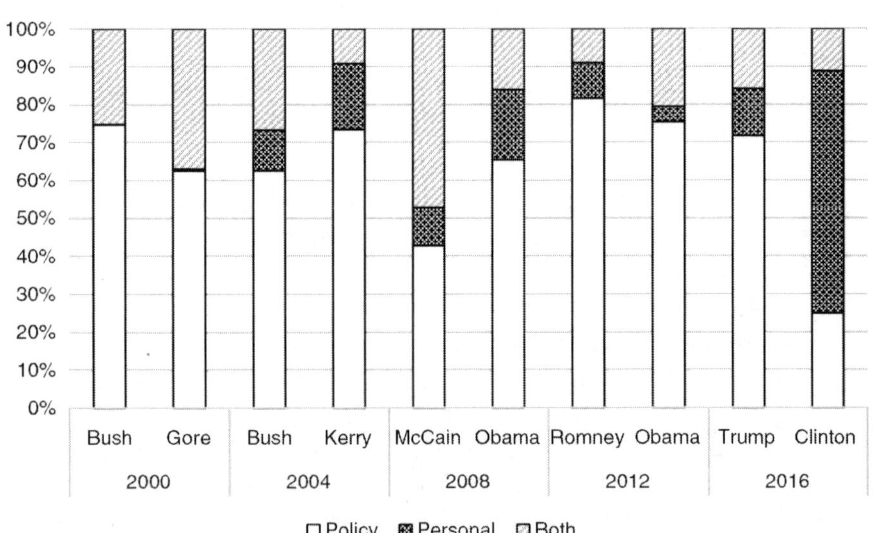

7.1: Personal and policy content of presidential campaigns. Source: Erika Franklin Fowler, 'Political advertising in 2016: The presidential election as outlier?' *The Forum*, Vol. 14, No. 4, December 2016.

over the course of two minutes.[40] This contrasts starkly with Trump's final campaign ad, in which raucous crowds are interposed with searing criticism of 'the establishment' and images of Goldman Sachs CEO Lloyd Blankfein. 'The only thing that can stop this corrupt machine is you. The only force strong enough to save our country is us', the candidate booms as the camera shows an enthusiastic rally.[41] Trump's ad has dark undertones, but it successfully constructs a collective subject, endows it with agency and steels it to charge against a common enemy.

While this strategy failed disastrously – in part because it relied on a candidate second only to Trump in her unprecedented unpopularity among voters – it is worth remembering that it was briefly hailed as extraordinarily deft. 'It's an argument that acknowledges, implicitly, that there are tens of millions of right-of-centre Americans who've never voted for a Democratic presidential candidate but didn't support Trump in the primary', journalist Matthew Yglesias noted. 'Clinton is pitching an argument aimed at those people – one designed to offer little ideological or policy content in hopes of appealing to 70 percent of the population rather than 51 percent.'[42] The strategy relied on a spectacular misreading of the country's political juncture.

Between the Scylla of violent antagonism and the Charybdis of a conflict-free vision of politics, Sanders managed to channel popular anger into progressive and democratic policies. Thus he delivered jeremiads against the one per cent and Wall Street greed, while refusing to run negative campaign ads and, famously, declining to join in the criticism of Clinton for her use of a private email server when Secretary of State.[43] This dynamic partially resulted from the senator's outsider status within the Democratic Party. Sanders could not afford to antagonise its favoured nominee, much less question the legacy of a president, Bill Clinton, who remained popular with its base. He therefore avoided personal clashes with his political rivals, while still deploying an agonistic campaign message.

Asked by an interviewer in 2016 to summarise his campaign, Sanders briskly defined it as 'standing up to the billionaire class'.[44] Indeed, the senator's well-known excoriations of 'the establishment' and 'millionaires and billionaires', often using a language that is uncommon in American presidential campaigns – his 2015 Georgetown address lambasted the country's 'ruling class' – were a defining feature of his campaign, and established a set of adversaries for his movement to mobilise against. These were the 'oligarchs': the one per cent and a host of parasitical industries – Wall Street, pharmaceuticals, big oil – that had 'rigged the economy', abetted by a political establishment that, in the wake of the 2010 Supreme Court's Citizens United resolution, has become increasingly subservient to moneyed interests.[45]

It has been noted that the 2016 Sanders and Trump campaigns shared a number of features, such as their claim to speak for frustrated voters, and their opposition to free trade deals responsible for offshoring American manufacturing jobs, such as NAFTA (North American Free Trade Agreement), signed by Bill Clinton in 1992, and Obama's Trans-Pacific Partnership.[46] But in contrast with Trump's construction of a people, which relied on the demonisation of a foreign Other and internal enemies, Sanders acknowledges that the articulation of his people-elites frontier requires the coming together of different democratic demands. In his writing and speeches, he frequently argues that Republicans win by dividing people on the basis of race, gender, religion, birthplace, and sexual orientation, and then go on to pursue an agenda that benefits their rich donors.[47] Opposing this dynamic requires coming together and rejecting these fault lines in favour of a struggle against 'the few'. This view was presented compellingly in 'Together', one of the 2016 campaign's most celebrated ads. Over the course of a minute, the clip juxtaposes a Sanders speech with a series of portraits of different Americans. It criticises the Republicans' divisive strategy and makes a call for unity; at the same time, it asks its listeners to unite *against the few*: 'When we stand together, as white and black and Hispanic and gay and straight and women and men – when we stand together and demand that this country work for all of us rather than the few, we will transform America!' A *Vox*/Morning Consult study (Figure 7.2) found that the ad played favourably with both liberal and Republican audiences, as long as the latter were not aware that it came from a Democratic candidate.[48]

In Chapter One, I noted how Laclau and Mouffe's framework for articulating democratic demands into a popular agenda offers a

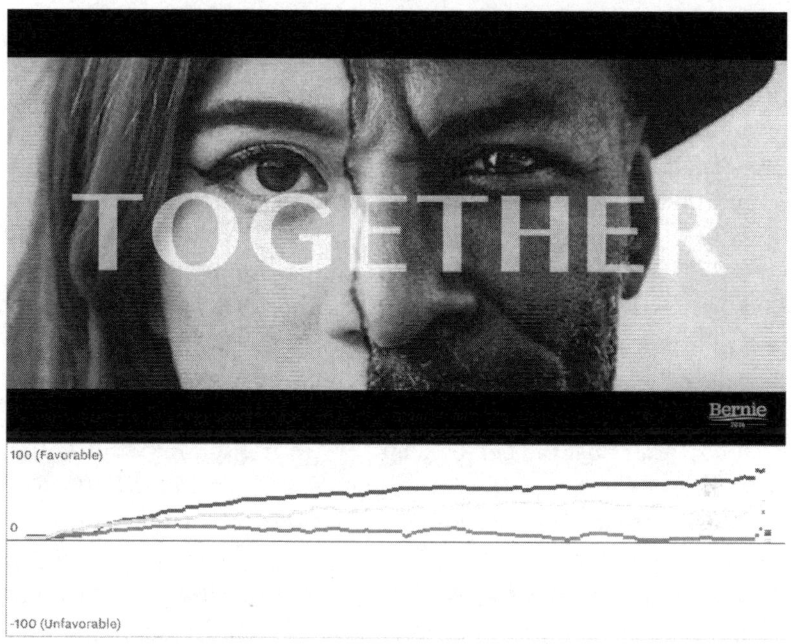

7.2: Jonathan Olinger's ad for the 2016 Sanders campaign, 'Together', generates positive responses among Democrats (black), Republicans (dark grey) and Independents (light grey). Source: https://www.vox.com/policy-and-politics/2016/3/14/11219138/bernie-sanders-ad-love-partisan

rhetorical alternative to a fragmentary brand of identity politics on the one hand, and class reductionism or essentialism on the other. It is useful to return to this as it highlights the ways in which left populists in different societies must devise discursive strategies to make their message resonate in their particular places. In Western Europe, where Mouffe centres her analysis, this often involves rejecting the wooden leftist jargon inherited from traditional communist parties, instead speaking for 'the people' in their fight against elites. In the US, however, progressive rhetoric is primarily attached to a somewhat baroque understanding of intersectional theory, which can make addressing large, structural problems in simple and compelling language inherently fraught, or 'problematic'. In this context, Sanders' inclusive but blunt and universalistic rhetoric represents a break with the dominant discursive practices of US progressives. Observers who stress the differences between Podemos' 'popular' discourse and Sanders' 'working-class' rhetoric therefore miss the larger point at stake in the latter's rhetorical break with the actually existing left. And, as I will show, Sanders succeeded – especially from 2020 onwards – in articulating a popular will behind his policy demands.

In Sanders' campaigns, the articulation of an internal frontier takes place along a top-down, rather than left-right, axis. Notwithstanding his identification as a socialist, Sanders discards leftist jargon in favour of a plainspoken approach that transmits moral outrage and claims a connection with everyday people feeling 'sick and tired' of politics as usual. Sanders himself has spoken of 'inject[ing] the radical concept of "morality" into the [2016] campaign'.[49] Clinton supporters argued that she could not afford to take his approach because an angry female candidate would have been the object of sexist pushback.[50] While there may be truth in this, the main point is surely that a candidate with her policy and personal record was simply incapable of running as a populist outsider. In contrast, Sanders' profile in 2016 was uniquely suited to this purpose, falling into the category of what political scientist Ignacio Sánchez-Cuenca calls 'old wine' political actors. Perceived by the public as having reached the end of their careers, these politicians – the UK's Jeremy Corbyn is another example – come across as cranky but incorruptible. Therefore – and in contrast to their younger counterparts in parties like Podemos – they are not negatively perceived as ambitious. Having spent decades as political outsiders rallying against elites, they are endowed with an aura of authenticity that stands in stark contrast with that of 'career politicians' like Clinton.[51]

The 2016 Democratic primaries

By late 2015, the battle lines for the Democratic Party's presidential primaries were drawn. Sanders had the support of a few progressive unions, such as National Nurses United and Communications Workers of America; left organisations such as Democratic Socialists of America (DSA) and Progressive Democrats of America; and a number of progressive publications, including *The Nation,*

Democracy Now!, and *Jacobin*. Sanders could also count on one other senator and a few members of the House. Against this, the Clinton campaign boasted endorsements from the remainder – i.e., the overwhelming majority – of the Democratic Party, backing from the country's leading union confederations and large advocacy groups such as Naral, La Raza,[52] Emily's List, and Planned Parenthood, and the sympathy of the editorial boards of leading press outlets, such as *The Washington Post* and *The New York Times*.[53] More importantly, Clinton surrogates controlled the Democratic National Committee and made sure to design a primary process that benefited their candidate.[54]

The candidates also had different bases of support. As a You Gov post-primaries study (Figure 7.3) shows, age and ethnicity were the defining factors of the race.[55] Black voters in the South voted overwhelmingly for Clinton, tipping the primaries in her favour from Super Tuesday onwards. Voters below the age of forty-five leaned toward Sanders, overwhelmingly so in the lower age brackets. Older voters, among other things put off by an avowedly socialist candidate, leaned toward Clinton.[56] Sanders also did better with non-registered voters, challenging the notion that most independents hover in a centrist no man's land between the Democratic and Republican primaries.[57] This source of support – or rather its absence – played to Clinton's advantage in critical primaries, such as those in New York, where only registered Democrats could vote and the local party apparatus set up a tilted playing field.[58]

Faced with these demographic cleavages, the Clinton campaign sought to frame its rival as heading a movement of young white men angry at Wall Street banks but unconcerned with gender or racial inequality, driven by misogynistic hatred of Hillary and her followers.[59] The concept of the 'Bernie bro', coined by a writer at *The Atlantic* who then complained that it had been subject to 'semantic drift', was loosely based on the fact that many left organisations in the US have an activist base that is younger and whiter than the national average.[60] Its application to the entirety of Sanders supporters, however, served to conceal the campaign's diversity. As the You Gov study shows, Sanders almost tied with Clinton among voters of colour below the age of forty-five, and actually overtook her among black millennials; Clinton, for her part, outperformed Sanders

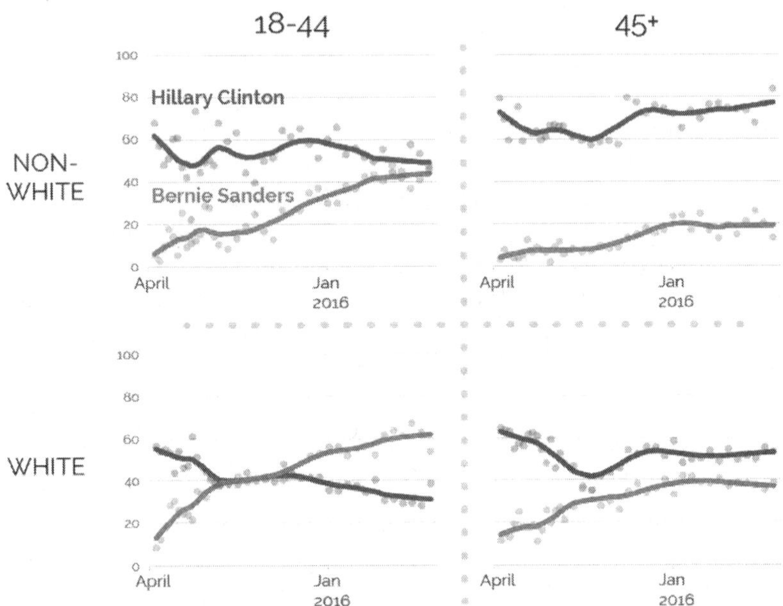

7.3: Breakdown of Clinton-Sanders voters according to race, age, and the evolution of the 2016 primaries. Source: YouGov/Economist poll April 2015-June 2016.

among old white voters.[61] Sanders also strongly outvoted Clinton among Arab and Muslim Americans – possibly as a result of his much more critical stances on US foreign policy – and won the caucuses of America's most diverse state – Hawaii – with a thirty-three-point margin.[62]

Sanders' failure to connect with black voters in the South is nevertheless worth examining, because it was a crucial factor in his failure to win the party nomination. Part of the explanation lies with the candidate's admitted lack of knowledge about the region.[63] This weakness was amplified in the face of the Clinton electoral machine, with its greater name recognition and strong links to black Democratic power brokers. As Michelle Alexander has pointed out, the Clintons retain a sentimental pull among older black voters, in spite of their policy record.[64] Sanders' stance on gun control, which as a senator from a rural state was laxer than Clinton's, played against him and was successfully exploited by the rival campaign.[65] Perhaps most importantly, Sanders in 2016 simply lacked name recognition. But these factors alone do not explain his failure to appeal to this constituency.

To use Laclau's terminology, in 2016 the Sanders movement failed to develop 'equivalential links' with black voters in the South. By late 2015 Sanders had effectively become a symbol for a number of popular demands, including socialised healthcare, free public college tuition, Wall Street regulation and a $15-an-hour minimum wage. He was not successful, however, in connecting these struggles to specific issues that affect black communities, such as police brutality and mass incarceration. 'If we broke the big banks tomorrow, would that end racism?' As Matt Taibbi has pointed out, this line of questioning from the Clinton campaign, presenting economic justice and anti-racism as mutually exclusive goals, may have been 'the line that won Hillary the nomination'.[66] Taibbi argues that the public associates 'Wall Street' with the stock market, which black voters generally mistrust. Because of this, and despite the evidence that the 2008 crisis had a disproportionate effect on poor black families, which financial institutions targeted with predatory schemes, 'Wall Street' can be presented as an issue that barely affects them:

> When Hillary Clinton used that line about breaking up the banks not ending racism, she opened a door for Bernie Sanders to talk about all of this. He could have talked about Wall Street not just as a symbol of international greed and corruption, but in terms of a more peculiarly American kind of ugliness. He could have begun with subprime and plausibly traced all the way back to 40 acres and a mule, explaining the modern problem of wealth inequality as (among other things) a still-extant failure of the Civil Rights movement, an ancient wrong still not corrected.
>
> But he didn't. Sanders I believe fundamentally sees the Wall Street corruption issue as a matter of class, i.e., rich vs. poor. He never found a way to talk about the special edge the financial sector brought/brings to the exploitation of non-white America.[67]

As Keeanga-Yamahtta Taylor has pointed out in her landmark study of the Black Lives Matter (BLM) movement, Sanders's understanding of black poverty, tied to the right wing of the American socialist tradition, also viewed the question through the somewhat narrow lens of economic distribution.[68] As a result, Sanders initially struggled to connect with BLM activists. The campaign eventually opened up to the movement's demands and presented a more comprehensive agenda against racial discrimination, aided by surrogates including Nina Turner, Cornel West, Killer Mike, and the late Erica Garner, who told the story of her father's killing – detailed in Chapter Five – in 'It's not over', by far the most moving ad aired in that electoral cycle.[69] By then, however, Clinton had consolidated a decisive firewall of older black voters in Southern states.

The left under Trump

Sanders' failure to win the Democratic nomination in 2016 should be analysed in the context of what he initially set out to achieve. Defeating Clinton would have been one of the greatest political upsets of recent times. The fact that it became a possibility for a brief period of time testifies to the campaign's success. More to the point, Sanders set out to build a political movement, rather than simply an operation to capture the White House. From 2016 onwards the contrast with Podemos became sharper: Sanders and his movement embarked on a promising long-term process while the Spanish party, which placed its bets on immediate electoral victory, stagnated.

The impact of Sanders' first campaign helped propel progressive movements in the age of Trump. The dynamics unleashed by Trump's presidency then restructured the terrain of political competition across the US in a way that presents considerable opportunities for the left. An immediate consequence of Trump's takeover in 2017 was a dramatic rise in social mobilisation, focused on opposition to his presidency. Many actions were spontaneous – for example, when protesters and cab unions collaborated to shut down New York's JFK airport following the administration's announcement that it planned to enforce a travel ban on a series of Muslim-majority countries.

Recent years have also witnessed a spike in labour activism. Unions have risen in popularity among the general public: according to Gallup, in 2019, they were viewed positively by 64 per cent of Americans, the third-highest approval rate since 1970.[70] Wildcat strikes in seemingly right-wing states with anti-union 'right to work' laws have delivered an important reminder that Democrats can compete with Republicans in the latter's traditional strongholds. Teacher strikes in Oklahoma have succeeded in wresting concessions from a profoundly hostile administration. In mid 2019, Kentucky coal miners – the demographic of working-class whites that establishment Democrats tend to portray as morally flawed Trump supporters – engaged in direct action to demand payment of stolen wages.[71] Although much remains to be accomplished – as detailed in Chapter Five, American organised labour has been systematically weakened for four decades – the signs here are promising.

Electorally, progressives have made advances at the local level. Left candidates such as Jackson, Mississippi mayor Chokwe Antar Lumumba are proving that it is possible for the left to make inroads in the red counties and states that traditional Democrats neglect. In Philadelphia, District Attorney Larry Krasner, backed by the Democratic Socialists of America (DSA), has made an ambitious attempt to end the city's 'war on drugs' and mass incarceration policies, in the face of vicious opposition from the state and federal governments. The DSA itself has grown exponentially, reaching 60,000 members in 2019, almost ten times its 2014 numbers, and 175 chapters across the US.[72]

Between 2016 and 2020, the most visible social mobilisation against the Trump administration was feminist. In the context of the #MeToo movement against sexual harassment and abuse, Trump's unabashed sexism, and the Republican Party's anti-choice agenda, women took a leading role in opposing the Trump administration. This effort began with the Women's March the day after Trump's inauguration: millions of protesters took to the streets in Washington, DC and other cities across the country, in what became the largest protest in US history.[73] Theda Skocpol and Laura Putnam have pointed out that in terms of scale of local mobilisation, this movement only finds a recent precedent in the Tea Party movement. But today's feminist mobilisation isn't funded by right-wing billionaires. Skocpol and Putnam also argue that women's increasing participation in politics explains two leading characteristics of the Democratic Party today: its capacity to compete against Republicans in right-wing districts, and the growing strength of its left wing.[74]

None of this is to say that the stars align for a full left takeover of US progressive politics. In the 2018 midterm elections, for example, the Democrats' success partly hinged on turnover in white, wealthy suburbs that have grown disenchanted with Trump.[75] But even in these kinds of areas, there are growing signs of left influence. As Ryan Grimm shows in his account of Jon Ossoff's – ultimately failed – campaign in Georgia's 6th congressional district, Democrats running in relatively wealthy, conservative districts adopt more progressive positions today than they would ten or even four years ago.[76] Across the Democratic Party, previously fringe policy positions such as full public healthcare ('Medicare for All') have become so popular that mainstream candidates are compelled to support them, at least nominally.

The 2018 midterms also brought to Congress an inspiring crop of progressive Democrats, many of them women from diverse backgrounds. The most famous among them include Rashida Tlaib, Ilhan Omar, and Alexandria Ocasio-Cortez, who defeated New York heavyweight Joe Crowley in a stunning primary upset. These newcomers reinforce the Democratic Party's left along a series of critical lines. Firstly, and much like the Madrid and Barcelona mayors once did for Podemos, they bring diversity to the movement's leadership, reaching constituencies Sanders might not (with the added advantage that their prominence challenges the stereotype of the socialist left as a preserve of young white men). They make innovative use of both social networks and House hearings: Ocasio-Cortez's plainspoken inquiries in House hearings, for example, have become as popular as Sanders' jeremiads. As with Sanders, part of the charisma of AOC resides not so much in her leftist credentials as in the plainspoken way in which she expresses her views and anger toward the status quo. As a co-founder of the progressive group Justice Democrats – which provided critical support for Ocasio-Cortez's campaign – has remarked, she is 'obviously a normal person. That might be a loaded term, but she was not a subcultural lefty or subcultural person of any weird little fringe subculture. She was a person that could communicate with anyone and make a connection with anyone.'[77]

Much of the rhetoric employed in Ocasio-Cortez's primary campaign can, in fact, be seen as an example of left populist discourse. Some of her advisors, such as the Justice Democrats' Waleed Shahid, have read Laclau, Mouffe, and Errejón closely, and have attempted to replicate Podemos' initial success in the US. This is not to say that their campaign simply mimicked a rhetoric that worked in Spain. In many ways they went beyond this discursive effort, combining a strong rhetorical strategy with the kind of ambitious grassroots organising that Podemos, with its media-driven approach, neglected. These similarities and differences are encapsulated in one of the opening scenes of the 2019 Netflix documentary about the campaign, *Knock Down the House*, as Ocasio-Cortez presents her pitch to a small New York audience:

> This is the work. I mean, *this is the work*. What I do is just talk to people all the time – just members of our community, all the time. And that is the organising and the work of running a grassroots campaign. This is not just about Democrats versus Republican, in fact it's so far away from that. It's not or left or right: it's up or down.[78]

While the last line echoes important elements of Podemos' discursive strategy, the emphasis on organising suggests a revealing difference. In order to be successful, candidates like Sanders and Ocasio-Cortez need to bring about a realignment in US political participation, mobilising the citizens who have given up on elections. Keep in mind that the US has consistently lower voter turnouts than Western European countries: in the 2012 and 2016 elections, roughly 61 per cent of the voting population turned out (in Spain, for example, turnout usually hovers above 70 per cent).[79] But mobilising the 'politically precarious', to use José Fernández-Albertos' term, requires building the capacity to reach them in the first place. The US left is doing so with ambitious digital fundraising and organising efforts, as well as outreach initiatives – canvassing, get-out-the-vote campaigns – that to this day do not form part of the Spanish left's operational repertoire. The numbers behind Ocasio-Cortez's campaign –120,000 doors knocked, more than 170,000 phone calls, over 175,000 text messages sent – speak to the intensity of this outreach effort.[80] As she notes in a maxim that challenges the Democratic mainstream's understanding of politics: 'big money is very lonely and we have people on our side'.[81]

Last but not least, the new congresswomen successfully pushed Sanders, the left's presidential candidate again in 2020, to adopt more progressive policies on a range of issues. Omar is an especially vocal opponent of the brutality of US foreign policy. Ocasio-Cortez's call for a Green New Deal has the potential to endow a left environmentalist agenda with widespread appeal in the US, and is currently being replicated in Spain.[82] The Green New Deal and Sanders' own ambitious agenda to combat climate change are especially valuable because they offer a pathway for articulating different social demands: green development can deliver not just environmental sustainability and a transition to clean energy sources, but well-paying unionised jobs, often in America's rural heartland.[83] This is critical given the scope of the challenge faced by the American left: ultimately, the defeat of the socio-economic circumstances that brought Trump to power in the first place.

Bernie Sanders' second campaign: Organisation without agonism

The aim of this book has been to identify the socio-economic reasons behind the emergence of left populism and, extrapolating from recent events, to imagine the political conditions under which it might successfully develop in future. Like his first run four years earlier, Bernie Sanders's second attempt at the presidency fell at the hurdle of the Democratic Party nomination. But, as we have seen, this is not only about the presidency. Part of the purpose of the 2020 campaign was, like that of its predecessor, to lay ground-work for US progressives in the coming years.

Sanders announced his second candidacy on February 2019. While the guiding themes were the same as those of his 2016 run, some of his stances – on foreign policy, on a Green New Deal, a call to abolish student debt, and a wealth tax for millionaires – had become significantly bolder.[84] The primaries were a rollercoaster. In early October, Sanders was struggling, unable to overtake Joe Biden as frontrunner and relegated to a third place by Elizabeth Warren – the other (more moderate) 'radical' in the field. That month, he suffered a heart attack, reminding voters of his old age. His bid was seemingly over, but endorsements from Ilhan Omar, Alexandria Ocasio-Cortez and Rashida Tlaib, and a high-octane rally in Brooklyn that drew 30,000 supporters,[85] marked the beginning of an upswing, in which he overtook Warren and reached the Iowa caucuses in February as a frontrunner in most early states.

The movement that Sanders and his allies built between 2015 and 2020 retained its skill at small-donor fundraising over that period, raising 87.5 million dollars in 2019 through average donations of eighteen dollars.[86] This financial capacity meant that only billionaire candidates like Michael Bloomberg could afford to outspend Sanders. The grassroots nature of this fundraising is notable: the largest employers of the people who donated to the campaign in 2019 were corporations like Amazon, Walmart, Starbucks, Target and the US Postal Service, suggesting that Sanders drew critical support from workers in the precarious and low-skilled sectors of the economy.[87]

Demographically, Sanders in 2020 moved well beyond his 2016 reach and assembled the most diverse coalition of all the 2020 Democratic contenders, becoming the strongest candidate among young non-white voters, as well as Asians and Latinos of all ages.[88] Below the age of forty-five, women constituted a larger part of his 2019 support base than men.[89] All of this means that Sanders' second campaign successfully engaged and mobilised the 'politically precarious' citizens who have been worst affected by neoliberalism, and who have as a result tended to be apathetic and wary of political engagement. The organisational prowess of the Sanders movement – an electoral 'war machine' with far more reach than the one Podemos' leaders set out to build – came into full view in weeks leading up to the 2020 Iowa caucuses. 1,700 volunteers from other states rushed to canvass and organise for their candidate, taking 10,000 door-knocking shifts and reaching 500,000 homes. Volunteers made ten million nationwide phone calls to reach out to potential primary voters.[90]

The makeup and potential of Sanders' 2020 coalition was made manifest in California – the country's most populous state and one of its most diverse – where early polls placed Sanders as the leading Democratic candidate among key demographic blocs: African American (31 per cent), Latino (38 per cent), Asian (24 per cent), non-college educated (35 per cent), under $60,000 annual income (34 per cent), union-affiliated (32 per cent), independent (35 per cent), and even conservative (23 per cent).[91] Sanders would go on to win the state in early March, suggesting that a combination of greater name recognition than in 2016, bolder policies, and repeated emphasis on the 'multi-generational, multi-racial, working class' nature of his coalition made a decisive difference.

Sanders' 2020 campaign has been a story of large-scale political organising, reinforced by a discursive operation designed to build a powerful repertoire of affective bonds among his followers. Beginning in spring 2019, the campaign started experimenting with a novel approach to communicating its message. Alongside his traditional jeremiads against the one per cent, Sanders put out a series of videos in which he visited US citizens who were struggling to make ends meet and coping with various troubles and anxieties. They show Sanders around their homes and explain their difficulties to the camera and the candidate. 'At many of his events, the antiseptic macro focus of the "oligarchy speech" had been replaced by the most intimate details of someone's life', journalist Ruby Cramer writes. 'The stories [Sanders] collects and broadcasts across the internet aren't just voter testimonials produced to validate the campaign or its policies ... they're aimed, in Bernie's mind, at people validating one another'.[92] Cramer describes how the process unfolds. It can be seen as a striking example of the aggregation and articulation of democratic demands into a populist agenda, described at length in Chapter One:

> His suggestion, by asking you to speak up about your private anxieties, many of them financial, is that you and the millions of people in the proverbial audience will begin to see your struggles not as personal failings, but systemic ones. He is less interested in explicitly presenting solutions than naming the problem ... mostly he'll just listen and nod, gaze lowered. Or he'll shake his head at the crowd, like *can you believe this?* And then, from the gut, a clipped scoff, like *of course you can believe*

it. That's the point. He has heard your story before, because it's all part of the same story: a broken system, driven by profit and greed, built to reinforce the notion that if you're bright enough, if you work hard enough, then you can travel the path to the middle class. And if you don't make it there…well, maybe you're the problem. And who wants to talk about that?

He is trying to change the way people interact with private hardship in this country, which is to say, silently and with self-loathing … He is imagining a presidential campaign that brings people out of alienation and into the political process simply by presenting stories where you might recognize some of your own struggles.[93]

Sanders's Twitter account similarly invited people to share experiences about their personal hardship. A typical tweet poses the question, 'What's the most absurd medical bill you've ever received?' A respondent – one among 14,000 – answers: '$480,000 for my Dad's spinal fusion surgery. That's more than we paid for our house.' Other Twitter users upload bills: $83,173 for heart surgery, $21,731 for a breast reduction as a preparation for a risk-reducing mastectomy.[94] The goal, again, is to highlight a common injustice while establishing affective bonds among those who are subjected to it, leading them replace anxiety or self-loathing with transformative political demands.

In October 2019, at his Brooklyn rally shortly after surgery following his heart attack, Sanders delivered a powerful expression of this new strategy. At a key point in his speech, he asked his supporters to look around and find someone who does not resemble them. Once they have done that, Sanders begins to kindle the notion of a popular will. He starts at the individual level, moving on to describe a transformative movement, and – at no point directly referencing himself – transforms his own person, through a chain of affective bonds, into a powerful symbol for popular demands, ready to carry them forward as a leader of 'the people':

Are you willing to stand together and fight for those people who are struggling in this country? Are you willing to fight for young people drowning in student debt even if you are not? Are you willing to fight to ensure that every American has health-care as a human right even if you have good healthcare? Are you willing to fight for frightened immigrants neighbours even if you are native-born? Are you willing to fight for a future for generations of people who have not even been born but are entitled to live in a planet that is healthy and habitable?

Because if you are willing to do that, if you are willing to love, if you are willing to fight for a government of compassion and justice and decency, if you are willing to stand up to Trump's desire to divide us up, if you are prepared to stand up to the greed and corruption of the corporate elite – if you and millions of others are prepared to do that, there is no doubt in my mind that not only will we win this election, but together we will transform this country.[95]

With such compelling messaging and an outstanding organisational infrastructure, Sanders seemed poised to win decisive results in the 2020 primaries. Indeed, throughout February his campaign led a fragmented pack of contenders, winning the popular vote in the Iowa caucuses – in spite of a vote recount process that some have viewed as fraudulent[96] – first place in New Hampshire's primaries, and an overwhelming victory in Nevada. The latter in particular spoke to the full potential of the Sanders coalition as it garnered young, working-class, Latino voters by overwhelming margins, against the objections of the power brokers in each state. This hat-trick of victories was unprecedented in the modern history of the Democratic Party. The primary field appeared in disarray: centrists Pete Buttigieg and Amy Klobuchar were incapable of drawing support from black and Hispanic voters; Michael Bloomberg's campaign spent half a billion dollars on publicity to little effect; and the expected frontrunner, Joe Biden, trailed in each and every state (fourth place in Iowa, fifth in New Hampshire, second in Nevada).

But a dramatic swing was underway – one that, unlike the October one, was to have devastating consequences for the Sanders campaign. The first signs appeared on 29 February, when Biden outperformed expectations and won an overwhelming victory in South Carolina, on the back of older, black voters, effectively putting him in the lead in terms of the popular vote. Between then and Super Tuesday (3 March), the Democratic field experienced an unexpected consolidation as Biden's campaign gained momentum. First came Buttigieg's resignation and endorsement of Biden; then those of Klobuchar and Beto O'Rourke, whose support was critical to ensuring Super Tuesday victories for Biden in Minnesota and Texas, respectively.[97] Elizabeth Warren, while lacking any clear path to victory at this point, refused to step down and support Sanders, ensuring a Biden victory in her home state of Massachusetts (where she came in third). While Sanders could cling to his important win in California, his hopes of ending the primaries in early March were shattered as Biden amassed a lead in popular votes and delegates.

Throughout March, a string of primary defeats followed a similar pattern. Against the increasingly fraught background of the coronavirus crisis, youth turnout was insufficient to push back the – older, moderate, suburbanite – voters that the Biden campaign mobilised to stop his opponent.[98] As Sanders' campaign struggled, other progressives remained equivocal, either actively damaging Sanders' chances – as in Warren's case – or unwisely waiting until Warren was out of the race to endorse him. The practical consequence of such dithering was to undermine the left's chances.

On 8 April, and under intense pressure from Democratic elite figures – in particular Barack Obama, whose behind-the-scenes support for Biden proved instrumental to harness momentum between his South Carolina victory and Super Tuesday – Sanders announced the end of his campaign. This was in part, the campaign said, to prevent danger to voters from Covid-19 – and, besides, his name would remain on the ballots of those states that had not yet voted. Six days later, however, Sanders endorsed Biden, sacrificing what leverage his campaign retained for the Democratic National Convention.[99] This anticlimactic gesture put an abrupt end to the 'political revolution' the candidate had been clamouring for until the previous month.

Explanations for the dramatic reversal in the campaign's fortunes fall into roughly three categories, none of which makes full sense on its own. When viewed in the round, however, these accounts offer a clearer picture of what went wrong.

The first line of reasoning is that Sanders was never going to win because his campaign faced insurmountable opposition from billionaires, the media, and the Democratic Party establishment. Even if Sanders had won the nomination, mainstream Democrats would have undermined his chances in November, much as the right wing of the UK Labour Party did with Jeremy Corbyn. This is an explanation with intuitive appeal, which rightly emphasises the structural hurdles in the way of the US left: hurdles exemplified by TV show hosts likening the Sanders campaign to coronavirus and the Nazis' conquest of France; party elites refusing to rally behind Sanders after successive victories; and oligarchs such as Michael Bloomberg being willing to spend hundreds of millions of dollars to stop his campaign.[100]

There are two problems with this line of reasoning. The first is that it is fatalistic. If the outcome was preordained, what is the point of trying in the first place? More importantly, if taken seriously, this argument raises the precise opposite question. If the forces aligned against Sanders were overwhelming, how was it possible that, in February, his victory became a real and tangible possibility? How did his campaign make it so far in the first place? This is an important question. It is the one we must pose of left populism more broadly at the present juncture – a moment when this movement has produced results well beyond initial expectations, yet has been disappointing in relation to the hopes it managed to raise along the way.[101]

The second argument is easier to dismiss. This states that Sanders and his supporters were overtly hostile to the Democratic Party, alienating its voters as much as its elites. It is, for the most part, an argument fielded by pundits and journalists who disliked key Sanders surrogates or supporters – such as his senior advisor David Sirota, National Press Secretary Briahna Joy Gray, journalist Glenn Greenwald, and the irreverent, left-wing hosts of the Chapo Trap House podcast – and it is easily dismissed by a slew of polls that ranked Sanders as one of the most, if not the most, popular primary contender among the Democratic base.[102] The issue was never Sanders's approval ratings, but an entirely different challenge: that of convincing primary voters that 'democratic socialism' was not just desirable, but both feasible and popular with independents and across swing states, such that Sanders would be both the most progressive candidate and the safest one to run against Trump.

To this end, certain decisions might have softened Sanders's image with the party base. An obvious one would have been for Sanders to actually register as a Democrat, rather than run in the primaries as an independent – even if it meant sacrificing a status that might have helped expand his base of support come November. As it was, his identity as an independent gifted a facile yet compelling line of attack to his critics: *Sanders isn't even a Democrat.* As part of such an effort, it might also have befitted Sanders to place less emphasis on his novelty as a democratic socialist – i.e., part of a tradition at odds with, and set to clash against, the party's mainstream – and instead present himself as an heir to Franklin Roosevelt and the New Deal, framing his opponents as the ones who had deserted the positions that the Democratic Party once stood for.[103] A discursive shift of this sort would have not required Sanders to give up any of his policies, much less denounce his brand of socialism – which, as I have argued, is rooted in the legacy of mainstream figures such as FDR and Martin Luther King. Paradoxically, this softer stance toward the party could and should have been combined with a less forgiving stance vis-à-vis particular candidates, Biden in particular.

This brings us to the third argument, which offers a more substantial critique than the previous two. If Sanders' attacks on Clinton in 2016 were mild, those against 'my friend Joe', as the socialist senator repeatedly presented his rival, were even more restrained. He repeatedly refused to present Biden as a weak candidate against Trump, or to seriously criticise his strikingly reactionary record. This record includes a host of sexism scandals, going back to Biden's involvement in the 1991 Senate hearings on sexual harassment allegations against Supreme Court nominee Clarence Thomas (the Anita Hill hearings);[104] sympathy for overtly racist Republicans, such as the segregationist Strom Thurmond; endorsement of punitive policies against and dismissive remarks about the problems faced by black communities; and sustained support for financial deregulation and failed overseas interventions, including the Iraq war, for which he lobbied as chair of the Senate Foreign Relations Committee. Sanders allowed his rival to present all of these as unfortunate mistakes, rather than as signs of something more fundamental. In a similar vein, a slew of farcical statements from Biden – including a false claim about getting arrested in South Africa trying to visit Nelson Mandela in prison – got a relatively free pass throughout the primary televised debates.[105]

This is the picture that emerges from the narrative of Sanders campaign advisors such as Sirota, who unsuccessfully attempted to steer Sanders and his inner circle – his wife, Jane Sanders, his long-time advisor Jeff Weaver, and campaign manager Faiz Shakir – toward taking a more confrontational approach towards Biden.[106] As in 2016, Matt Taibbi has offered the clearest dissection of the decisions that damaged Sanders' chances. In a column published shortly after Super Tuesday, the *Rolling Stone* journalist pointed out that:

> The reluctance to engage strongly with Biden speaks to the larger issue of Bernie's attitude toward the Democratic Party. Sanders clearly sees the Party's flaws and rails against its susceptibility to corporate influence, but has trouble understanding that the current leadership will never truly accept him and his message, unless forced. He's been reluctant to use his mass appeal as a cudgel, preferring to focus on making a case to the public.[107]

It would be unfair to claim that the campaign's defeat rested upon this decision. But it is worth pointing out that in addition to the construction of 'a people', in order to effectively mobilise, left populists must also define an adversary. In this regard, Sanders' excoriation of 'millionaires and billionaires' was insufficient, given that he was unwilling to take the necessary steps to frame Joe Biden as a representative of such interests. Internal polls suggested that drawing a stronger contrast with Biden, emphasising his track record of supporting racist policies and his repeated attempts to cut Social Security, could have weakened his support by double-digit numbers among key constituencies: for example, with the black and older voters who proved essential for his comeback from South Carolina onwards.[108] Ultimately, the responsibility for taking an insufficiently agonistic stance against such a vulnerable candidate rests with Sanders himself.

Meanwhile, the Democratic Party itself proceeded with its own momentum and strategies. While clearly unappealing to younger and more progressive voters – as witnessed by the dramatic cleavages by voters' age throughout the primaries – the party's electoral strategy has been relentlessly focused on mobilising older, suburban moderates: first against Sanders, then, perhaps, against Republicans. This discursive operation – amplified by mainstream media – is heavily reliant on projecting Trump simply as a Russian asset and on framing the attack on the president in terms of character, rather than policy.[109]

Above all, the Democrats seemed eager to avoid the kind of fragmented, prolonged primaries that in 2016 allowed Trump to emerge as the Republican nominee. In order to do so they were willing to pull out all the necessary stops: overlooking possible electoral fraud in Iowa, encouraging people to go out and vote in the midst of a pandemic, and rallying behind a manifestly uninspiring, even frail, candidate. The party, it would seem, has neither learned nor forgotten anything from the last four years: in the words of historian Quinn Slobodian, in 2016 the Democrats 'lost because they suppressed an insurgency in their own party; [Republicans] won because they failed to'.[110] But the Democratic Party establishment should not be underestimated: in key primary states and among important groups of voters – for example, older black voters in Southern states – it retains a remarkable capacity to direct its base toward its preferred candidates.[111]

In the age of Trump, the Democratic Party has chosen to prolong the rightward drift it has undergone for almost half a century. Whether the US left can work within this party and influence it in the aftermath of the Sanders campaigns remains an open question. If it hopes to do so, the 2016 and 2020 campaigns offer meaningful – and sometimes painful – lessons.

Notes

1. Bernie Sanders, *Our Revolution: A Future to Believe in*, Profile: London, 2016, p87.
2. Jacob S. Hacker and Paul Pierson, *Winner-Take-All Politics: How Washington Made the Rich Richer – And Turned its Back on the Middle Class*, Simon & Schuster: New York, 2010, p252.

3. Quoted in Ryan Grimm, *We've Got People: Jesse Jackson to AOC, the End of Big Money and the Rise of a Movement*, Strong Arm Press: Washington, DC, 2019, p302.

4. 'Bernie Sanders' campaign rally on Lake Champlain', www.c-span.org, 26 May 2015.

5. Criminal justice reform, a comparatively neglected issue at first, would receive greater attention after Sanders was pressured by Black Lives Matter activists.

6. www.c-span.org, *2015*.

7. Russell Berman, 'Bernie Sanders launches his Vermonster campaign', *The Atlantic*, 26 May 2015.

8. *Ibid.*

9. Jennifer Agiesta, 'Poll: New speed bumps for Clinton', cnn.com, 2 June 2015.

10. 'Democratic National Convention Day One: Bernie Sanders tells supporters, "Hillary Clinton must become the next president of the United States"', *LA Times*, 26 July 2017.

11. Sanders 2016.

12. See, for example, Agiesta, 'National poll: Clinton, Sanders both top Trump', cnn.com, 2 March 2016.

13. See Grimm 2019. Jackson and Sanders have been allies since the latter's 2016 run. Dean abandoned his progressive credentials to become a healthcare lobbyist.

14. Max Ehrenfreund, 'A majority of millennials now reject capitalism, poll shows', washingtonpost.com, 16 April 2016.

15. Sanders 2016.

16. 'Bernie Sanders defines democratic socialism in Georgetown speech', www.georgetown.edu, 19 November 2015.

17. Franklin D. Roosevelt Presidential Library, 'State of the Union Message to Congress', www.fdrlibrary.marist.edu.

18. Sanders 2016, p21.

19. Dan Mangan, 'Medicare, Medicaid popularity high: Kaiser', www.cnbc.com, 16 July 2016

20. Sanders 2016, p21.

21. Stephanie Kirchgaessner, 'Bernie Sanders stresses "common good" in Vatican attack on capitalism', *The Guardian*, 15 April 2016.

22. Sanders 2016.

23. 'Remarks at the Liberty University Convocation', berniesanders.com, 14 September 2015.

24. Patrick Iber and Mike Konczal, 'Karl Polanyi for President', Dissent, 23 May 2016.

25. *Ibid.*

26. Leonardo Boff, 'El Papa Francisco y la economía de la exclusión', https://leonardoboff.wordpress.com, 31 December 2013; Michael Burawoy, 'Facing an unequal world', *Current Sociology*, Vol. 63, No. 1, pp5-34.

27. Laura Galaup, 'Guillermo Fernández Vázquez: "La derecha radical europea está muy interesada en hacer caer a este Papa"', www.eldiario.es, 17 August 2019.

28. Tara Golshan, 'Read: Bernie Sanders defines his vision for democratic socialism in the US' vox.com, 12 June 21019.

29. *Ibid.*

30. Sanders 2016.

31. Chantal Mouffe, 'Why the left needs a political adversary not a moral enemy', https://transversal.at, January 2001.

32. In its initial stages, the campaign was directed by Trump confidant and former Nixon adviser Roger Stone. On his trajectory and personality, see Dylan Bank and Daniel DiMauro's 2017 documentary, *Get Me Roger Stone*.

33. Mouffe, *The Democratic Paradox*, Verso: London, 2000, p104. .

34. 'US hate crimes up 20 percent in 2016, fueled by election campaign: Report', www.nbcnews.com, 14 March 2017.

35. Jonathan Allen and Amie Parnes, *Shattered: Inside Hillary Clinton's Doomed Campaign*, Penguin Random House: New York, 2017, p18.

36. Doug Henwood, *My Turn*, OR Books: New York, 2016.

37. Libby Nelson, 'Democrats have stolen the GOP's best rhetoric – and Republicans have noticed', vox.com, 28 July 2016; see also Nathan Schneider, 'Democrats' claim that "America is already great" just borrows Republican's rhetoric', *The Guardian*, 4 August 2016.

38. Jim Geraghty, 'Chuck Schumer: Democrats will lose blue-collar workers but gain in the suburbs', *National Review*, 28 July 2016.

39. Erika Franklin Fowler, 'Political advertising in 2016: The presidential election as outlier?', *The Forum*, Vol. 14, No. 4, December 2016.

40. Kristina Monllos, 'Here are Donald Trump and Hillary Clinton's final 2-minute ads', *Adweek*, www.adweek.com, 7 November 2016.

41. *Ibid.*

42. Matthew Yglesias, 'Hillary Clinton rolled out the anti-Trump argument that could deliver a landslide', vox.com, 2 June 2016. On Clinton's popularity, or lack thereof, see Eliza Collins, 'Clinton, Trump, most unpopular candidates ever', usatoday.com, 31 July 2016. See also John McCormick, 'Finally, a poll Trump will like: Clinton is even more unpopular', Bloomberg.com, 18 July 2017.

43. Elizabeth Bruenig, 'Bernie Sanders will have to fight dirty', *The New York Times*, 24 January 2020.

44. Mic Check, 'Bernie Sanders says "billionaires"', youtube,com, 17 January 2016.

45. Sanders 2016.

46. See, for example, Thomas B. Edsall, 'The Trump-Sanders fantasy', *The New York Times*, 24 February 2016.

47. Sanders 2016.

48. Alvin Change, 'Democrats and Republicans both loved this Bernie Sanders ad', vox.com, 14 March 2016.

49. Sanders 2016, p88.

50. For an example, see Rebecca Traister, 'Hillary Clinton is furious. And resigned. And funny. And worried', nymag.com, 26 May 2017.

51. Ignacio Sánchez Cuenca, 'El nuevo liderazgo político: ensaladas de plástico y vino añejo', infolibre.es, 19 July 2017.

52. Renamed UnidosUS in 2017.

53. On *The New York Times*'s anti-Sanders outlook, see Matt Taibbi, 'How *The New York Times* sandbagged Bernie Sanders', rollingstone.com, 15 March 2016. The *Washington Post*'s coverage was unabashedly hostile. See Adam Johnson, 'Washington Post ran 16 negative stories on Bernie Sanders in 16 hours', https://fair.org, 8 March 2016.

54. Michael Sainato, 'Wikileaks proves primary was rigged', https://observer.com, 22 July 2016.

55. William Jordan, 'Age and race in the 2016 Democratic primary', https://today.yougov.com, 7 June 2016.

56. Sanders 2016.

57. Dan Hopkins, 'Why Sanders does better with independents', *FiveThirtyEight*, 18 April 2016.

58. Heather Gautney, 'Dear Democratic Party: It's time to stop rigging the primaries', www.theguardian.com/commentisfree, 11 June 2018.

59. Robinson Meyer, 'It's not just Bernie bros', *The Atlantic*, 5 February 2016.

60. As *Jacobin* magazine publisher Bhaskar Sunkara pointed out at the 2017 People's Summit, a gathering of progressive and leftist organisations that had supported Bernie Sanders' 2016 campaign, in organisations like the Democratic Socialists of America, this trend is related to the party's lack of a base in the US working class, which is blacker and browner than the American average. On the myth of the Bernie bro, see Robinson Meyer, 'It's not just Berniebros', theatlantic.com, 5 February 2016.

61. https://today.yougov.com 2016; Perry Bacon Jr, 'Huge split between older and younger blacks in the Democratic primary', nbcnews.com, 28 May 2016.

62. Emma Bowman, Colin Dwyer, Camila Domonoske, 'Bernie Sanders

sweeps caucuses in Washington, Alaska, Hawaii', npr.org, 26 March 2016; see also Zaid Jilani, 'Bernie won America's largest Arab community by being open to them', https://theintercept.com, 9 March 2016.

63. Sanders 2016, p104.

64. Chris Hayes, 'Extended interview: Alexander on why Clinton doesn't deserve the black vote', msnbc.com, 4 January 2016.

65. See Patrick Healy and Jonathan Martin, 'Bernie Sanders a virtual unknown among black voters', nytimes.com, 24 June 2015.

66. Matt Taibbi, 'The line that may have won Hillary the nomination', rollingstone.com, 28 April 2016.

67. *Ibid.*

68. Keeanga-Yamahtta Taylor, *From Black Lives Matter to Black Liberation*, Haymarket: Chicago, IL, 2016.

69. 'Bernie Sanders: It's not over', www.youtube.com, 17 February 2016.

70. Jeffrey M. Jones, 'As Labor Day turns 125, union approval near 50-year high', gallup.com, 28 August 2019.

71. Cal Winslow, 'No neutrals in Harlan County', jacobinmag.com, 14 August 2019.

72. Germán López, 'The Trump Justice Department's war on progressive prosecutors, explained', vox.com, 16 August 2019; Jamiles Lartey, 'A revolutionary, not a liberal: Can a radical black mayor bring change to Mississippi?', *The Guardian*, 11 September 2017.

73. Lara Putnam and Theda Skocpol, 'Women are rebuilding the Democratic Party from the ground up', *The New Republic*, 21 August 2018.

74. *Ibid.*

75. Jorge Tamames, 'Elecciones en Estados Unidos: ¿Normalidad excepcional?', http://agendapublica.elpais.com, 8 November 2018.

76. On this subject, see Grimm 2019.

77. *Ibid.*

78. Alexandria Ocasio-Cortez, speaking in Rachel Lears (dir.), *Knock Down the House*, www.netflix.com, 2019.

79. Thom File, 'Voting in America: A look at the 2016 presidential election', census.gov, 10 May 2017.

80. See Miriam Bensman, 'They had money, we had people', *Dissent*, 9 July 2018.

81. *Ibid.*

82. See for example Emilio Santiago and Héctor Tejero Franco, *¿Qué hacer en caso de incendio? Manifiesto por el Green New Deal*, Capitán Swing: Madrid, 2019.

83. On this subject, see Thea Riofrancos, 'Plan, mood, battlefield – Reflections on the Green New Deal', viewpointmag.com, 16 May 2019.

84. On foreign policy, see Peter Beinart, 'It's foreign policy that distinguishes Bernie this time', *The Atlantic*, 21 February 2019. On the Green New Deal, see Riofrancos 2019; see also Umair Irfan and Tara Golshan, 'Bernie's Green New Deal, explained', vox.com, 22 August 2019. On student debt, see Emily Cochrane, 'Bernie Sanders unveils education plan to eliminate student loan debt', nytimes.com, 24 June 2019; on the wealth tax, see Gabriel Zucman, 'Sanders wealth tax', http://gabriel-zucman.eu.

85. Eoin Higgins, '"I'm willing to fight for someone I don't know": Sanders speech becomes viral rallying cry', www.commondreams.org, 21 October 2019.

86. Higgins, 'Because of small donations, Sanders "out-raised literally everyone else in the field" in 2019', www.commondreams.org, 30 December 2019. See also Rebecca Lai, Josh Katz, Rachel Shorey, Thomas Kaplan and Derek Watkins, 'The donors powering the campaign of Bernie Sanders', nytimes.com, 1 February 2020.

87. Hayley Peterson, 'Bernie Sanders' campaign says more of his donors work for Walmart than any other company', businessinsider.com, 2 July 2019.

88. Golshan, '2020: Bernie Sanders's real base is diverse – and very young', vox.com, 7 March 2019; Ruobing Su and Walt Hickey, 'There are just 6 weeks until the first primary. Here's where the Democratic contenders stand based on gender, race, age, and geography', businessinsider.com, 21 December 2019.

89. Marie Solis, 'Young women actually make up more of Bernie's base than men do', vice.com, 20 September 2019.

90. Lissandra Villa, 'Inside Bernie Sanders' Iowa ground game', time.com, 1 February 2020.

91. See Mark DiCamillo, 'Tabulations from a January 2020 survey of likely voters in California's Democratic presidential primary election', Institute of Government Studies, University of California, Berkeley, January 2020.

92. Ruby Cramer, 'You don't know Bernie', buzzfeed.com, 16 December 2019.

93. *Ibid.*

94. See 'What's the most absurd medical bill you have ever received?', https://twitter.com/BernieSanders, 14 September 2019.

95. Higgins, '"I'm willing to fight for someone I don't know": Sanders speech becomes viral rallying cry', 2019.

96. On Iowa and its flawed electoral recount, see Meagan Day, 'Bernie won Iowa', *Jacobin*, 6 February 2020.

97. *Ibid.*; see also Tamames, 'Nostalgia', politicaexterior.com, 11 March 2020.

98. See Jamelle Bouie, 'Bernie Sanders and the case of the missing youth vote', nytimes.com, 13 March 2020.

99. Lauren Gambino, 'Bernie Sanders, who reshaped US politics, ends 2020 presidential run', theguardian.com/us, 8 April 2020; Sydney Ember and Katie Glueck, 'Bernie Sanders endorses Joe Biden for president', nytimes.com, 16 April 2020.

100. Michael M. Grynbaum, 'Chris Matthews apologises to Bernie Sanders for remarks on Nevada win', nytimes.com, 24 February 2020; Jon Queally 'CNN Host Michael Smerconish rebuked for comparing Sanders surge to spread of coronavirus', commondreams.org, 29 February 2020.

101. For a lucid and constructive, if somewhat fatalistic, account of the flaws of left populism, see Anton Jäger, 'We bet the house on left populism – and lost', jacobinmag.com, 25 November 2019.

102. See, for example, Courtney Subramanian, 'USA TODAY/Ipsos poll: For voters, Bernie Sanders outranks other Democrats – and Trump – on values, empathy', eu.usatoday.com, 16 February 2020.

103. This is, for example, the contention of Thomas Frank's book, *Listen Liberal: Or, Whatever Happened to the Party of the People?* Picador: New York, 2016.

104. On Biden's role during the Anita Hill hearings, see Li Zhou, 'The Joe Biden and Anita Hill controversy, explained', vox.com, 29 April 2019.

105. Veronica Stracqualursi and Sarah Mucha, 'Biden acknowledges he wasn't arrested in South Africa despite earlier claims', cnn.com, 28 February 2020.

106. David Sirota, 'The tyranny of decorum', https://sirota.substack.com, 15 April 2020; see also Alexander Burns and Jonathan Martin, 'How it all came apart for Bernie Sanders', https://www.nytimes, 21 March 2020.

107. Matt Taibbi, 'To rebound and win, Bernie Sanders needs to leave his comfort zone', rollingstone.com, 6 March 2020.

108. Interview with Claire Sandberg, April 2020.

109. On this subject, see Matt Taibbi, *Hate, Inc.: Why Today's Media Makes Us Despise One Another,* OR Books: New York, 2020.

110. Quinn Slobodian, https://twitter.com/zeithistoriker/status/796536927470161920.

111. In South Carolina, for example, the endorsement of Congressman James Clyburn, who supported Biden, appears to have been key to making up the minds of 61 per cent of primary voters. See Zeeshan Aleem, 'Rep. Jim Clyburn's endorsement gave Biden some serious momentum in South Carolina', vox.com, 1 March 2020.

Hopes and Prospects for Left Populism

Imagination is both the fabric of social life and the motor of history. Real needs, real resources and interests act only indirectly, because they do not figure in the consciousness of crowds ... The state of imaginations sets the limits within which power can be effectively exercised to get a grip upon reality, in any given instance. In the next instance, those limits will have moved.[1]

– Simone Weil

The fragmented political scene continues to be haunted by the absent ghost of – not *the* Party (there are plenty of those) but of 'party' in the Gramscian sense ... This failure to find a basis for political education is part of a larger political crisis: the crisis of political organisation that has afflicted the left since Leninism lost its magic in 1956, and since 1968, when to be radical meant, by definition, to be 'radically against *all* parties, party lines and party bureaucracies' ... This problem of 'party' presents an unsurpassed limit in the problems of the left today: a line we seem neither able to return to nor pass across. But we shouldn't mistake this dilemma for a solution![2]

– Stuart Hall

Marx says that revolutions are the locomotive of history. But perhaps it is quite otherwise. Perhaps revolutions are an attempt by the passengers on this train – namely the human race – to activate the emergency brake.[3]

– Walter Benjamin

This book set out to examine the links between economic trans-formations and the emergence of left populist movements in Spain and the US. Because dominant approaches to the question of populism struggle to contextualise its rise, and frequently do so from a position of normative hostility, it is in our interest to understand the phenomenon as best as possible. Equipped with the evidence provided by the analysis of Podemos and the Bernie Sanders movement, we can now turn back to the questions posed in the opening pages.

I have argued that, to be adequately understood, the rise of populism requires a long-term approach that takes political economy into serious consideration, examining not just the impact of the 2008 crisis but also the social and political cleavages generated by economic transformations that took place during the preceding decades. Karl Polanyi's work offers an effective framework for understanding this phenomenon: mainly through his concept of the double movement, but also through his recognition of the global nature of commodification processes, the emphasis he placed on the spontaneous nature of societal – as against narrowly class-based – countermovements, and his perception of both the cultural and material disempowerment brought upon by rapid economic transformations. This is not to say that the rise of populism is preordained, of course. On the contrary, it depends on the interplay of historical, political, and institutional variables, as well as the decisions taken by individual men and women at specific critical junctures. Populists adopt rhetorics and make organisational choices that have lasting consequences. Even as they exercise their political agency, their projects are affected – and afflicted – by a considerable degree of chance. To quote Machiavelli, left populists can 'second fortune, but not oppose it; they can weave its warp but not break it'.[4] In Spain and the US they have made history, but not under conditions of their own choosing, and they have not always achieved the results for which they originally strove.

I have sought to capture this balance of structure and agency in the image of the earthquake. Along the fault line of neoliberalism, the slow grind of socio-economic dynamics has pushed our societies into increasingly precarious terrain, weakened by economic – and, more and more often, climatic – shocks. The landslides, when they finally take place, jeopardise existing political architectures. But they do so in different ways. Remember the geologists' observation: 'When an earthquake happens deep underground, a crack will start to open on a pre-existing line of weakness in the Earth's brittle crust.'[5] After the impact of the 2008 crisis was mismanaged, each country's pre-existing lines of weaknesses presented diverging avenues for political action.

In Spain, the *indignados* harnessed outrage in a progressive, emancipatory direction; from 2017 onwards, however, the constitutional crisis generated by the Catalan government's bid for independence provided an opportunity to reconfigure the crisis along reactionary, punitive lines. While this dynamic was ultimately contained, it helped to inhibit Podemos' rise. In the US, Sanders' 2016 defeat at the hands of the Democratic establishment helped to open up the route for Donald Trump to exploit a different set of lines of weakness: racism, Islamophobia, nativism, and sexism. Hillary Clinton was a weak candidate, all the more so at a populist moment. As Quinn Slobodian observes, the Democrats lost because they supressed an insurgency within their own ranks, and the Republicans won because they failed to do so.[6] Ultimately, however, the Republican Party remains electorally competitive thanks to the distorting effects of the Electoral College on the American voting system at a national level, and widespread anti-democratic activity – gerrymandering, voter ID laws – on the part of local and state governments.[7] At the time of writing, both Spain and the US appear stranded in what Gramsci termed an organic crisis: an interregnum where the old is dying and the new cannot be born.

Polanyi also realized that the move to the market could generate both democratising and undemocratic countermovements. I have examined the rise of left populist movements because, unlike their radical right counterparts, their proposed solutions to the crises that their societies face address the root causes of the problems at hand. Their approaches stand in stark contrast to the twin perils of antagonism – embodied in violent, xenophobic rhetoric and action – and a politics without a *them,* characterised by blandness and reluctance to acknowledge the existence of profound societal – as against simply personal – divisions. Thus, it is not possible to answer the question of whether populism per se threatens liberal democracy. Radical right populism poses a threat to pluralism and civil liberties, but left populism has arisen as a response to a neoliberal order that fragments and disempowers a majority of citizens. These parties and movements seek to redemocratise their states and societies, even as, in the process, they identify political adversaries and politicise profound societal divisions. This is, of course, a confrontational attitude toward the existing state of affairs. It views conflict as embedded within and inseparable from democratic politics. But, as Margaret Thatcher famously inquired, 'whoever won a battle under the banner "I stand for consensus"?'[8]

What is clear, in any event, is that mainstream accounts of populism fail to understand the question at hand when they present populists as demagogues duping voters through mass psychology, as an embodiment of democratic excesses that threaten liberal societies, or as incomprehensible catastrophes that beset the citizenry. Many of the dominant narratives offered by media and academics on the subject are also counterproductive, because condescension fuels the very phenomenon they seek to contain. It is the radical right that has exploited this juncture with greatest success, and which benefits most from lazy analyses of its rise. As a result, left populist parties and movements remain under-examined in dominant accounts of populism. Analysing them serves to highlight the limitations of such approaches.

It is no coincidence that the emergence of left populism coincides with the ongoing crisis of social democracy, brought about by its neoliberal reinvention. Left populists in Spain and the US have broken the centre left's hold on progressive politics, but neither has proved capable of surpassing it thus far. While the strategies employed were different in each case – launching an independent party and adopting a confrontational attitude in Podemos' case; working within the Democratic Party and maintaining a semblance of civility in Sanders' – their mutual travails suggests that a modus vivendi must be reached between left populists and traditional social democrats or US Democrats. This relationship will prove challenging, but it is necessary if progressives expect to curtail both the advance of the radical right and the structural forces that propel it.

Needless to say, the operation will only be feasible to the extent that left populists retain an organisational and electoral edge, surpassing or at the very least becoming powerful enough that the centre left cannot afford to ignore them. If they remain hostile to pressure from the left, European socialists and US Democrats will never become an effective force against the rise of the radical right, much less regain the hegemonic position they held in the post-war period.

Left populists need to approach the centre cautiously to avoid co-optation. This is the threat and opportunity that Podemos faces by entering government as a junior partner to the PSOE. Parties of the centre left, in turn, will have to recalibrate and defend the positions they stood for before their neoliberal reinvention. Here the PSOE's dilemma, as expressed by the differing positions of its former prime ministers, is instructive. Felipe González, who oversaw Spain's transition to embedded neoliberalism, has repeatedly voiced his opposition to the Podemos-PSOE alliance; José Luis Rodriguez Zapatero, whose attempts to combat the 2008 crisis without resorting to austerity were cut short by external coercion, defends it. To date, the only countries in Western Europe that have witnessed a recovery of traditional social democracy are those where it has opened up, however timidly, to pressure and ideas from its left, with Spain and Portugal as paradigmatic examples. I am not advocating for a return to embedded liberalism, however, as twenty-first century societies make demands that the post-war order could not have fulfilled, or in some cases even recognised.

Podemos: A critical reflection

Chapter Six detailed some of the errors and challenges that blunted Podemos' advance. These included changes in messaging and policy; short-term manoeuvring that made the party come across as capricious; infighting among its different factions and inability to handle internal dissent; and the 2017 Catalan crisis, which put Podemos in an inherently difficult position and was then handled clumsily. These observations are frequently presented as morality tales, in which different factions of the party are blamed and chastised for Podemos' travails. To draw helpful lessons for parties and movements fighting for emancipatory change, in Spain, the US, and elsewhere, we must push beyond the blame game and analyse Podemos' reversals more dispassionately.

Podemos' mistakes should be understood first and foremost as the result of organisational and institutional choices. Maurice Duverger once remarked that just as people retain the marks of childhood throughout the rest of their lives, political parties suffer the enduring influence of their origins.[9] In its foundational congress, Podemos constituted itself as a 'swift and powerful armoured vehicle', driven by a small group of intellectuals set on 'storming the heavens' of the post-Franco regime. This structure sacrificed the horizontalism of the *indignados* movement in favour of a tight and seemingly efficient chain of command capable of delivering immediate electoral victory. The decision delivered impressive electoral results, unprecedented for a left party in the history of Spanish democracy. What it failed to do is make Podemos Spain's leading political party in the space of two years, as its leaders envisioned.

In retrospect, this outcome seems unsurprising. Discursive operations, however brilliant, do not exist in isolation from political economy. Íñigo Errejón's populist hypothesis overestimated the extent to which Podemos could shatter the country's political system in the space of two years. Spain is a European parliamentary regime with party structures that, in spite of significant erosion and delegitimation, remain more robust than those of, say, the Latin American societies to which Podemos strategists looked. The same is true of social stratification. In spite of Podemos' capacity to mobilise well beyond the confines of the traditional Spanish left, it remained associated with the classic demographics of progressive parties: culture-sector professionals, young, urban voters, and disgruntled centre-left supporters (many of whom returned to the PSOE in 2019), while failing to make inroads among older and rural constituencies.[10] Territorial diversity and tensions also constituted significant obstacles. Adopting a reactive strategy to maintain its position in Catalonia – and, to an extent, the Basque Country – Podemos alienated both supporters and opponents of independence (the first viewing the party as untrustworthy on the matter, the second judging it to have surrendered to separatist nationalism). Finally, it was not possible to sustain the party's calculated ambiguity along the left-right axis following the appearance of the centre-right party Cs, which effectively framed Podemos as a progressive force that was nevertheless different from both IU and the PSOE. The endurance of the left-right cleavage as a predictor of voting behaviour from 2016 onwards speaks to this critical fact.

Spain is not a Latin American country, but it is not Greece either. In spite of the 2008 crisis and the 2010 turn to austerity, Spanish citizens did not face the same level of material hardship that Greeks were subjected to from 2010 onwards. Spanish public administration, in spite of budget cuts and corruption at higher levels of political management, remains relatively efficient. Far from sharing the fate of Greece's main centre-left party, PASOK, which disintegrated under the pressure of that country's financial crisis, the PSOE proved capable of withstanding a significant amount of pressure. Pablo Iglesias and his entourage erred in their identification of the socialists as their main rivals. Their heavy-handed attempts to splinter the PSOE in 2016-2017 by exacerbating its internal contradictions backfired: they soured Podemos' image not only among the other party's elites but also among a significant part of its base, which Podemos needed to appeal to in order to remain competitive. Subsequent attempts to develop a cooperative relationship did not change Podemos' image as an untrustworthy partner – a convenient state of affairs for the PSOE, which remains profoundly uncomfortable with the existence of a large political party to its left. It remains to be seen whether both parties can overcome their entrenched differences now that they share power in a coalition government, and whether Podemos can extract meaningful concessions from the PSOE in its present state. If the past is any guide, the alliance will prove fraught. But there is enough at stake should they fail – the possibility of the radical right entering government, the likely impossibility of building another left coalition for many years to come – to hope that both parties play to each other's strengths rather than exacerbate their differences.

Iglesias also struggled to effect a transition from a populist to a republican moment. His firebrand style was hugely successful at first, but it wore thin with time and constant media exposure. From 2016 onwards, it became counterproductive – as seen in his collapsing approval ratings.[11] A talented orator, Iglesias was able to project a more tempered profile when circumstances demanded it. But recurrent shifts in his disposition toward the PSOE, coupled with Podemos' current communicational style – which often presents him as an enemy of the system and a victim of vicious press and elite hostility – have made him equally as heroic to party loyalists as unappealing to the majority of the electorate.[12] To the extent that the existence of leaders with a strong personal appeal and an affective bond with their supporters is essential for left populism, Bernie Sanders proved more successful at developing a pluralistic, broad-based movement, in which he was cherished as a means to an end, rather than an end in itself. Paradoxically, this has the effect of concentrating as much, if not more, symbolic power around his person. The point here is not to establish contrasts between Sanders and Iglesias as individuals so much as compare distinct rhetorical and organisational choices – which are themselves responses to each country's particular institutional architecture, party structures, electoral system, and political culture.

The limitations of the hierarchical, electoral-machine approach adopted by Podemos at its 2014 congress at Vistalegre began to be apparent in late 2015, when the model yielded strong electoral results but failed to deliver absolute victory. Acknowledging these limitations would have meant discarding Podemos' original strategy and concluding that the road to power required a different set of priorities: establishing alliances with civil society and social movements, expanding the party's base, developing policymaking experience, and strengthening its internal organisation – at the time, the *círculos* (party base organisations) that the original model marginalised were still popular among members. In short, it would have required developing the kind of organisational capacity that the Sanders movement built up between 2015 and 2020, capacity that is essential for the left to remain electorally competitive beyond the populist moments of heightened social mobilisation, which can neither be prolonged indefinitely nor summoned into existence by party leaders at a given juncture.

In early 2016 a few voices within the Podemos leadership, perhaps aware of the change that had taken place regarding the possibility of immediate electoral victory, suggested that allowing the PSOE to govern with Cs would be a more constructive way to highlight the centre left's contradictions, while granting Podemos time to stabilise and organise. But most party members – myself included – voted against this proposal, viewing it as an unnecessary concession at a time when Podemos could still expand electorally and overtake the PSOE in a second general election.[13] In retrospect I believe I was wrong, or at the very least overconfident in Podemos' capacity to garner support by doubling down on a seemingly compelling narrative – namely, that the PSOE had 'sold out' to the centre-right. To reiterate, this criticism is formulated retroactively. There was no clear path for the party to follow from its inception or at that particular juncture. Mistakes were inevitable, and if correctly assessed might have provided a learning process for the party's leaders and supporters.

Unfortunately, such introspection never took place. Instead, Podemos' leadership clung to its founding goal of aiming for, and achieving, a conclusive electoral victory in a short period of time, and it attempted to prolong the circumstances of political exception under which this goal was developed. It should also be noted, in their partial defence, that this approach demanded a set of skills – elaborating discourses, designing innovative political communications, quick manoeuvring, exploiting the news cycle – that Podemos leaders excelled at, in comparison to which developing the party's structure and outreach must have seemed a thankless ordeal.

From mid 2016 onwards, it became clear that the 'Vistalegre model' had run out of steam. Still the party leadership failed to recalibrate, instead engaging in an internal struggle that ended with Errejón – and many other of the party's founding figures – sidelined, a takeover by new Iglesias loyalists, and a degradation of the party's discursive and communicational capacity. Worst of all, the original Vistalegre vices became ingrained. The party remained rigidly hierarchical, its talent and creativity now sapped by internal suspicion and a working culture that prized a narrow conception of loyalty as its cardinal virtue. Geared for immediate victory, Podemos' restless, self-referential disposition generated frustration as soon as its supporters were – as it were – demobilised. For a party in which Antonio Gramsci remains a universal reference, the necessity of distinguishing between a war of manoeuvre and a war of position – between jockeying for electoral gains in the short term, and acquiring broader discursive and organisational strength in the long term – seems oddly alien.

Podemos did not fail to realise its early promise because it became another 'old left party', with Iglesias lapsing into the political grammar of IU, the traditional communist grouping in the Spanish Parliament – as some critics who saw Errejón as holding true to the original project would have it. As Laura Chazel and Guillermo Fernández Vázquez point out, both Iglesias and Errejón subscribed to the populist hypothesis, but they made diverging and ultimately incompatible interpretations of Ernesto Laclau and Chantal Mouffe's work.[14] Podemos today is not simply a larger version of IU: unlike Spain's traditional left, it lacks a strong historical and organisational mooring. 'Podemos is not really a party', journalist Enric Juliana writes. 'It is a movement polarised by Iglesias' strong personality.'[15] Errejón's breakaway party faces similar organisational dilemmas. Following a promising start in the Madrid regional elections, its rushed campaign in the November 2019 elections gathered 2.3% of the vote – far less than its leaders had expected.

Podemos' leaders grasped that Spain's economic crisis opened a window of opportunity for their project – in other words, that Polanyi's double movement led to a populist moment – and they designed a discursive and electoral strategy suited for this juncture. They reflected less, however, on the extent to which economic transformations have also transformed political party systems – the move from catch-all to cartel parties theorised by Peter Mair and described in Chapter Three. Their organisational model, paradoxically, could be seen as an extreme variant of the cartel party brought about by neoliberal transformations: highly mediatised, with a small leadership that bypasses intermediate structures and members, and with weak organic links to other social or institutional actors. In the absence of immediate victory, Podemos' leaders were left ruling a void.[16]

Against this background, Podemos' main innovation regarding party organisation was holding online primaries and referenda on specific issues, making it an example of what Paolo Gerbaudo has termed a 'digital party'.[17] But this model only made the initial lack of pluralism worse. As César Rendueles and Jorge Sola write:

> The direct election resulted in massive participation in the electoral processes of Podemos and made it appear as a more democratic party. However, it weakened the organic links

(between the party base, its cadres and public representatives), granted enormous power to the leaders – who maintained de facto control over the lists – and favoured a functioning more based on imposition than deliberation. In other words, the model had a marked plebiscitary character.[18]

To the extent that Podemos is a representative example, the 'digital party' amounts to a cartel party with voting apps and online forums. Perhaps the solution to this state of affairs is not to be found in horizontalism – which poses its own problems for developing political action – but in a more structured organisational culture, with stronger checks and balances, a truly collegial leadership, genuine deliberation mechanisms, and a more open and permeable disposition towards civil society and social movements. Whether such pluralism is reconcilable with the populist hypothesis, which places strong emphasis on leadership and the development of affective bonds between voters and the party's leader – and thus can circumvent the party's officials and structures – remains an open question. While pluralism was certainly incompatible with the Vistalegre model, Podemos could have democratised its internal culture while retaining the populist style and rhetoric it employed: Sanders and the movement behind his candidacy suggest this balancing act is achievable.

Three profound problems now face Podemos. The first is its incapacity to amass the technical and organisational capacity that it requires if it expects to deliver transformational change. The second is a party leadership that devotes excessive attention to internal, short-term jockeying for power, at the expense of thinking and planning strategically. The third is a communication strategy that lurches from one proposal to another without a long-term set of priorities. 'Sometimes I think that the only lesson [Iglesias] drew out of the populist hypothesis is that a sudden discursive shift can be useful electorally', a former Podemos MP pointed out.[19] A succession of sudden and often contradictory shifts will, however, put any party's credibility on the line.

Changing the party's priorities is important because Spain today has moved away from the brief political juncture in which elections were the key site for challenging tests of strength for politics-as-usual. Following a period in which electoral competition and manoeuvring took centre stage, the country is experiencing a return of social mobilisation along a series of promising fronts. A transformative strand of feminism has been on the rise since 2018, gathering massive crowds every 8 March.[20] Labour activists have won small victories in the new, highly exploitative sectors of the gig economy. Climate change has become a concern for public opinion, in a country that faces desertification if temperatures continue to rise. Demands for rent controls are increasing. Against this backdrop, the economic agenda of Spain's right-wing parties amounts to tax cuts and upward economic redistribution. Unless heavily pressured from the left, the PSOE will be tempted to administer only cosmetic patches to the country's problems. If it expects to turn the country's unfulfilled demands into electoral support for its more radical agenda, however, Podemos will need to overhaul the stifling structure it inherited from both Vistalegre congresses.

Towards the left's next reinvention

A left populist strategy can make use of a given political juncture, expanding a party or movement's support well beyond its traditional confines. What it cannot achieve, however, is brisk electoral victory in an advanced capitalist democracy, where formulating cross-class coalitions and articulating complex social blocs remain necessary in order to achieve lasting victory. In the absence of a full-blown state crisis like the ones that beset Greece in the 2010s or Latin America in the 1980s, Spanish society remained too diverse to be flattened into a 'people versus elites' dichotomy in the space of twenty-four months. In 2014, the ground beneath post-Franco democracy began to shake and left populism destabilised its traditional political parties. Ultimately, however, the edifice proved resilient in the face of this tremor.

Setbacks and false starts should be expected. The case of the British Labour Party under Jeremy Corbyn and Jean-Luc Mélenchon's France Insoumise are sharp reminders. Viewed in light of these experiences, Podemos' post-2017 trajectory remains noteworthy. Its initial discursive strategy, on the other hand, is perhaps the clearest example of left populism's immense potential in Western societies ravaged by neoliberal transformation. In its early phase, Podemos captured the imagination of progressives and leftists across the world: it effectively became, in the space of two years, the most promising force of the European left. Perhaps its way forward today, then, lies in learning from allies elsewhere. As Spain transitions away from its populist moment, the impressive organisational efforts and infrastructure developed by the US Bernie Sanders movement between 2015 and 2020 provide a useful departure point for the Spanish left to draw inspiration from.

Combining a left populist discourse with strong organisational capacity is essential for parties and movements seeking lasting change. To use Stephanie Mudge's terms, they must develop the kind of cultural, intellectual, and technical infrastructure that underpinned social democracy's hegemony in the mid-twentieth century, as well as reflecting on their capacity for social intermediation in the twenty-first century. In the latter period, neoliberal economists, wonks, and spin doctors have failed to gather popular support around their agenda, but the figure of the Keynesian economic theorist – with its capacity to act as an intermediary between the worlds of labour, academia, and party politics – cannot be conjured from the past.

Recovering the left's *raison d'etre* demands refusing its neoliberal reinvention. Making a left project meaningful and appealing today requires combining the left's original, transformative ethos with the confident praxis it expressed throughout the post-war period. There is reason for cautious optimism. During the onset of neoliberalism, progressives and the left struggled against a coherent, well-structured assault on embedded liberalism and the post-war Keynesian consensus. Today they find themselves in a different setting. Neoliberalism has lost traction since the 2008 crisis. New economic ideas today – on the relationship between inequality and meritocracy; on the nature of value and the public sector's role in its creation; on how to tax wealth and combat climate change in an effective way – come from the left, not the radical right or the centre. What is needed is a lever to enact this agenda of radical social democracy, politically as well as culturally.[21]

In a well-known poem, Bertold Brecht tells the story of the tailor from Ulm, who in 1592 designed a device that would allow people to fly. Challenged by the bishop to prove its usefulness, he strapped the contraption to his back and jumped from the roof of the town's church. It was a premature attempt to storm the heavens, and it ended with the tailor flattened against the pavement. But this gesture, Brecht suggests, was not in vain. Four centuries later, humankind learned to soar across the skies.[22]

The parable is touching, but it requires an update in light of present attempts to storm the heavens. The political, economic, and environmental transformations our societies must undergo if we expect to have a future worth living cannot be postponed for another four hundred years. Given liberalism's indifference and the centre left's reluctance, left populists must provide the critical impulse for this paradigm shift.

Notes

1. Simone Weil, 'Meditations on a corpse', *New Left Review*, 111, May-June 2018.
2. Stuart Hall, *The Hard Road to Renewal: Thatcherism and the Crisis of the Left*, Verso: London, 1990, pp180-1.
3. Quoted in Michael Löwy, *Fire Alarm: Reading Walter Benjamin's 'On the Concept of History'*, Verso: New York, 2016, pp66-7.
4. Quoted in Chantal Mouffe, *For a Left Populism*, Verso: New York, 2018.
5. British Geological Survey, 'Seismic waves', www.bgs.ac.uk/discoveringGeology/hazards/earthquakes/seismicWaves.html.
6. https://twitter.com/zeithistoriker/status/796536927470161920.
7. The Electoral College system makes states, rather than individual voters, the unit that determines who wins the presidency. States have electors allocated to them following census guidelines, but they operate through a winner-takes-all system. Consider two states with an identical number of electors. In one of them Republicans win 51 per cent of the vote; in the other, Democrats obtain 99 per cent of the vote. The Democrats have almost three times more votes, but the result is a tie in electors. The effect of the Electoral College is to introduce a bias in favour of small, rural states, which traditionally lean Republican.
8. Quoted in Robin, 'The Obamanauts', *Dissent*, Fall 2019.
9. Maurice Duverger, *Los partidos políticos*, Fondo de Cultura Económica: México, DF, 1957, p15.

10. See José Fernández-Albertos, *Los votantes de Podemos. Del partido de los indignados al partido de los excluidos*. Madrid: Catarata, 2015.

11. 'Pablo Iglesias, el líder nacional peor valorado en pleno debate interno de Podemos', cadenaser.com, 7 February 2017.

12. His tendency to morally excoriate his rivals also damaged Iglesias and his deputy and partner, Irene Montero, when they decided to buy a large house in Madrid's north-western suburbs. The decision – taken after their endless denunciations of Spanish elites for abandoning their constituencies to pursue secluded lifestyles, as well as repeated accusations that Errejón and his followers were privileged, reformist pushovers – blew a hole in his credibility, for understandable reasons. The matter was brought before a digital party vote, which asked whether the couple should refrain from buying the house and resign. The vote effectively became a plebiscite on Iglesias' leadership. For a critical account, see Santiago Alba Rico, 'Pasar vergüenza', www.eldiario.es, 23 May 2018.

13. While Errejón was repeatedly framed as the party's leading moderate, he adopted a noncommittal stance as this debate unfolded.

14. Laura Chazel and Guillermo Fernández Vázquez, 'Podemos, at the origins of the internal conflicts around the "populist hypothesis": A comparison of the theoretical production, public speeches, and militant trajectories of Pablo Iglesias and Íñigo Errejón', *European Politics and Society*, 18 February 2019.

15. Enric Juliana, 'Gana Sánchez, sin Madrid', www.lavanguardia.com, 27 May 2019.

16. The problems posed by this model manifest themselves in a number of ways. Following a hesitant and ultimately failed attempt to set up an affiliate union, and even though it provided steadfast support for workers in both the traditional and new, precarious sectors of the economy, Podemos to this day lacks a clear internal agency tasked with establishing and overseeing a substantive exchange with organised labour. Policy work also came to be neglected in favour of media soundbites, both in Parliament and in the party's think tank, Instituto 25-M, which saw its activity jeopardised by party infighting. Throughout the Catalan crisis, the party never drafted a comprehensive proposal for reforming Spain's territorial administration. Instead, it repeated its 2014 calls for plurinationality and a referendum on independence – a somewhat simplistic solution, given the scope of the question at hand – and a nationwide referendum on the monarchy: a seemingly important decision that was subsequently shelved and is rarely mentioned today.

17. For a brief overview, see Paolo Gerbaudo, 'One person, one click: Is this the way to save democracy?', *The Guardian*, 13 February 2019.

18. César Rendueles and Jorge Sola, 'Strategic crossroads: the situation of the left in Spain', Rosa Luxemburg Stiftung, June 2019, p29.

19. Interview with author, 15 March 2019.

20. For an overview of the subject, see Beatriz García, Nuria Alabao, and Marisa Pérez, 'Spain's Feminist Strike', *New Left Review* 110, April 2018, pp35-7; see also Clara Serra and Alba Pez, 'Un feminismo para el 99%', *Política Exterior* No. 188, March-April 2019, pp130-7.

21. See Jorge Tamames, 'Paradigmas', politicaexterior.com, 29 November 2019.

22. Quoted in Lucio Magri, *El Sastre de Ulm: El comunismo en el siglo XX. Hechos y reflexiones*, El Viejo Topo: Barcelona, 2010.

Index

academic coverage of populism 10-11

adversarial conception of politics 12

agonism 144, 172, 208-9

Alesina, Alberto 119

Alexander, Michelle 216

Allen, Jonathan 209

Alternative for Germany (AfD) 29

American Enterprise Institute 144

Americans for Tax Reform 152

Anderson, Perry 10, 47, 106, 120, 167

antagonism 208

anti-austerity mobilisations 169-70

Anti-capitalist Left party 172

anti-segregation movements 205

anti-system candidates 15

anti-systemic movements 17

'apologetics for terrorism' 131-2

Arditi, Benjamín 45

'articulation' 46-7

asset footprints 116-17

Atkinson, Anthony 80

The Atlantic 202, 206

Aufstehen movement 56

August 1914 (Tuchman) 26-7

austerity 11, 116, 117-18, 173-4, 244

authoritarian and exclusionary agendas 13

'authoritarian populism' (Hall) 101

Axelrod, David 156

Aznar López, Jose Maria 112

Balzac, Honoré de 92

Ban, Cornel 17-18, 85, 86, 109, 110, 111, 113, 122

Bannon, Steven 69

Basque Country 180, 243

belle epoque 26

Benjamin, Walter 238

Berlusconi, Silvio 29

Berman, Sheri 66, 115

Bernanke, Ben 154, 156

'Bernie bro' 215 *see also* Sanders, Bernard (Bernie)

Biden, Joseph Robinette, Jr (Joe Biden) 16, 122, 155, 226-7, 229-30

billionaires 88

black Americans 150, 157-8

Black Lives Matter (BLM) 139, 160, 218

black voters 215, 216-18

Blair, Tony 41, 98, 99

Block, Fred 63, 66

Bloomberg, Michael 209, 226, 228

Blum, León 62

Blyth, Mark 77, 80, 85, 94, 117

Boff, Leonardo 206

Bolsonaro, Jair Messias 12

Bowling Alone (Putnam) 93

'bracket creep' 146 *see also* tax cuts

Brazil 12

Brecht, Bertold 250-1

Breitbart, Andrew 69, 170

Bretton Woods system 67, 78-9, 84

Brexit 59

British Geological Survey 53, 56-7

Brooklyn rally (2019) 223, 225-6

Brown, Michael 139

Buffett, Warren 141

Bundesbank 114

Burawoy, Michael 61, 67, 68, *68*, 69, 206
Bush, George W. 43, 153-4
Bustinduy, Pablo 177
Buttigieg, Pete 226

California 223-4, 227
campaign funding 144
Cano, Germán 173
Capital in the Twenty-first Century (Piketty) 88-9
Carmena, Manuela 185
Carnation Revolution (Portugal) 108
Carroll, Lewis 26
cartel parties 96, 110
Carter, Jimmy 138, 142-3
Carter-Reagan years 4, 19, 140
Case, Anne 157
Catalonia 33, 57; Podemos' policies 243; secessionism 180-1, 190-1
catch-all parties 94, 95-6
caudillista tactics 172
'causal pathways' 94
central bank independence 95, 114-15
Centre for Sociological Research (Spain) 125
centre-left parties 95
Chazel, Laura 247
Chigurh, Anton, *No Country for Old Men* 43
Chile 42
CIA-sponsored coups 82
citizen tides (*mareas*) 130, 171
Citizens United v. Federal Election Commission (US Supreme Court 2010) 147-8
Ciudadanos (Citizens, Cs) 39, 181, 184
climate change 55
Clinton, Bill 5, 138, 140
Clinton, Hillary 15, 155; campaign 2016 209-11; Democratic primaries 2016 214-18; differences with Sanders 208; response to aggressive nativism 209; weak candidate 240
Club for Growth 152
Colau, Ada 185
Cold War 82
colonial wars 82
Comisiones Obreras (CCOO) 109
commercial openness 86
commodifying dynamics 79
Common Agricultural Policy (EU) 86
communism 81
compensatory neoliberalism 5, 106-7, 111, 150
conspiracy theories 39
consumer credit 93 *see also* financial crisis 2008
consumption-driven growth model 83
'coordinated market economies' 87
Corbyn, Jeremy 13-14, 214, 249
'cordons sanitaires' 33
Coriolanus (Shakespeare) 9
Corporate Political Action Committees (PACs) 144
'corporate socialism' 207-8
'corrupt elites' 2
counterhegemonic communication projects 171
countermovements: and double movements 59-60; markets 61; as a populism 63-6; post-war 77
Covid-19 virus pandemic 18, 227
Cramer, Ruby 224-5
Credit Suisse Global Wealth Report 88
Crockett, Molly 31
cross-border financial flows 79
Crowley, Joe 220
cultural grievances 64
cultural vs economic demands 65
cyclical theory of change 67

Dale, Gareth 69
dating apps 94
de Gaulle, Charles 82, 84
de-regulation 86
De Sousa Santos, Boaventura 173
de-unionisation 146-7 *see also*
    labour unions
Dean, Howard 203-4
Deaton, Angus 157
debt reduction 116
Deliveroo 94
demagogues 11
demands 45-7
democracy 40-2
Democratic Congressional Campaign
    Committee (DCCC) 155-6
Democratic Leadership Council
    (DLC) 149
Democratic National Convention
    209
The Democratic Paradox (Mouffe)
    40-1
Democratic Party 4-5, 148-53; age
    and ethnicity of voters 215,
    216; black voters 215, 216-18;
    campaign 2016 208-14; fiscal
    discipline and activism 145-6;
    fringe policies 220; neoliberal
    drift 159; neoliberal reinvention
    19, 149; opposition to Bernie
    Sanders 228-9; party of urban
    professionals 157; in power
    1933–53 76; primaries 2016
    214-18; primaries 2020 231;
    rightward drift 231; social
    polarisation 152-3; third-way
    politics 19; and the working
    class 145
'democratic regression' 39-40
democratic socialism 203, 207, 228
Democratic Socialists of America
    (DSA) 21, 219
democratic values 4
democratisation processes 107-8

demos 48
D'Eramo, Marco 30, 48
deregulation 4, 92-3
destruction of private wealth 80
Deutsche Bank 116-17
Deutsche Mark 115
'digital parties' (Gerbaudo) 247-8
digital spread of misinformation 54
Dijsselbloem, Jeroen 117
disciplinary neoliberalism 150,
    157-8
discursive strategies 1-2, 3, 16, 45
disembedded economies 20, 23, 94,
    148
disrespectful treatments 42
The Divide (Taibbi) 158
'double movement' (Polanyi) 3, 47,
    59-63; and countermovements
    59-60, 239; historical
    perspectives *68*; interaction
    between markets and society 54;
    and orthodox Marxism 67; and
    Podemos 247; and populism 11,
    63-6 *see also* Polanyi, Karl
'double withdrawal' (Mair) 147
Downton Abbey 81
Draghi, Mario 124
Drezner, Daniel 140
Dutch elections (2017) 36
Duverger, Maurice 243

earthquakes 53-4, 239-40;
    metaphor for social change
    55; time horizons of cause 55;
    Western politics 17, 18
economic anxiety 64
economic change 65-6
economic crisis 1929 77
economic crisis 2008 *see* financial
    crisis 2008
economic inequality 11, 43
economic management 56
Economic Recovery Tax Act (ERTA
    1981) 144-5

economic theorists 95
economic transformations 55, 58
Edward VII of England 26-7
Eisenhower, Dwight 76, 82
Electoral College 43, 240
'elephant chart' (Lakner and
    Milanovic) 90, *91*
'elephant chart' (World Inequality
    Database) *91*
'the elites' and 'the people' frontier
    45
'emancipation' as third movement
    (Fraser) 68-9
Emanuel, Rahm 155-6, 201
embedded liberalism 4, 78-83;
    and Bretton Woods system 79;
    catch-all parties 94; faltering
    84-5; hardware and software 85;
    and neoliberalism 2-3, 83, 99;
    post-war reconstruction 81-2;
    unmet social demands 82
'embedded neoliberalism' (Ban) 18
Emily's List 147
epidemics 33
equality 4
'equivalential links' 172
erosion of parliamentary norms 54
Errejón, Íñigo 167, 168-9, 171;
    background 170; 'catastrophic
    draw' 187; 'electoral war
    machine' 179; green party 193;
    and Podemos 175-6, 188, 189;
    populist hypothesis 243, 247
essentialist narratives 117
Essex School of discourse analysis
    44
established politics: breakdown 33,
    55; opposition to 10
'eurocritical' middle road 120
European Central Bank (ECB) 115,
    116, 124, 156
European Commission 116
European federalism 120
European Monetary System 114

European Monetary Union 62
European Parliament elections 167-8
'European troika' 183
European Union (EU) 86, 114-15,
    119, 156
Eurosceptics 120
Eurozone 107, 116-19
explanatory power 14
extreme right parties 20

'fake news' 33, 54, 182
Falklands war (1982) 100
fascism 20, 30, 64
fault lines 58
Federal Reserve 156
feminist mobilisation 219-20
Ferguson, Missouri 139
Fernández-Albertos, Jose 93, 147,
    221, 223
Fernández Vázquez, Guillermo 20,
    247
15 May movement (15-M) 19, 128-
    31, 168, 169, 177, 191
Fight For 15 movement 140
finance capitalism 3-4, 158
financial crisis 2008 11, 19; cheap
    consumer credit 93; EU and US
    responses 156-7; and financial
    deregulation 150, 153-4; lines
    of weaknesses 240; Obama's
    first term 140; and the rise of
    populism 43; Spain 107, 121
financial deregulation 150
financial liberalisation 4, 88
financialisation 92-3
fires 54
First World War 63, 77
fiscal capacity 80
Fishman, Robert 108
Five Star Movement 29, 56
Flint, Michigan 158
For the People (Tamames) 2-3
Fordist model of capitalism 67, 93
fortress liberalism 159

'four freedoms' (Roosevelt) 61

France 14; 'cordon sanitaire' 33; *dirigiste* state 81-2; dollar reserves in gold 84; and Eurozone elites 10; *'les trente glorieuses'* 81; welfare chauvinism 64

France Insoumise 13, 29, 249

Francis, Pope 205, 206

Franco dictatorship 108-9

Frank, Thomas 153; *Listen, Liberal* 143; *What's the Matter with Kansas?* 36

Fraser, Douglas 142-3

Fraser, Nancy 10, 68-9

free enterprise 145

French New Deal 62

French Revolution 30

Friedman, Milton 86

'friend-enemy' distinction (Schmitt) 37

'friendly Leninism' 179

funding electoral campaigns 147-8, 223

Garner, Eric 139

Garzón, Alberto 184

Gates, Robert 155

Geithner, Timothy 155

Gellner, Ernst 29

Gerbaudo, Paolo 247

Germany 117, 118-20

Gillespie, Richard 110

Gingrich, Newt 145, 152

Glass-Steagall Act 150

global distribution of incomes 90

globalisation: losers from 90; social consequences 4

gold 84

gold standard 62-3

González, Felipe 106, 110, 132, 242

Gopnik, Adam 158

Gramsci, Antonio 45, 47, 69, 86, 170-1, 246

grassroots fundraising 223

Great Lisbon earthquake (1755) 56

Great Society programme 84

The Great Transformation (Polanyi) 3, 27, 53, 59-61, 63-9

Greece 14, 116, 183-4, 244

Green New Deal 222

Greenspan, Alan 153-4

Grimm, Ryan 155-6, 203, 220

growth models 107, 125

The Guardian 32-3

Hacker, Jacob S., *Winner-Take-All Politics* 141, 142-4, 147, 159

Hall, Peter 98-100

Hall, Stuart 100, 101, 145, 238

'hardware' (specific managing institutions) 85

Hayek, Friedrich 19

hegemony 170

Helgadóttir, Oddny 119

Henwood, Doug 209

Heritage Foundation 144

Hindu nationalism 12

Hobsbawm, Eric 22, 100

Hochschild, Arlie 32

Hofstadter, Richard 30, 75-6

Holder, Eric 155

Hopkin, Jonathan 59, 85, 94, 118

'horizontalist' strategies 5

Horn, Heather 206

How Democracies Die (Levitsky and Ziblatt) 41-2

Hungary 12

Iber, Patrick 206

'ideational' approaches 34

ideological eco-chambers 94

Iglesias, Pablo 167, 168-9, 174; appeal to *la patria* 175; firebrand style 244-5; groundwork for Podemos 170, 171-2; media hostility 182; media profile 171-2; 'the people'

against 'the caste' 175; Podemos'
set backs 188; polarising figure
179; populist hypothesis 247;
Vistalegre II 189-90
income inequality 88-92, *91*, 141-2
see also wealth inequality
India 12
indignados movement 5, 16, 19,
129-30, 168, 171, 177, 240
individual liberty and social equity
19
Industrial Revolution 65
inflation 84
ING 117
Inglehart, Ronald 64
internal devaluation 118
international economic order 58-9,
78
International Monetary Fund 85,
116
internationalisation of production
and finance 79
intersectional theory 213
Ionescu, Ghita 29
Italy 116

Jackson, Jesse 203
Jackson, Mississippi 219
Jacobin magazine 160
Johnson, Lyndon 84
Joseph, Keith 99
journalistic coverage of populism
10-11
Juan Carlos, King of Spain 178
Judt, Tony, *Postwar* 81
Juliana, Enric 188, 247
Justice Democrats 220-1

Kahn, Alfred 143
Kalecki, Michał 83
Kaltwasser, Cristóbal Rovira 47;
*Populism in Europe and the
Americas* 34-5
Karp, Matt 159

Katz, Richard 96
Kelsen, Hans 37
Kemp, Jack 145
Kentucky coal miners 219
Keynes, John Maynard 75, 78-9
Keynesian 'economic theorists' 95
Keynesianism 2-3, 12, 82-3
King, Martin Luther, Jr 204-5, 229
Klein, Naomi 173
Klobuchar, Amy 226, 227
Knock Down the House documentary
(Netflix) 221
Konczal, Mike 206
Krasner, Larry 219
Krastev, Ivan 29
Krugman, Paul 121
Kuhn, Thomas 100

labelling processes 10
labour activism 219
labour arbitrage 94
Labour Party (UK) 13-14, 249
labour unions 93, 94, 146-7
Laclau, Ernesto 11, 19, 101,
247; agonistic rhetoric 172;
'articulation' 46-7; framework
for democratic demands 212-
13; and Polanyi 66; populism
28, 45; *On Populist Reason* 1,
44, 47; theory of populism 28;
'vagueness and indeterminacy'
67
Lakner, Christoph 90, *91*
Latin America 173-4, 182
Le Bon, Gustave 30-1
left anti-establishment parties 37-8
left populism 11-12, 13-17, 19,
47-8, 241-2, 249, 250 *see also*
Podemos; Sanders, Bernard
(Bernie)
Leftism Reinvented (Mudge) 110-11
Lega Nord 29, 120
Levitsky, Steven 43; *How
Democracies Die* 41-2

Lewinsky, Monica 152
LGBT rights 148
liberal democracy 20, 43, 240-1
liberalism: and democracy 40-1; hubristic and precarious foundations 60; meaning 19; plebiscitary forms 43
lines of weakness 57, 140, 240
Linz, Juan 14, 39, 108
Listen, Liberal (Frank) 143
Loach, Ken 81
lobbying 144, 147
Lombroso, Cesare 31
London School of Economics (LSE) 30
'low-information' voters 33
Luban, Danial 59
Lumumba, Chokwe Antar 219

Maastricht Treaty (1992) 18-19, 62, 114, 115-16
Machiavelli, Niccolò 239
Macmillan, Harold 81
macro-structural developments 80-1
Macron, Emmanuel 32
Madrid bombings 39
Maestre, Antonio 193
mainstream media discourses 33
Mair, Peter 44, 75, 94, 97; 'double withdrawal' 147; 'Ruling the void' 96-7; *Ruling the Void* 97-8
Manaugh, Geoff 53, 57
market liberalisation 100
Martin, Trayvon 139
Marx, Karl 31
'material' vs 'identitarian' approaches 65, 147
Matthijs, Matthias 119
Mazower, Mark 120
Mazzucato, Mariana 87
McCain, John Sidney, III 27-8, 43
McGovern-Fraser Commission (1968) 143
McNamara, Kathleen 115

media 33, 36
'Medicare for All' 220
Megabyzus (Persian satrap) 9
Mélenchon, Jean-Luc 13, 249
Merkel, Angela 106, 117
meteorological analogies 55
#MeToo movement 219-20
middle classes 81
middle-range theories 15
midterm elections 2018 220
Milanovic, Branko 90, *91*
Mill, John Stuart 14
Milward, Alan 120
miners' strikes 100, 219
Mises, Ludwig von 19, 65
Mitra 151, *151*
mobilising disenfranchised citizens 12
Modi, Narendra 12
Moncloa pacts 109
Monedero, Juan Carlos 170, 179, 182-3, 188
Monereo, Manuel 59
monetarism 86
monetary union 114-15
Monica Lewinsky scandal 152
Monnet, Jean 21, 120
Moore, Stephen 152
Morales, Evo 32
'morally upstanding people' 2
Morozov, Evgeny 40
'most different systems' model 14
Mouffe, Chantal 11, 19, 44, 101, 247; agonism 144, 172, 208, 209; antagonism 208, 209; 'articulation' 46-7; *The Democratic Paradox* 40-1; framework for democratic demands 212-13; and Polanyi 66; populism 28, 45; populist hypothesis 47
Moulder, Nicholas 120
Mounk, Yascha, *The People vs Democracy* 39-40, 41

move toward the markets 151
Mudde, Cas 29, 34-6, 47; *Populism in Europe and the Americas* 34-5
Mudge, Stephanie L. 19, 85, 94-5, 250; *Leftism Reinvented* 110-11
Müller, Jan-Werner 32; *What is Populism?* 37
The Myth of Solid Ground (Ulin) 54, 55-6

NAFTA 150
name recognition 216-17
Napoleon III 31
Narodniks movement 30
national sovereignty 119
National Union of Mineworkers 100
nativism 57, 208-9
neo-fascists 20
neoliberal globalisation 3
neoliberal 'reinvention' (Mudge) 19
neoliberalism 83-92; ascent of 85; and catch-all parties 95-6; 'causal pathways' 94; defining 85; and embedded liberalism 2-3, 83, 99; fault lines 239; hardware and software 85; ideology with global reach 17-18, 86-7; measurable effects 94; segmentation and atomisation 94; since 2008 crisis 250; social and economic effects 87-8; Spain 5; United States (US) 140; wealth and income inequality 88
Netflix 94
Netherlands 36
networks 144
New Deal 204; abandonment 143; Carter-Reagan years dismantling 4, 140; prospering after gold standard 62; and Richard Nixon 142; and Sanders 229; and Second World War 78

'The new populism' (*The Guardian*) 32-3
nineteenth century: countermovements 65-6; liberalism 60, 81; 'peace interest' 63; revolts 61
Nixon, Richard Milhous 38, 84, 142, 143
No Country for Old Men (Chigurh) 43
Norquist, Grover 69, 152
Norris, Pippa 64

Obama, Barack Hussein 27; bipartisan consensus 158-9; faults 42-3; first term 153; healthcare reform 156; 'The new populism' (*The Guardian*) 32; Republican opposition to 38-9; social spending cuts 157; structural racism 139; support for Joe Biden 227
Obama for America 154-5, 158
Ocasio-Cortez, Alexandria (AOC) 201, 220-1, 222, 223
Occupy Wall Street movement 5, 12, 19, 140, 159-60
Oesch, Daniel 96
Oklahoma teacher strikes 219
'Old Testament justice' 155
oligarchisation 92
Omar, Ilhan 21, 220, 222, 223
On Populist Reason (Laclau) 1, 44, 47
O'Neil, Cathy 40
Orbán, Viktor 12, 40
ordoliberalism 119
organic crises 240
organised labour 219
Organize for America 154-5, 158
O'Rourke, Beto 227
Ortega y Gasset, José 10, 115
orthodox Marxism 65-6
Ossoff, Jon 220
Oxfam 88

p-waves 56
Pantaleo, Daniel 139
paradigm shifts 98-9
'paradigmatic' democracy (Linz) 14
Paris Commune 30
parliamentary monarchy 15
Parnes, Amie 209
party affiliation 96-7
PASOK 244
'peace interest' 63
'the people' and 'the elites' frontier 45
The People vs Democracy (Mounk)
    39-40, 41
People's Party (Spain) *see* PP
    (People's Party)
People's Party (US) 30
Perez-Rubalcaba, Alfredo 178
personal hardships 225
'personal responsibility' 150
Philadelphia 219
Pierson, Paul 17; *Politics in Time* 55;
    Winner-Take-All Politics 141,
    142-4, 147, 159
Piketty, Thomas 80, 92, 206;
    *Capital in the Twenty-first
    Century* 88-9
Pinochet, Augusto 42, 173
Platform for People Affected by
    Mortgages (PAH) 130-1
plebiscitary forms of liberalism 43
'pluralism' 19
Podemos 4, 5, 29, 167-95,
    242-9, 249-50; alliances
    (*confluencias*) 181; ambiguity
    of left-right axis 243; another
    'old left party' 245-6; axis of
    opposition 174-5; candidates
    in elections 172; challenges and
    contradictions 178-84; 'digital
    party' 247-8; elections 2015
    185-7; elections 2016 187-
    8; elections 2019 21-2, 192;
    electoral results 16; electoral
    stagnation 169; electoral

volatility *194*; emergence as a
    party 13; European elections
    2014 168; founding team
    170; and French radical right
    37-8; grassroots associations
    (*círculos*) 177; image as an
    untrustworthy partner 244;
    independence movements 240,
    243; independent party 14; 'left'
    populists 19; local concerns and
    regional autonomy 181; media
    173, 181-2; as the 'monarchic
    bloc' 190; as a movement 247;
    'onslaught' (blitzkrieg) 178;
    patriotism 181, 190-1; policy of
    electoral victory 246; political
    challenges 15-16, 248-9;
    post-2017 trajectory 249-50;
    relationship with PSOE 189,
    190; strategic underpinnings
    171; Syriza as allies 182-3; tax
    scandals 182-3; Vistalegre I
    178-9, 189; Vistalegre II 188-
    91; Vistalegre model 245, 246,
    248; voters 176-7, *176*
Polanyi, Karl 11, 59-69, 138;
    background 69; and Bernie
    Sanders 205-6; 'Bolshevik
    soul' and 'Fabian muzzle' 67-
    9; commodifying dynamics
    79; de-regulation as regulation
    86; fascism 62, 63, 64; focus
    on 'society' 67; gold standard
    and fascism 62; minor edits
    68; move to the market 240;
    orthodox Marxism 65-6; self-
    regulated markets 64, 67;
    socialism 63-4; spontaneous
    nature of revolts 61; 'theorist
    of discontinuity' 63; theorist
    of the 'primacy of politics' 66;
    US subordinating markets
    to social imperatives 77;
    worldview 66 *see also* 'double

movement' (Polanyi); *The Great Transformation* (Polanyi)
Polanyian frameworks 3, 59, 90
policy wonks 96
political apathy 43
political discontent 18
political elites 96, 107
political volatility 14-15
'politically precarious' (Fernández-Albertos) 93, 147, 221, 223
politics 5
Politics in Time (Pierson) 55
'politics without frontiers' (Mouffe) 47
Popular Party (PP) *see* PP (People's Party)
popular passions 30
popular sovereignty 4
popular will 37, 225-6
populism: academic and journalistic coverage 10-11; challenge to liberal order 28; constituting unity of a group 45; constructing a political subject 48; as a countermovement 63-6; defining 1, 19, 29-30; as an epidemic 33; as an existential threat 44; as fascist 30; history of the term 28, 29; 'ideational' approaches 34; mainstream accounts 241; normative hostility 30; as a pathology 44, 55; as a political logic 44-8; and politics 47; psychological accounts 31-2; rise of 11; as a rising tide or tsunami 33-4; in Spain 174; and technocracy 37, 98; 'thin-centred ideology' 35; threat to liberal democracy 240-1; as a tornado 17; understanding quantitatively 32; *us* and a *them* logic 11
Populism in Europe and the Americas (Mudde and Kaltwasser) 34-5
'populism studies' 1
populist countermovements 203
populists: adversarial conception of politics 12; anti-pluralists 37; discursive strategies 45; mobilising disenfranchised citizens 12; morality tales 183-4
Portugal 82, 108, 111
post-war Keynesianism 82-3
post-war reconstruction 80, 81-2
post-war settlement 79-80
Postwar (Judt) 81
PP (People's Party) 16, 39; austerity policies 123; European elections 2014 167, 169; general election 2015 187; general election 2016 188; impervious to change 178; as 'populist' 38; and PSOE 112, 123, 127, 131; and Spanish patriotism 175, 181
Prasad, Monica 144, 145
pre- and re-distributive policies, 92
precarious jobs 93-4, 124
prediction 56
presidential campaigns *210*
presidential democracies 14-15
prevention 56
privatisation 4
progressive advocacy groups 147 *see also* lobbying
progressive movements 140
'progressive neoliberalism' (Fraser) 10
progressive politics 101
protectionism 64, 86
PSOE-Podemos government 192
PSOE (Spanish Socialist Workers' Party) 16; cartelisation 110; centre-left party 20; and Ciudadanos (Cs) 181, 245-6; defeat 2011 131; elections 2014 178; electoral victories 110-13; European elections 2014 167; general election 2015 186-7;

general election 2016 187-8;
Madrid bombings 39; and
Podemos 169, 190, 193, 242,
244; and PP (Popular Party)
112, 123, 127, 131
public healthcare policies 220
public research 87
Puerta del Sol protests 128
Putnam, Laura 219-20
Putnam, Robert, *Bowling Alone* 93

racism 57, 138-9, 150-1, 157-8
'radical right' 20
radical right anti-establishment
parties 37-8
radical-right populism 12, 13
'radical social democracy' 19
'rainbow coalition' (Jackson) 203
Rajoy, Mariano 123-4, 131
ranking political processes 32-3
The Reactionary Mind (Robin) 38
Reagan, Ronald 3, 38, 64, 86, 141-
8
real estate bubbles 107, 113
regional (*autonomías*) elections 185
regulation and de-regulation 86
Rendueles, César 129, 171-2, 247-8
Rennwald, Line 96
rentiers 92, 94
Republican Party: electorally
competitive 240; fiscal
discipline and activism
145-6; 'malaise' 1970s 144;
opposition to Barack Obama
38-9; plutocratic interests 145;
radicalisation 42, 152; social
polarisation 152
'the revolt of the masses' (Ortega y
Gasset) 10
revolts 61
'rhizomatic revolution' 129
Rice, Tamir 139
Ridgecrest tremors (California
2019) 57

rise of populism 11, 239
Rivera, Albert 184
'the roaring nineties' (Stiglitz) 114-
15
Robin, Corey, *The Reactionary Mind*
38
Romer, Christina 156
Roosevelt, Franklin Delano (FDR)
76, 78, 206; 'four freedoms' 61;
New Deal 62, 204, 229; Second
Bill of Rights 204
Rosa, Isaac 182
Royo, Sebastián 110
RTVE 181-2
Ruggie, John 79
rulers and ruled 98
'Ruling the void' (Mair) 96-7
Ruling the Void (Mair) 97-8
Russia 33

Saez, Emmanuel 80
Salgado, Elena 121
Salvini, Matteo 120
San Francisco earthquake (1906)
53-4, 56
Sánchez-Cuenca, Ignacio 125, 214
Sánchez, Pedro 178, 187, 190, 192,
194
Sanders, Bernard (Bernie) 4, 5, 201-
31; appeal 203; and black voters
217; Brooklyn rally (2019)
223, 225-6; California 223-4;
campaign ad *213*; defeat by
Democratic establishment 240;
democratic socialism 13, 206-8,
228-9; developing a political
movement 218; fundraising
223; as an independent 229;
and Joe Biden 227, 229-30;
media reaction 202; mobilising
'politically precarious' 223; not
a populist 38; and Podemos 14;
'political revolution' 57; and
Pope Francis 205-6; presidential

election campaign 2016 201-3, 211-18; presidential election campaign 2020 222-31; 'radical reforms' agenda 20; shared campaign features with Trump 150, 212; South Carolina primaries 226-7; symbol for popular demands 217; Twitter account 225; universalistic rhetoric 213-14; use of 'socialist' label 204; volunteers 223

Sanders, Jane 230

Sanders movement 16, 19, 21, 218

Scandinavia 87

Scargill, Arthur 100

Schmitt, Carl 37, 40-1

Schumer, Chuck 210

Second Bill of Rights 204

Second World War 77, 78, 80

'secular stagnation' (Summers) 92

segmentation 94

seismic activity 57-8

self-regulating markets 60-1, 64, 67

La Sexta 173

Shahid, Waleed 220

Shakespeare, William, *Coriolanus* 9

Shakir, Faiz 230

shock absorbers 157

Simón, Pablo 35

Sirota, David 228, 230

Skocpol, Theda 219-20

Slobodian, Quinn 85, 231, 240

small-donor fundraising 223

social atomisation 43, 93, 94

social democratic parties 95-6

social embeddedness 94-5

social equity 19

social fragmentation 43, 94

social mobilisation 218, 219-20

social networks 40, 94

social polarisation 152

social science 31-2

socialism 63-4

'socialists' 20

socio-economic patterns 18

socio-economic processes 28

'software' (policy commitments) 85

Sola, Jorge 129, 171-2, 247-8

Solchaga, Carlos 114

Somers, Margaret 66

South Carolina primaries 2020 226-7

southern European countries 117, 118

'Southern strategy' (Nixon) 38, 145

Soviet Union 81

Spain 106-32; abortion rights 131; austerity measures 116, 122-3, 125, 244; autarchic economic model 108; bailouts 116, 123-4; bi-party system 109-10; Centre for Sociological Research 125; compensatory neoliberalism 5, 106-7, 111, 150; constitution of 1978 108, 123; constitutional crisis 2017 33; construction industry 113; countermovement 2011-2013 125-32; crisis and austerity 121-5; democratisation processes 107-8; developmental path 111; developmental programme 108-9; economic recovery 111, 124-5; elections 2015 and 2016 184-8; elections 2019 192; electoral stagnation 2016 15; electoral volatility *194*; embedded liberalism 82; embedded neoliberalism 107-13; established political structures 193; euro accession 107; European integration 114, 115-16; European Monetary System 114; Eurosceptics 120; 'fake news' industry 182; financial crisis 2008 62, 107, 121; government-opposition system 126, *127*; growth model 107, 125; international economic

order 58-9; left populism 13-
17; media 181-2; national
discontent 132; national identity
180; 'paradigmatic' democracy
14; plurinational country 181;
political elites 107; political
parties 14; populism 174, 193;
protests 2011 57, 61, 128;
public trust in politics 125-6,
126; real estate bubble 107, 113;
resilience of the left-right axis
194-5; restructuring 110; shock
absorbers and countermeasures
18; stimulus programme 121-
2; transition to democracy
115; unemployment 111, *112*;
voting intentions 127, *128*; as a
'zombie democracy' 132
spin doctors 96
The Spirit of '45 (documentary) 81
spontaneous protests 61-2
stagflation 84, 144
Standing Rock environmental
protests 140
'starve the beast' theory 146
states' structural capacities 80
statism 82
steel tariffs 64, 86
Steinmo, Sven 77, 80
Stepan, Alfred 39, 108
Stiglitz, Joseph 114-15, 121-2
Streeck, Wolfgang 120
Suárez, Adolfo 109
Summers, Larry 92, 155
Sunkara, Bhaskar 20
Super Tuesday (2020) 227
Syriza 14, 29, 37-8, 40, 183

Taibbi, Matt 139, 217, 230; *The
Divide* 158
Taine, Hippolyte 31
Tamames, Jorge 4, 109; *For the
People* 2-3
Taub, Amanda 31

tax cuts 144-5, 146
tax havens 92
Taylor, Keeanga-Yamahtta 218
Tea Party movement 159-60
teacher strikes 219
Thatcher, Margaret 3, 75, 98-102,
241
theory of hegemony (Gramsci) 170
theory of state design 85 *see*
neoliberalism
'thin-centred ideology' 35
'third way' politics 12-13, 19, 41,
98, 112, 140
'tidal' metaphors 33-4
Tilly, Charles 32
time 28
time horizon of causes and
outcomes (Pierson) 55
Tlaib, Rashida 220, 223
Tooze, Adam 58, 116
Tormey, Simon 132
tornados 17, 55
Torreblanca, José Ignacio 29, 172-3
La transición 107-8
transnationalised, finance-oriented
economists (TFEs) 95-6
Traub, James 9
'les trente glorieuses' 81-2
Trichet, Jean-Claude 122, 156
Truman, Harry 76
Trump, Donald John 10, 15,
75; brand of populism 38;
campaign and victory 2016
63, 211, 212; conspiracy
theories against 39; 'corporate
socialism' 207-8; exploiting
lines of weakness 140, 240;
John McCain's memorial service
28; losing the popular vote 43;
misinformation campaigns 182;
nativism and structural racism
57; neoliberalism 64; polarising
candidacy 208-9; protectionism
86; restructuring political

competition 218; shared campaign features with Sanders 150, 212; voting base 31
Tsipras, Alexis 183
tsunami metaphors 33-4
Tuchman, Barbara, *August 1914* 26-7
Tucker, Robert C. 31
La Tuerka ('The Screw' TV series) 171
Twitter 225

Uber 94
UGT 110
Ulin, David 57; *The Myth of Solid Ground* 54, 55-6
undemocratic liberalism 40
unemployment 84
Unidas Podemos (UP) 187-8
United Kingdom (UK) 15, 99-100
United Left (IU) 115, 131, 167
United States (US) 138-60; crime bill 150; disciplinary neoliberalism 150, 157-8; economic supremacy 1945 84; elections 2016 33, 36; financial crisis 2008 18, 156-7; fiscal stimulus 2009 156; governed by demagogues 75-6; income inequality 89, 141-2; inflation 145-6; labour activism 219; labour unions 146, 219; left populism 13-17; 'liberals' 19; 'lines of weakness' 57, 140; midterm elections 2018 220; move toward the markets 151; neoliberalism 140; norms and civility 42; police killing of black people 139; populist moments 15, 28, 153; progressive advocacy groups 147; progressive rhetoric 213; protectionism 86; subordinating markets to social imperatives

77; two-party system 14; welfare cuts and securitisation *151*
University of Chicago 205
upwardly mobile professionals 145
urban poverty 65
US dollar 84

Varuna 151, *151*
Vázquez Montalbán, Manuel 108
Venezuela 183
Ventotene Manifesto 120
Vietnam war 84
Villacañas, José Luis 179
viruses 33
Vistalegre I 178-9, 189
Vistalegre II 188-91
Vistalegre model 245, 246, 248
Volcker, Paul 86
volunteers 223
Vox (radical-right party) 22, 191, 193
Vox (website) 31

Wall Street 150, 155, 217
Wallerstein, Immanuel 58
Warren, Elizabeth 21, 227
wealth inequality 80, 88 *see also* income inequality
wealth redistribution 79-80
Weaver, Jeff 230
Weber, Max 5
Weil, Simone 238
welfare chauvinism 64
welfare reform 150
Western Europe: communism 81; welfare states 157
Western politics 17
Western societies 18, 90
What is Populism? (Müller) 37
What's the Matter with Kansas? (Frank) 36
white evangelicals 145
White, Harry Dexter 78-9
wildcat strikes 219

Wiles, Peter 26
Winner-Take-All Politics (Hacker and Pierson) 141, 142-4, 147, 159
Wolf, Martin 118
Women's March 219
working class 145
Works Progress Administration (WPA), 77
World Bank 85
World Inequality Database 90, *91*, 124

World Inequality Report 88
World Wars: countermovements 77; destruction of private wealth 80; and Trump's victory 63; US public spending 78

Zapatero, José Luis Rodríguez 39, 113, 121-3, 242
Ziblatt, Daniel 43; *How Democracies Die* 41-2
Zimmerman, George 139
Zizek, Slavoj 47